THE EXTENT OF THE ROMAN · EMPIRE · AT THE DEATH OF AUGUSTUS · 14 A.D.

SARMATIA

HUNS

GOTHS

DANUBE RIVER

BLACK SEA

MOESIA

SINOPE

PARTHIAN EMPIRE

THRACE

BITHYNIA and PONTUS

ACEDONIA

GALATA

PROVINCE OF ASIA

CAPPADOCIA

PHARSALUS

IONIA

CILICIA

SYRIA

EUPHRATES RIVER

TIGRIS RIVER

ACTIUM

ATHENS

CORINTH

SPARTA

RHODES

CYPRESS

CRETE

JERUSALEM

EAN SEA

ARABIA

ALEXANDRIA

CYRENE

CYRENAICA

EGYPT

NILE RIVER

GULF OF ARABIA

T O   1 4   A. D.

AUGUSTUS

BOOKS BY JOHN BUCHAN

CAESAR AUGUSTUS
(Vatican)

AUGUSTUS

By JOHN BUCHAN

Immensa Romanae pacis majestas

Illustrated

HOUGHTON MIFFLIN COMPANY · BOSTON
The Riverside Press Cambridge
1937

The Riverside Press
CAMBRIDGE · MASSACHUSETTS
PRINTED IN THE U.S.A.

TO MY FRIEND

WILLIAM LYON MACKENZIE KING

FOUR TIMES PRIME MINISTER OF CANADA

PREFACE

THIS book is an attempt to understand a little part of the mind of a great man. In my youth I was fascinated by Julius Caesar, and was ready to believe, with Mommsen and his school, that the constructive ideas commonly attributed to his great-nephew were born of his genius. As my studies progressed I felt this view to be untenable, and not less that other which seems to be taking its place today, and which would make Agrippa the true architect of the Roman empire. I came to see that Augustus, while he had able colleagues — and one of his gifts was his power to choose collaborators — was always the master designer and the chief executant. I seemed to find in his work a profound practical intelligence which is even rarer in history than a seminal idealism. Consequently since my undergraduate days Augustus has inspired me with a lively interest, which has been sustained by such experience as I have had, under varied conditions, of those problems of government which are much the same in every age. Two Canadian winters have enabled me to complete a task begun many years ago.

Gibbon complained that he had to 'collect the actions of Trajan from the glimmerings of an abridgment or the doubtful light of a panegyric.' The authorities for Augustus are scarcely more satisfactory. The chief contemporary sources are lost: the thirteen books of Augustus's own autobiography; the three books of the correspondence between him and Cicero; the memoirs of Agrippa; the works of Asinius Pollio and Messalla Corvinus; the thirty books of Livy which covered the period

from 44 to 9 B.C.; the pamphlets of men like Oppius and
Julius Saturninus, and most of Nicolaus of Damascus.
Much of our material, too, for the understanding of Roman thought and society is gone: nearly all the minor
poets; a good deal of Cicero; the plays which were not
paraphrases from the Greek, after Plautus or Terence,
but true transcripts of Roman life. Some of these lost
sources are no doubt embodied in the work of later chron-
iclers, but it is impossible to know what is an authentic
borrowing and what is the author's gloss. Apart from
minor contemporaries like Strabo and Velleius, we are
chiefly dependent on authors who lived from half a century to two centuries later — Plutarch, Appian, Suetonius, the two Plinys, and Dio Cassius, and these were
moralists or gossip-writers, with little historical conscience. The one man of genius, Tacitus, also wrote long
after the event, and, as was said of Carlyle, he 'preferred
seriousness to truth.'

Happily the imperfect literary sources can be supplemented by important archaeological and epigraphical
matter. Since the envoys of the Emperor Ferdinand II
first copied the Monumentum Ancyranum in 1555, every
century has brought new discoveries. Papyri have made
clear many points in the administration of Egypt, and
inscriptions containing laws, edicts and senatusconsults
have extended our knowledge of provincial government.
The brilliant work of the excavators has shed new light
upon Augustan sculpture and architecture. But, when
all has been said, we have still scanty materials to estimate the man and his work. A principal guide must still
be tradition; we know that succeeding ages believed certain things about him, and a long-continued belief cannot be without warrant.

A great scholar has written of the fallibility of all historical reconstruction: 'The tradition yields us only

ruins. The more closely we test and examine them, the more clearly we see how ruinous they are, and out of ruins no whole can be built. Tradition is dead; our task is to revivify life that has passed away. We know that ghosts cannot speak until they have drunk blood, and the spirits which we evoke demand the blood of our hearts. We give it to them gladly, and if they then abide our question something from us has entered into them.' [1] I am conscious that my interpretation of Augustus is a personal thing, coloured insensibly by my own beliefs. But, since the historian is most at home in an age which resembles his own, I hope that the convulsions of our time may give an insight into the problems of the early Roman empire which was perhaps unattainable by scholars who lived in easier days.

I have been compelled to make large drafts on the kindness of my friends in Europe, and would especially thank for their generous assistance Professor Hugh Last of Oxford and Count Roberto Weiss.

J. B.

GOVERNMENT HOUSE, OTTAWA.

[1] Wilamowitz, *Greek Historical Writing and Apollo*, 26.

CONTENTS

ILLUSTRATIONS

ABBREVIATIONS

A. J. Phil.	*American Journal of Philology.*
Aegypt.	*Aegyptus; rivista italiana di egittologia e di papirologia.*
App.	Appian, Ῥωμαικά (*Bella Civilia*).
App., *Illyr.*	Appian, *Illyrica.*
Augustine, *Civ. Dei*	St. Augustine, *de civitate Dei.*
Augustine, *Confess.*	St. Augustine, *Confessions.*
Aul. Gell.	Aulus Gellius, *Noctes Atticae.*
Bull. de C. hell.	*Bulletin de correspondance hellénique.*
Bull. del. C. A.	*Bullettino della commissione archaeologica communale di Roma.*
C. A. H.	*Cambridge Ancient History.*
C. I. G.	*Corpus Inscriptionum Graecarum.*
C. I. L.	*Corpus Inscriptionum Latinarum.*
Cic., *ad Att.*	Cicero, *Epistulae ad Atticum.*
Cic., *ad Brut.*	Cicero, *Epistulae ad Brutum.*
Cic., *ad Fam.*	Cicero, *Epistulae ad Familiares.*
Cic., *ad Q. Fr.*	Cicero, *Epistulae ad Quintum fratrem.*
Cic., *in Verr.*	Cicero, *in Verrem.*
Cic., *Phil.*	Cicero, *Philippics.*
Cic., *pro Marc.*	Cicero, *pro Marcello.*
Cic., *pro Planc.*	Cicero, *pro Plancio.*
Cic., *de Leg.*	Cicero, *de Legibus.*
Cic., *de Nat. deorum*	Cicero, *de Natura deorum.*
Cic., *de Off.*	Cicero, *de Officiis.*
Cic., *de Rep.*	Cicero, *de Republica.*
C. Q.	*Classical Quarterly.*
C. P.	*Classical Philology.*
Claudian, *in Rufin.*	Claudian, *in Rufinum.*
Claudian, *de cons. Stilich.*	Claudian, *de consulatu Stilichonis.*
Dessau	*Inscriptiones Latiniae Selectae* (1892–1916).
Dio	Dio Cassius.
Dio Chrys.	Dio Chrysostom, *Orationes.*
Diod.	Diodorus Siculus.
Ferrero	G. Ferrero, *Grandezza e decadenza di Roma* (1902). Eng. trans., *The Greatness and Decline of Rome* (1907).
Florus, *Epit.*	Florus, *Epitome de Gestis Romanorum.*
Gaius, *Inst.*	Gaius, *Institutiones.*
Gardthausen	V. Gardthausen, *Augustus und seine Zeit.* (1891–1904).

Hor., *Ars Poet.*	Horace, *Ars Poetica.*
Hor., *Ep.*	Horace, *Epistulae.*
Hor., *Epod.*	Horace, *Epodes.*
Hor., *Od.*	Horace, *Odes* (*Carmina*).
J. R. S.	*Journal of Roman Studies.*
Josephus, *Ant.*	Josephus, *Jewish Antiquities.*
Josephus, *in Ap.*	Josephus, *in Apionem.*
Juv.	Juvenal, *Satires.*
Livy	Livy, *History of Rome* (*Annales*).
Livy, *Epit.*	Livy, *Epitome* (covering the lost books).
Lucan, *Phars.*	Lucan, *Pharsalia.*
Macrob., *Saturn.*	Macrobius, *Saturnalia.*
Malcovati	H. Malcovati (ed.), *Augusti operum fragmenta* (Turin, 1928).
M. Aurelius, *Med.*	Marcus Aurelius, *Meditations.*
Mart.	Martial, *Epigrams.*
Mél. de l'É. F.	*Mélanges d'archéologie et d'histoire de l'École française de Rome.*
Momms., *Staatsr.*	T. Mommsen, *Römisches Staatsrecht* (1887–1888).
Mon. Anc.	*Monumentum Ancyranum.* (ed. E. G. Hardy, 1923).
N. Ant.	*Nuova Antologia.*
N. J. cl. Alt.	*Neue Jahrbücher für das classiche Alterthum.*
Nic.	Nicolaus of Damascus (in Jacoby, *Fragm. Graec. Hist.*).
Ovid, *Ars amat.*	Ovid, *Ars amatoria.*
Ovid, *Fast.*	Ovid, *Fasti.*
Ovid, *Met.*	Ovid, *Metamorphoses.*
Pauly-Wissowa	Pauly-Wissowa (ed.), *Real-Encyclopädie der classischen Alterthumswissenschaft* (1894 *sqq.*).
Periplus	*Periplus maris Erythraei* (in *Geog. Graec. Min.*).
Pliny, *N. H.*	Pliny the elder, *Naturalis Historia.*
Pliny, *Ep.*	Pliny the younger, *Epistulae.*
Pliny, *Pan.*	Pliny the younger, *Panegyricus.*
Plut., *Ant.*, *Cic.*, etc.	Plutarch, *Parallel Lives* — *Antony*, *Cicero*, etc.
Plut., *Mor.*	Plutarch, *Moralia.*
Polyb.	Polybius, *History of Rome.*
Procop. *Bell. Goth.*	Procopius, *de bello Gothico.*
Rend. I. L.	*Rendiconti del reale Istituto Lombardo.*
Rend. Linc.	*Rendiconti della reale Accademia dei Lincei.*
Res Gestae	see *Mon. Anc.*
Rev. des E. L.	*Revue des études latines.*
Rev. de P.	*Revue de philologie, de littérature, et d'histoire anciennes.*
Rev. Hist.	*Revue Historique.*
Rice Holmes	*The Architect of the Roman Empire* (1928).
S. H. A.	*Scriptores Historiae Augustae.*
Seneca, *Controv.*	Seneca the elder, *Controversiae.*
Seneca, *Cons. ad Helviam*	Seneca, *de consolatione ad Helviam matrem.*

Seneca, *de clem.*	Seneca, *de clementia ad Neronem Caesarem.*
Seneca, *Ep.*	Seneca, *Epistulae Morales.*
Seneca, *Nat. Quaest.*	Seneca, *Naturales Quaestiones.*
Strabo	Γεωγραφικά (*Geographica*).
Suet., *Div. Jul.; Div. Aug.,* etc.	Suetonius, *de vita Caesarum; Divus Julius,* etc.
Suet., *Vit. Hor.*	Suetonius, *Vita Horatii.*
Tac., *Agr.*	Tacitus, *Vita Agricolae.*
Tac., *Ann.*	Tacitus, *Annales.*
Tac., *Dialog.*	Tacitus, *Dialogus de oratoribus.*
Tac., *Germ.*	Tacitus, *de moribus et populis Germaniae.*
Tac., *Hist.*	Tacitus, *Historiae.*
Tertullian, *adv. Marc.*	Tertullian, *adversus Marcionem.*
Tertullian, *Apol.*	Tertullian, *Apologeticum.*
Tyrrell	Tyrrell and Purser (eds.), *Correspondence of M. Tullius Cicero.*
Ulpian, *Dig.*	Ulpian, in Justinian's *Digesta.*
Val. Max.	Valerius Maximus, *Exempla.*
Vell.	Velleius Paterculus, *Historiae Romanae.*
Virg., *Aen.*	Virgil, *Aeneid.*
Virg., *Ecl.*	Virgil, *Eclogues* (*Bucolica*).

OCTAVIUS

BOOK ONE

I. WINTER AT APOLLONIA

(45–44 B.C.)

The homespun cloak that muffled half his cheek
Dropped somewhat, and I had a glimpse — just one!
One was enough, whose — whose might be the face?
That unkempt careless hair — brown, yellowish —
Those sparkling eyes beneath their eyebrows' ridge
(Each meets each, and the hawk-nose rules between)
— That was enough, no glimpse was needed more!

BROWNING, '*Imperante Augusto*'

I

THE town of Apollonia on the Illyrian shore, an old colony of Corinth, was in the spring of the year 44 B.C. the centre of a varied life. It was a busy port, for it was one of the debauchments on the Adriatic of the great Via Egnatia, the high road from Rome to the East; it was a military station; and for some years its bland air and its position as a half-way house between East and West had drawn to it scholars whose fame brought them many pupils. As seaport, garrison, and university town, it was a pleasant dwelling-place for youth.

Among those who walked its streets in the mild March weather there was one on whom many turned to look a second time, for he was the great-nephew of him who was now master of the world. But he was a young man who on his own account would anywhere have attracted notice. His name was Gaius Octavius Thurinus,[1] and

---

[1] The cognomen, which he never used, was given him in memory of his father's victory over a band of runaway slaves at Thurii. Suet., *Div. Aug.*, 7.

he had come to Apollonia in the previous autumn to
complete an education which had been interrupted by
the wars in Spain. He was now half-way through his
nineteenth year, having been born on the 23rd of September, 63, in the consulship of Cicero. In build he was
small and slight, not quite five feet seven, but he was
well-proportioned, and his short stature did not catch
the eye. His features were so delicately modelled as to
be almost girlish, for the Julian strain had a notable fineness, but the impression left on the spectator was not
one of effeminacy. The firm mouth and the high-bridged
nose forbade that, but above all the steady, luminous
grey eyes. Wonderful eyes they were, so penetrating, so
intense in their regard, that those on whom he bent them
had to avert their gaze.[1] His complexion was pale, for
he had always been a delicate boy, but now and then he
would flush delightfully. His voice was quiet and pleasant, and his whole air was of calm and self-control, with
just a hint of suffering. For his years he seemed prepos-
terously mature, and he had few youthful irregularities;
he drank little wine, and ate no more than a bird, having
a miserable digestion. But, though nothing of a boon
companion, there was a grace about him which charmed,
and a hint of latent power which impressed.

He looked the scholar which he had been since his
childhood. He had declaimed orations when scarcely out
of his cradle, and during his teens he had been a serious
student of what went in Rome by the name of philosophy.
Like all the Roman youth he had given much time to rhetoric, the science which taught literary style and the arts
of persuasion; but he had not been one of the younger set
that Cicero despised, whose craze was for extravagant

'geminas cui tempora flammas
laeta vomunt.'
Virg., *Aen.*, VIII, 650.

tropes and novel idioms. Like his great-uncle he had a dry taste in letters, preferring the Attic to the Corinthian manner. This same austerity appeared in his philosophical interests. An indifferent Greek scholar, he was not a devotee of any Hellenic master, but after the Roman fashion was something of a free-lance and an eclectic. Like his great-uncle again, he had fallen under the spell of Posidonius,[1] a Stoic who borrowed from many schools, and who tried to marry the thought of Greece and the East with Roman tradition, seeking what might be a universal creed for a universal empire. Unlike many of his young contemporaries, Octavius had no contempt for ancient Roman ways or any undue love of the exotic.

This discreet young man had brought with him a tutor, one Apollodorus, an ancient *savant* from Pergamum, whose chief task was to improve his halting Greek. But his friends were not limited to his fellow-students at the Academy. Six legions were quartered in Illyria and Macedonia, and, as befitted one who had been appointed to Julius's staff, he lived a good deal in military society. He was popular among the officers, for he could tell them at first hand of the recent Spanish campaign, and he had the glamour of his kinship and friendship with the chief soldier of the age. Also there was about him an air of high destiny, and the omens which had accompanied his birth and childhood were common talk in the mess-rooms. Once at Apollonia he had visited the astrologer Theogenes, who had been so overwhelmed by the splendour of his horoscope that he had flung himself in worship at his feet. The boy had in him a vein of superstition, and the incident had increased his self-confidence, as it had greatly enlarged his popular prestige.[2]

---

[1] For Posidonius see Bake's edition of the fragments (Leyden, 1810); Schmekel's *Die Philosophie der mittleren Stoa* (1902); and Bevan's *Stoics and Sceptics*, ch. III.

[2] Suet., *Div. Aug.*, 94.

Besides his tutor Apollodorus, and another *savant*, one Athenodorus of Tarsus, he had several intimates of his own age. One was Salvidienus Rufus, whose friendship was destined to have a tragic end. Closer to him was Gaius Cilnius Maecenas, a man a few years his senior, who claimed to be sprung from the old royal house of Etruria. Maecenas was a striking figure, with hollow eyes, and strong, harsh features that lacked the Roman modelling. His manner, in spite of his rugged appearance, was oddly effeminate; sometimes his dress was fantastic, and his chief interest appeared to be in letters and connoisseurship. But Octavius valued his advice, given always with complete candour, and he had no doubt about his affection. The ambition of Maecenas seemed to be never for himself but only for his friends.

Closest of all was his exact coeval, Marcus Vipsanius Agrippa. Of no particular family, Roman or Etruscan, Agrippa had been already the comrade of Octavius in his brief campaign, and had won a love and confidence which were to remain unshaken for thirty years.[1] He was a most impressive young man, with his straight eyebrows, his deeply sunk penetrating eyes, his massive jaw, and his mouth as delicately modelled as that of Julius himself.[2] He had all the sagacity of Maecenas, but already it was clear that he was more than a counsellor and diplomatist, and in a crisis might be a leader of men. The officers in the mess-rooms respected his military judgment, and found in him a spirit after their own hearts, and his devotion to Octavius exalted the latter in their esteem. He was not the great-nephew of the world's master, but he was himself the stuff of which masters of the world were made. This stripling of eighteen was one of the most

[1] It seems probable that these young men of humble origin, Agrippa and Salvidienus Rufus, had already attracted the attention of Julius, who had attached them to Octavius. Other examples were P. Ventidius Bassus and Cornelius Gallus.

[2] See especially the Butrinto bust, *C.A.H.*, iv (Plates), 154.

competent of living men, but all his powers were laid on the altar of friendship. He is the supreme example in history of a man of the first order whom loyalty constrained to take the second place.

Octavius had been born in Rome, in a house at the east end of the Palatine, but his family was of the provinces. His grandfather, a member of the plebeian Octavian clan, had been a banker in the Volscian town of Velitrae, a profession which in Roman eyes did not dignify those who followed it. His father, however, had raised the family into the official nobility, for he had served the state as quaestor, plebeian aedile, and praetor, and had governed Macedonia with honesty and competence, fighting several successful little campaigns against hill tribes.[1] More, he had allied himself by marriage with one of the proudest of the patrician houses, the Julian, for his wife Atia was the daughter of a Velitran bourgeois, M. Atius Balbus, and Julia, the sister of Gaius Julius Caesar. He might have been consul, had he not died in 58 at his villa at Nola, when his son was not yet five years old. The boy was brought up in the country, mainly at Velitrae, but also at the other country houses of his well-to-do family. Presently Atia married again, the consular L. Marius Philippus, a son of the famous orator of that name, and a close friend of Cicero. But this association with the larger life of Rome was not allowed to interfere with the strictness of Octavius's upbringing. He was held close to his books, the regime of his life was Spartan, and he was rarely permitted to visit the capital. Once only before he assumed the dress of manhood did he appear in public, when at the age of twelve he delivered the customary eulogy at the funeral of his grandmother Julia, and Roman society looked with interest at the modest,

[1] For the elder Octavius see Suet., *Div. Aug.*, 3; Vell., ii, 59; Cic., *ad Q. fr.*, i, 21, 27; *C. I. L.*, 279.

handsome child, kin to a great man who had no son of his own.

For in those years Julius was striding towards the first place in the world. While Octavius was with his tutor at Velitrae or Nola or at his stepfather's Campanian villa, the struggle with Pompey was at its height. The step-father was a moderate Pompeian in sympathies, but his family connections kept him neutral, and the household was never drawn into the war. When, in 49, Julius crossed the Rubicon the boy was fourteen, living in the depth of the country; but, as the campaign proceeded and Italy fell into the conqueror's hands, he was brought more often to Rome and treated with some of the respect due to a prince of the blood. After Pharsalus, when scarcely sixteen, he officially entered upon manhood, and about the same time was elected to the college of pontifices, a significant honour for so young a man. He now undertook certain public duties, occasionally presiding, as the pontifices were entitled to do, in the praetorian courts, but he still lived a retired life under his mother's stern eye, and this seclusion and mystery increased the popular interest. For he was now very generally regarded as the heir apparent of one who had made himself to all intents the monarch of the world.

It was a situation which might well have turned a lighter head. But the young man kept his own counsel and appeared content to be dutiful and obscure. Yet his mind was very full of his great-uncle and he longed ardently for his return. In all his life he had scarcely seen him, for Julius had gone to Gaul when he was still a little child, and it is not likely that the two met in the feverish months before the former embarked for the campaign that ended at Pharsalus. But when the victor returned from Alexandria in the autumn of 47 there was a meeting, and the heart of the older man went out to the handsome youth, who was the chief male left of his race. He would have taken Octavius with him to Africa, and Octavius longed to go, but his health at the time was weak and his mother forbade the journey. After Thapsus, however, he became virtually a member of the dictator's household, though he was not as yet formally adopted.[1] He shared in his triumph, riding in a chariot close behind him; he induced him to pardon Agrippa's Pompeian brother, who had been made prisoner in Africa; he stood by his side at the sacrifices and sat by him in the theatre; he took precedence of all his suite, and seemed destined, in spite of his years, to be the dictator's constant associate and his virtual chief-of-staff.

But his health served him ill. The hot weather in Rome brought on a fever, and he was a sick man when Julius started for Spain in December 46 to fight his last battle. Early in the new year he was sufficiently recovered to follow him, and after a dangerous and difficult journey he joined him at Calpe on the morrow of Munda. With him he crossed to Carthage, and shared in the preliminary councils about the new ordering of the empire. He returned alone to Rome, where he had now to walk discreetly, for he was courted on all sides as the intimate of the conqueror. A Parthian campaign was in prospect, and as one of the two masters of the horse he was in the heart of the business. Moreover, the Senate, at Julius's request, had made him a patrician. But in those difficult months Octavius moved so warily that he made no enemies, and committed himself to no faction or intrigue. He was Julius's great-nephew, but he was only a youth, he said, with his education still to complete, and all business must wait on Julius's return. For a moment in September he met the master of the world, when he came

---

[1] In spite of Nicolaus, 8, it seems clear that Julius never adopted him in his lifetime. Cf. Dio, xlv, 3; Vell., ii, 59; Livy, *Epit.*, 116.

home to see about the reconstruction of the empire. But presently he left with his tutor for Apollonia — probably by his own desire. He had become the object of a great man's affection and the confidant of his schemes, but his mind was still in a turmoil. He needed leisure to reflect upon those tremendous problems of government of which he had now an inkling, and on what seemed to be his own high but unpredictable destiny.

II

The world at that time appeared to most men a tangle of knots waiting to be cut by the sword, but Octavius had imbibed sufficient philosophy to distrust the sword as a cure for all ills. He had in his bones the Roman sense of the past, and his mind in those quiet months had been working back upon the long record of his people, and striving to assess the many elements upon which Rome's future depended.

He saw behind him one of the miracles of history. A little fortified town, the centre of a community of yeomen, had within four centuries of her foundation made herself the mistress of all Italy. Two centuries later she controlled the shores of the Mediterranean and a large part of the empire of Alexander; her inconsiderable hills had become as famous as the Acropolis or the Pyramids; the mountain torrent which washed her walls was a name as familiar to men as the River of Egypt; and her commercial expansion had kept pace with her conquests. The hammer-blows of fate seemed not to weaken but to temper her strength, and to quicken it to fresh achievements. But in this amazing development there had been no corresponding adjustment of her constitution.[1] She still

[1] It should be noted that the failure of the Republic to govern an empire was due to defects in the administrative machine, not in doctrine and principle. The special court,

maintained the antique forms of the old city-state, forms continually transgressed or disregarded, but still in theory inviolate. A municipality attempted to govern half the world, and a most curious and delicately balanced municipality at that. The extension of her boundaries had been achieved rather by accident than by design, for it was her desire to be secure in Italy that had forced an empire into her reluctant hands. Her settled policy had always been anti-expansionist, which explains her slowness to revise her mechanism of government.

In that government the cardinal principle, since the Law of the Twelve Tables, was the sovereignty of the Roman people. But the people were only the ultimate authority, and they reigned rather than governed — inevitably, since in practice they meant only the half-million dwellers within the city boundaries. Their power lay in the choice of magistrates, and the actual work of government was in the hands of these magistrates, and of the Senate which represented the collective wisdom and the essential tradition of Rome. The old distinction of patrician and plebeian had now little meaning; the new aristocracy was a nobility of office, made up of those families which had held high posts in the state. The aversion of such a body to foreign conquests is intelligible enough when it is remembered that a new province meant an additional governor, and that an increase in magistrates by swelling its numbers diminished its exclusive pride and effective control.[1]

Destiny proved too strong for the Senate, and undesired conquests tumbled into its lap, for there was in

administering the *jus gentium*, was established as early as 242 B.C. The theory behind this remarkable innovation will be found in Cicero's famous definition of true law, *de Rep.*, III, 2, one of the few passages in the work which, previous to the discovery of the Vatican palimpsest in 1822, was known to the world through its quotation by Lactantius.

[1] This point has been fully treated by Prof. Marsh in *The Founding of the Roman Empire*, ch. I.

Rome a fierce instinct of growth which defied limits. It made halting efforts to preserve its ancient prestige. The number of praetors was increased, and the system of pro-magistracies enabled it to give the existing officers double duties. But this did not solve the problem, for the number of foreign governorships soon exceeded the desired quota. If human ingenuity fails in an urgent task, fate may take a hand. There was still a residuum of power in the Roman Assembly, and in a crisis which seriously affected them the Roman people could insist on appointing some favourite general or politician to a special and overruling command. With this innovation the Republic in its strict sense came to an end. The new empire had grown too big and too difficult for the old machine. When the Senate or People appointed a great man to meet some urgent need and gave him an army, the ancient governance was sapped in its foundations. An emergency expedient, tacked on to the old forms, proved more potent than them all.

These were facts which every thinking Roman of the day admitted. A vast empire had been unwillingly won, an empire of which the natural frontiers were recognized as destined sooner or later to be the Atlantic, the African desert, the Euphrates, the Danube, and the Rhine. In the East there was the menace of Parthia, and the thunder-cloud of the Germanic peoples hung darkly in the North. Inside the Roman bounds many of the provinces were muttering volcanoes. No serious mechanism of provincial government had been evolved. There was no permanent civil service. The governors were changed annually, and it depended wholly on their individual characters whether their terms of office were equitable or oppressive. The revenues from the provinces, which were the chief source of Rome's income, were farmed out to joint-stock companies of Roman capitalists. There was inadequate control by the Senate; indeed, the fact that money and men could be got from the provinces without the Senate's authority was a direct peril to the Senate's prestige. The Roman people had no craving for a dapper uniformity, and, being raw to the business, were content to accept any system that would work; 'they value,' said one of their later historians, 'the reality of empire and disregard its empty forms.' [1] But some principles there must be, however elastic, and serious system there was none. 'All the provinces are mourning,' Cicero told his countrymen; 'all the free peoples are complaining.... The Roman people can no longer withstand ... their complaints, their lamentations and their tears.' [2]

Rome herself had been for a century the arena of a struggle between the Optimates, the conservative nobility of office which desired to perpetuate the rule of the Senate, and the Populares, the radical reformers who sought change by the medium of the Assembly. Both claimed a constitutional warrant for their deeds; both consistently crashed through the fundamentals of the constitution. The chief weapon of both was the emergency appointment of a High Command, a special magistrate with dictatorial powers,[3] a Sulla, a Pompey, a Caesar — always permissible in a crisis, but now a regular practice. The extreme medicine of the constitution, in Burke's phrase, had become its daily bread. For four hundred years the centre of gravity had been in the Senate; now it was shifting no man could say whither. 'The accretions of ages had changed a curious but comparatively simple type of polity into a jumble of constitutional law and custom, through which even the keen eyes of a Roman jurist could not pierce, and which even his capacity for fictitious interpretation and the invention of compromises could not

---

[1] Tac., *Ann.*, xv, 31.　　　[2] *in Verr.*, iii, 87.
[3] For the extraordinary commands see Hammond, *The Augustan Principate*, 14 *sqq.*

reduce to a system.'[1] But the theoretic anomaly mattered little compared with the practical breakdown. The Assembly could not govern at all, and the Senate, with the twin tasks of administering an empire and curbing the new democracy, failed in both. Slowly it was realized that the necessary reforms could only come from the quarter where the true power now resided — the High Command, the individual who had been given an overriding authority and had an army behind him.

It must come in the end to the sword — this the most pacific and legally-minded had been forced to admit. Between the conservatives who would not bow to the logic of facts, and the radicals who demanded changes which they did not clearly envisage, there was no hope of compromise. Armies, a new kind of army, had become the only arbiter. In old days every citizen had been a soldier, who served unpaid in the little wars. According to Livy, the protracted siege of Veii first compelled the payment of troops. The struggle with Carthage and the consequent Spanish wars inaugurated a long-service system; the defeat of Hannibal imposed on Rome the penalty of an empire, and grandiose campaigns for which the citizens were most unwillingly conscripted. Marius accordingly made the army a volunteer force, enlisted under a particular general for a particular campaign, and so fundamentally changed its character. The fortunes of the soldiers were now linked with those of their commander; he alone could procure them their due reward, and their loyalty was owed to him rather than to the State. A popular general who could raise men and attract their allegiance had a weapon so potent that it wholly upset the balance of the constitution. Rome had no standing army in Italy and only small forces in the provinces; when an emergency came an army had to be improvised; only a

[1] Greenidge, *Rom. Public Life*, 146.

general of repute could get recruits, and for that service
he could make his own terms. The Senate had no hold
upon an army's loyalty. The High Command, ever since
distant wars began, had become a recognized part of the
state machinery. Sulla, Pompey and Julius had revealed
it as the major part. Was the ancient civic constitution
destined to give way to a military satrapy?

Octavius — he was not for nothing the scion of banking stock — looked beyond the political conundrum to
the economic problems of the land. These in the stress
of wars and tumults had been forgotten, but they were
there in the background, an eternal irritant. The Roman economy was unbalanced. The importation of cheap
grain had ruined the old peasant proprietors. Some had
turned successfully from wheat to olives and vines, but
many had gone under, and what had once been arable
land was now rough pasture, farmed by joint-stock companies or individual capitalists by means of slave labour.
Rome was not self-supporting, and depended precari-
ously for her food upon the continued command of the
sea. The system of corn doles had pauperized her citizens. The city itself was a centre of world-wide financial
operations — as a banker's grandson he knew them well
and although the north side of the Forum was a nest of
banks and stock exchanges, her industrial life was meagre,
and her commerce, at least in Roman hands, was on a
narrow scale. The merchant had little purchase in the
State, for he had never succeeded in getting the harbour
at Ostia improved, and for his larger vessels was compelled to use Puteoli, a hundred and fifty miles away;
moreover, most people did not think him quite respectable. In a slave-owning society trade and industry are
always at a discount. The public finance was grotesque.
In Italy there was no direct taxation; the revenue came
from the rents of public lands, the salt monopoly and one

or two small duties: the bulk of the state income was provincial tribute collected on so preposterous a system that scarcely half of what the provincials paid came to the exchequer. The total Roman income was perhaps three million pounds, and the meagreness of the result was commensurate with the crudity of the methods. Octavius was enough of a financier to have little respect for Rome's financial apparatus.

He was enough of a moralist and philosopher, too, to be uneasy about less ponderable things. In the lower classes the old Roman stock was nearly extinct, and the men who voted in the Assembly were a conglomerate of all races. It has been calculated that some ninety per cent were of foreign extraction,[1] and their source of origin was largely the East. The poorer citizens were little more than parasites, fed with free state bread, amused by free state shows, superb material for the demagogue. The middle classes were rarely industrialists or merchants in the honourable sense; the rich among them made their fortunes chiefly by farming the state rents and taxes, by army contracts, by dealing in slaves, and by a kind of banking which might be better described as speculative money-lending.[2] The aristocrats by birth had either joined the 'new men' in the race for wealth, or had become stiff relic-worshippers and pedants of ancestry. As sprung himself from the bourgeoisie, Octavius had suffered from their loutish arrogance. Except in the rural districts and a few old-fashioned city homes the traditional Roman 'gravitas' and 'pietas' had become things of the past.

It was not a pleasing picture to contemplate for a young man, country-bred, gravely educated, a lover of a life that seemed to be vanishing and of a past separated

[1] This is the view of Tenney Frank (based upon vol. VI of the *C. I. L.*), *Econ. Hist. of Rome*, 213. Cf. Cic., *pro Flacco*, 17.

[2] See Ward Fowler, *Soc. Life at Rome*, ch. III. The *locus classicus* is Polyb., VI, 17.

by a great gulf from the present. One thing was clear. The elaborate checks and balances of the constitution had resulted only in the loss of all responsibility. That constitution was 'the chaotic result of attempts to arrest internal revolution, and of feeble and undirected efforts to adjust the relation of outworn powers. A state in which three popular assemblies has each the right of eliciting the sovereign will of the people, possesses no organization which can satisfy the need for which constitutions exist — the ordered arrangement of all the wants of civic life by means of a series of acts possessing perpetual validity.'[1] The position of the Senate was no less anomalous and impotent. The power of the holders of successive High Commands was a return to barbarism. The whole of Rome's government had broken down, and what was to replace it? Could it ever be replaced? Could a people that had failed to rule a city rule the world? Had not Rome's success been her ruin?

He had heard the Senate's defence, put magisterially by Cicero and angrily by the ordinary conservative. It was simply that the Republic had worked well enough till the machine was put out of gear by the triumvirate of Julius and Pompey and Crassus. The constitution was a balanced thing, as the Greek Polybius had long ago argued, an adroit mingling of monarchy, aristocracy and democracy. The magistrates, with their right of initiative in Senate and Assembly, had ample executive powers, which were tempered by the Senate's authority in matters of policy. The veto of the tribunes protected the individual. The Senate represented the embodied ability and experience of the state, while the popular election of magistrates gave public opinion a constitutional means of expressing itself.[2] Let Rome return to the beaten

[1] Greenidge, *op. cit.*, 261.
[2] Cicero in his *de Republica* and *de Legibus*, basing himself upon Panaetius and Polyb-

track, to the old ways, and all would be well. But to the young man's clear mind it was plain that there could be no such returning. The traditional machine had been cranky for a century and was now damaged past repair. So long as there was an empire the High Commands must remain, and with them the dictatorial armies with whom the power lay. Was there any solution? Must the choice lie between the dynasts and the bombasts, between barbarism and muddle?

These were academic meditations, Octavius suddenly reminded himself, for he had forgotten Julius. The dynast, who was his great-uncle, had driven all others from the field, and had the Senate awed into stillness by his shadow and the world quiet under his hand. This man had a new way of life for Rome. Octavius had heard him expound it during late watches in the camp, in his quiet reedy voice, when the eyes in the lean face seemed in the lamplight to have the masterful luminosity of Jove's eagle. He had heard the matter discussed by Julius's friends. Word had come during later weeks to Apollonia of edicts which were the first steps in the new policy. He tried to piece the fragments into a body of doctrine.

Law and order must be restored. The empire must be governed, and there must be a centre of power. The Roman world required a single administrative system. This could not be given by the People, for a mob could not govern. It could not be given by the Senate, which had shown itself in the highest degree incompetent, and in any case had no means of holding the soldiers' loyalty. Only a man could meet the need, a man who had the undivided allegiance of an army, and that the only army.

ius, found the nearest approach to the ideal 'mixed' polity in the pre-Gracchan Republic — 'Tenuit igitur hoc in statu senatus rem publicam temporibus illis ut in populo libero pauca per populum, pleraque senatus auctoritate... gererentur, atque uti consules potestatem haberent tempore dumtaxat annuam, genere ipso ac jure regiam.' de Rep., II, 56. Cf. Polyb., VI, 3, 7, 11.

A general without an army was a cypher, as Pompey had found, and, since an army was now a necessity, he who controlled it must be the master of the state. The idea of a personal sovereign, which had come from Greece and the East and had long been hovering at the back of Roman minds, must now become a fact, for it was the only alternative to anarchy.

This was Julius's cardinal principle. It followed from it that the old autocracy of the Optimates and the Senate must disappear. That indeed had happened. Julius had always denied — it was one of the few charges which annoyed him — that he had destroyed the Republic; he had only struck at the tyranny of a maleficent growth which had nothing republican about it. He had already quietly shelved the Senate, though he treated it with elaborate respect. He and the new civil service which he was creating would be the mechanism of rule. He himself would appoint all the provincial governors and would be responsible for their honesty and competence. He would rebuild the empire on a basis of reason and humanity.

It was to be a new kind of empire. Something had been drawn from the dreams of Alexander, but for the most part it was the creation of his own profound and audacious mind. There were to be wide local liberties. He proposed to decentralize, to establish local government in Italy as the beginning of a world-wide system of free municipalities. Rome was to be only the greatest among many great and autonomous cities. There was to be a universal Roman nation, not a city with a host of servile provinces, and citizenship in it should be open to all who were worthy.[1] The decadence of the Roman plebs would be redeemed by the virility of the new peoples.

[1] He gave the franchise to Cisalpine Gaul, while it remained a province, which shows that he saw no inconsistency between provincial status and full Roman citizenship. For the very different attitude of Augustus see the story of Suet., *Div. Aug.*, 40.

It was a great conception, and, as expounded by
Julius's eager, winning voice, with his famous 'facultas
dicendi imperatoria,' it had at first fired the young man's
fancy. It was practical too, not the whimsy of a philosopher but the policy of an experienced statesman. Combined with it were elaborate legal and financial reforms.
There was a broad scheme of economic development, of
which Octavius was getting word from correspondents
who knew his interest in such things; colonizing on the
grand scale, state help for Italian agriculture and empire
commerce, new ports and harbours, the reclamation of
waste lands, a ship canal through the isthmus of Corinth,
the rebuilding of derelict cities which were commercial
key-points. The spirit which had conquered a world was
busy re-shaping that world.

The first impact of this policy on Octavius's mind had
left it in bewildered and docile admiration. But, as he
thought over it during the winter months, he had begun
to doubt not the wisdom but the feasibility of some of it.
He did not care greatly for the imperial citizenship idea.
He believed that the Italian race was immeasurably the
superior of any other, and he did not wish to see it lost in
a polyglot welter. He came of a business stock which
prided itself on its *tact des choses possibles*. Conservative
stock, too, for at least half of his kin had been on the side
of the Optimates. He loved the old ways of the land, and
had no natural craving for revolution. Militarism in
itself he distrusted. So did Julius, who had often declared that no nation could be permanently ruled by
martial law; but was the military element not dominant
in his great-uncle's plan? He had cordially disliked the
wild talk he had heard in the camp from excited soldiers
and in Rome from Caesarian demagogues. As he read
the case, the world demanded peace and law, not liberties
and privileges. That meant a return to the settled ways

with which men were familiar, which in turn meant the restoration in some form of the Republic. Now to the ordinary Roman the Republic was meaningless without the Senate, and the Senate Julius had turned into a farce. There was a deep-seated public opinion which even genius could not flout with impunity. If Julius had not had this preponderantly on his side after he crossed the Rubicon he would never have defeated Pompey. In the long run popular sentiment would wear down the glory of any conqueror. The tough, exclusive urban conservatism of the old city-state was still a potent thing. Was it wise to begin by neglecting it? Could not some way be found to preserve at any rate the old forms, and to conciliate the aristocracy, for some governing class there must be, even if it were on a new and better basis? He found himself almost in agreement with old Cicero, whom Julius was apt to treat with a kindly contempt.

As Octavius puzzled over the matter one reflection haunted his mind. His great-uncle had already begun his work. Many things had been achieved which could not be undone. Rome was committed to a course which involved some kind of personal sovereignty. Julius was now a man of fifty-eight, and the ailments of age were crowding upon him. On a day not too far distant the gods would send for him. Who would succeed him in the government of the world? Rome would not tolerate a hereditary monarchy in the ordinary sense, but it was certain that Julius must nominate a successor, and many little things of late had suggested on whom his choice would fall. With a thrill in which pride and fear were mingled the young man realized that the world's next master might be himself.

III

On an afternoon in late March a freedman of his mother's household arrived in Apollonia with a letter for Octavius. It contained fateful news. The date was the 15th of March, and it told him that on that very day Julius had been murdered in the Senate House. It did not say by whom, only by 'his enemies.' 'The time has come,' Atia wrote, 'when you must play the man, decide, and act, for no one can tell the things that may come forth.' Grave words for one who did not use inflated speech.

The news leaked out, in an hour the town was full of it, the soldiers heard it, and that evening Octavius's lodgings were thronged by those who proffered help. The citizens promised him a safe asylum, the troops their help to avenge the murdered Julius and win the heritage that was his by right. Gently he put them by, and till late in the night he was closeted with his friends. Some, like Agrippa and Salvidienus Rufus, would have had him strike at once, and march on Rome at the head of the Macedonian legions.[1] Others — perhaps Maecenas was among them — counselled him to play for safety, to go forthwith to Italy and spy out the land before committing himself. He chose the latter course. It took a day or two to get a ship, and when found, it was a poor one, and it was over yeasty seas that he crossed to Hydruntum (Otranto), the nearest point on the Calabrian shore. Already he had adopted a policy of caution, for he avoided the populous Brundisium.

The day on which Atia's freedman brought the letter was the last of Octavius's youth. The news shattered his ease and fevered his mind. For the great Julius he had felt something more than the hero-worship of a boy

[1] Vell., ii, 59, 5; App., iii, 10; Nic., 16.

OCTAVIUS AT SIXTEEN
(British Museum)

and the pride of a kinsman; he had formed for him one of the rare affections of a nature not easily kindled to love. The thought of him, pulled down like a noble stag by curs, maddened him and made his first impulse one of hot revenge. That passion he curbed at once. Revenge there would be, but it must be a careful and calculated thing. At present he knew little. He did not know who were the murderers, and he suspected that he might find strange figures in the conspiracy. He did not know if he was Julius's heir; he was his next of kin, but there had been no formal adoption. He put aside the entreaties of Agrippa and the legions, for he knew little of war, and had no reason to think that he had any special military talent. To appear in Italy as an amateur dynast might end in a grim fiasco. He realized that he stood on a razor edge. He was resolved to win through to fortune, but he must first discover his tools. Somehow or other he would wear the Caesarian mantle, but he must wait for the right moment to don it. Infinite caution, tight-lipped, unshakable patience, these must be his rule.

Up till now he had been open in manner, easy of access, a little quick of temper but readily appeased, with an engaging boyishness which matched well with his handsome face. Now the gaiety of youth died in him. His countenance became a mask. As a token of mourning he let his beard grow,[1] and did not shave for six years. His health declined and his skin grew blotched. He buttoned himself up, and kept his thoughts secret from even his dearest friends. The seal which he used bore the image of a sphinx.[2] All the forces of his being were massed behind one imperious resolve.

[1] That is to say, he postponed the ceremony of the 'depositio barbae,' which in the great Roman families accompanied the attainment of manhood.

[2] Suet., *Div. Aug.*, 50.

II. THE DISPUTED INHERITANCE

(April 44 B.C.—July 43 B.C.)

Je suis jeune, il est vrai: mais aux âmes bien nées
La valeur n'attend point le nombre des années.

CORNEILLE, *Don Rodrigue.*

I

WHEN Octavius, not yet nineteen, landed in Calabria
on a day in mid-April,[1] he had one fixed resolution; but
it was an emotion and not a policy, for he had as yet no
exact knowledge.[2] He was resolved to avenge the one
great man he had ever known, a man of his own blood
who had treated him with a father's tenderness and had
kindled his imagination by his dreams. He was determined, also, himself to play a major part in Roman
affairs, for Julius had awakened his ambition. But that,
with Julius dead, would be no easy matter. He was conscious that, without the Caesarian mantle to dignify him,
he was only a provincial bourgeois with a tincture of
noble blood; well-to-do, but not with one of the great
fortunes; without powerful connections, inexpert in the
business of politics, and deplorably young. His was the
case of a stripling advancing against giants. The thought
of his impotence maddened him, but, if we may judge the

---

[1] Gardthausen, I, 52–53.

[2] For the mind of Octavius during this year we have little direct evidence. The chief
sources are Cicero's general correspondence, and a few references in the *Res Gestae*.
Suetonius is fairly informative, but Plutarch's lives of contemporaries like Cicero,
Brutus and Antony cast little light on the main figure. Dio is rhetorical and diffuse.
For actual events Appian is the best guide, since he used not only the memoirs of
Augustus but the lost work of Asinius Pollio.

youth by the man, he gave no sign of it to his intimates, but awaited fuller news with a frozen calm.

That news, which reached him when half-way to Brundisium, was startling enough. The murder had been shared in by Julius's old companions in arms, like Decimus Brutus and Trebonius, but the leaders had been the ambitious *arriviste* Gaius Cassius, and Marcus Brutus, Cato's nephew, whom Julius had respected for his portentous gravity. When the deed had been done, the assassins' nerves had cracked and they had fled to the Capitol. Mark Antony, the senior consul, had taken charge of the city with the assistance of Lepidus, the master of the horse. Calpurnia had handed over to him her husband's papers and ready money, and he had summoned a meeting of the Senate for March 17, which had proclaimed a general amnesty and ratified Julius's decrees, both those enacted and those only proposed. That very day, too, he had entertained the murderers at dinner. But wild doings had followed. At the funeral three days later, the veterans of the Caesarian armies had taken charge of the proceedings. The ivory bier had been brought to the Forum, with singers chanting the verse of an old poet, 'I saved those who have been my death.' Then Antony from the Rostra had spoken words which roused the mob to fury.[1] A pyre had been raised in the Forum itself, and the body of Julius became ashes in the midst of such a scene of frenzy and lamentation as Rome had rarely witnessed. Thereafter there had been savage rioting, led by a bogus nephew of Marius, and a hasty exodus of all who had something to lose — Brutus and Cassius, Cicero, Cleopatra, and a medley of nobles and senators.

[1] Suetonius (*Div. Jul.*, 84) denies that Antony made a speech, and Ferrero (III, 27 *n.*) accepts his denial on the ground that Cicero does not mention it in his contemporary letters. But see *ad Att.*, XIV, 10. All other historians accept the speech: App., II, 143–47; Dio, XLIV, 35–49; Plut., *Ant.*, 14.

Antony was in control, and he was playing a subtle game. He had stirred up the mob, and then chastised it. He seemed determined to be no man's enemy. He cultivated the Caesarians, allowing Dolabella to succeed Julius as consul, though he had once violently opposed the appointment, and winning the support of Lepidus by procuring his irregular election as Pontifex Maximus. But he was also conciliatory to the Senate; he himself proposed a decree abolishing the dictatorship for ever; he secured for Brutus permission to be absent from Rome beyond the statutory time permitted to the urban praetor; he even made friendly overtures to Cicero. But he was busiest in another way, for he had much of Julius's wealth in his hands, and from his papers he was perpetually finding new enactments which the Senate had by anticipation given the force of law, which enriched him and consolidated his power, but which most men believed to be forgeries. The more Octavius thought of Antony's doings the less he liked them.

But there was one item of news which outweighed all others. Julius by his will had adopted him as his son. After providing for lavish bequests to every Roman citizen, he had left him three-fourths of his huge fortune, the remaining fourth going to his other great-nephews, Lucius Pinarius and Quintus Pedius.[1] Antony, Decimus Brutus and several others were named as alternate legatees, in case any or all of the nephews declined the bequest. The tidings moved Octavius deeply; the great man, whom he was already sworn to avenge, had singled him out as his successor, the legatee, as he saw it, not only of his name and his wealth, but of his dreams. The Caesarian mantle was now on his shoulders, and no man should pluck it from him.

---

[1] They surrendered their shares to Octavius, having no wish for such a *damnosa hereditas*.

His resolution was soon put to the test, for at Brundisium he found letters from his mother Atia and his stepfather Philippus, urging him to refuse the inheritance.
His mother begged him to come at once to her. Philippus
was an old Pompeian, and a timorous being; to him he
replied that he could not disgrace the name of which
Julius had thought him worthy. Atia, whose counsel
meant much to him,[1] he answered in the famous words in
which Achilles replied to his mother Thetis: 'Now go I
forth that I may light on the destroyer of him I loved:
then will I accept my death whensoever Zeus and the
other immortals will to accomplish it.'[2] But he hastened
to fulfil her commands. She and Philippus were at Puteoli; so also was Cicero, and Caesarians like Balbus and
Hirtius and Pansa, and a crowd of Roman notables. He
would go there and spy out the land. Meantime he must
walk warily. He was the heir of Julius, but none the less
a person of small account, and Antony was in power and,
said rumour, busy helping himself to that part of his inheritance which Julius had deposited in the temple of
Ops to his private order. He was already encumbered
by offers of help from Caesarian veterans who thronged
around him and begged him to lead them to avenge the
murder. He gently put aside such appeals. His first business was to go to Rome to give notice to the urban praetor
that he accepted the inheritance, declare in a public
assembly his plans for administering the will, and have
his adoption officially ratified. One important step he
did take with a view to future possibilities: as Julius's
heir, he sent to Asia for the treasure which Julius had
stored there for the Parthian campaign. For the rest he
was a private citizen, concerned only with his personal

---

[1] Tac., *Dialog.*, 28. The *Dialogus* appears anonymously in the manuscript which con-
tains *Germania* and *Agricola*, but I incline to its Tacitean authorship. Cf., however,
C. Marchesi, *Tacito* (1924), 301 *sqq.*

[2] *Iliad*, XVIII, 98 *sqq.*

rights and duties. His 'pietas,' his devotion to his kinsman's memory, was the flag under which he must enter
public life.[1]

To Puteoli he journeyed by the Appian Way, receiving
on the road embarrassing attentions from colonists and
veterans, some of whom continued in his train. He was
obliged to allow himself to be addressed as Caesar. He
reached his stepfather's villa about the 18th, and found
that, though Philippus was still opposed to his course,
his mother's heart was with him. Next day he met Balbus
and told him his intentions; that loyal Caesarian was the
first outside his family circle to know of them. That day,
too, he called upon Cicero, and the statesman of sixty-two
and the stripling of nineteen delicately manœuvred for
position, and sought to read each other's minds.

Cicero was the last of the philosophic republicans. For
a time he had been Julius's friend; had he not once written, 'I burn with love for him'? In the final struggle he
had half-heartedly gone over to Pompey, because his
cause was more or less the cause of the Senate: but after
Pharsalus Julius had treated him kindly, and the old man
had turned to letters in a new fever of composition.
Julius's death had opened vistas to a mind which had
little contact with reality. He had passionately approved
the murder, made gods of Brutus and Cassius, and laboured to stiffen the purpose of the bewildered conspirators. But Antony's sinister figure had blocked the road
to a restored republic, and now he sat in his country villa,
hurling letters at a multitude of friends, sometimes buoy-
ant with hope, oftener shrill with despair, striving to
steady his thoughts by writing his treatise on 'Old Age,'
planning with his inexhaustible zest a new work on 'Duty,'
a philosopher who had lost all philosophic balance. He

[1] M. A. Levi, *Ottaviano capoparte*, I, 88 ff. On the meaning of Julius's will, see *C. A.
H.*, IX, 724–26.

was consumed with most human hates, and tantalized by dreams of being once again, as in Catiline's day, his country's saviour. Octavius had known him slightly in Rome, had studied his *de Republica* and his *de Legibus*, and had learned from them certain doctrines which he was always to remember.[1] As a student himself of Panaetius and Posidonius, he revered a master in their craft. There was much in Cicero's creed with which he agreed, and he hoped to get from him some notion of the purpose and strength of the faction which had been the death of Julius.

So, as a respectful youth who had no thought beyond his family duties, he approached the old statesman. He addressed him as 'father,' avoided all controversial matters, sadly declared that the present situation was intolerable, and humbly sought guidance. He made a favourable impression, which was somewhat lessened by his entourage of noisy Caesarians. Cicero wrote to Atticus that the young man seemed quite devoted to him, though he could not see how it was possible for one with such antecedents to be a good citizen. He considered him harmless and colourless; it maddened him to think that this youth could go to Rome in safety while his heroes, Brutus and Cassius, dare not show their faces there: but he found a slightly malicious comfort in the thought that he would have a tussle with Antony before he got his inheritance.[2]

From Cicero Octavius got more enlightenment than he gave. He realized that he himself was still an inconsiderable person, a mere claimant who had to translate his rights into facts. The republicans were not greatly concerned about him; the humbler Caesarians might crowd around him, but the Caesarian leader, Antony, was plun-

---

[1] For the influence of Cicero's thought upon Augustus, see A. Oltramare's 'La réaction ciceronienne et les débuts du Principat' in *Rev. des E. L.* (1932), 58–90.

[2] Cic., *ad Brut.*, I, 17, 5; *ad Att.*, XIV, 10, 11, 12.

dering his heritage. Cicero had been cordial, because he
saw in this stripling a wedge which might split the faction
of his enemies. The task which he had entered upon had
suddenly taken on a new magnitude. He would have to
fight, not only the assassins, but the friends of Julius.
Wariness was more than ever his duty. In the long run
he must range himself implacably against the 'liberators,'
but first he had to checkmate Antony, and for that the
republicans might be useful temporary allies. Therefore
he must keep close to Cicero, in whom new qualities
seemed to have been born. The latter's conservatism,
partly a lawyer's reverence for ancient things, partly the
sentiment of a provincial for the old aristocracy, had become a fighting creed. He had lost his former dream of a
concordia ordinum, and had become a furious partisan.
His personal vanity had been transmuted into something
nobler, an ambition to save the state a second time from
brigandage, and for that end to face the uttermost risks.
Courage, a desperate courage, was already, in spite of
temporary hesitations and fears, becoming the breath of
the old man's being. Beyond doubt Cicero must not be
neglected.

Octavius went on to Rome, which he reached by the
end of the first week of May. He found the city quiet for
the moment, and was warmly greeted by the mob, who
were beneficiaries under Julius's will and who looked to
his heir for the money, and by old soldiers of the Gallic
wars. A halo round the sun, as he entered the city, seemed
to promise the favour of the gods. There were three An-
tonies in office, Marcus the consul, Gaius the praetor, and
Lucius the tribune. To Gaius he formally announced his
acceptance of the adoption, while Lucius introduced him
to the statutory public meeting. There he made a discreet speech, promised to pay every citizen at once the
bequest of Julius, and to celebrate, if necessary at his

own expense, the games in July appointed for Julius's victories. On the amnesty to the murderers he was silent, thereby grievously disappointing Cicero.[1] Nothing untoward occurred except that at some games postponed from April he was forbidden by a tribune to use Julius's gilded chair, and the applause of the middle-class spectators told him that the republicans had still many well-wishers in Rome. Lucius Antonius, too, proved curiously obstructive in the matter of the law required to ratify his adoption.

But it was the conduct of Mark Antony that gave him concern. The consul had shown his view of the unimportance of Octavius by leaving the city in the last week of April [2] before his arrival. He was now busy in Campania, recruiting a bodyguard of veterans and Syrians, some of whom he was sending on in batches to Rome. Octavius must await his return to get cash to pay Julius's legacies. He had a large fortune of his own, and he could also draw upon his mother, but in view of what the future might require he was not inclined to deplete his private account. He was now the owner of the bulk of his great-uncle's estate, but most of it was in real property and slaves, and threatened, too, with many claims at law. The ready money was that deposited in the temple of Ops, and the big sum which Calpurnia had handed over on the night of the murder; the latter Antony had annexed, and the former he was using to pay his debts and purchase partisans. He must have an early settlement with this man who now straddled his path like a Colossus.

The character of Mark Antony is no easier for the historian to assess than it was at that moment for Octavius. The latter had met him often, for Antony had patched up his quarrel with Julius, had ridden by the conqueror's side after Munda, had been his colleague in the consul-

<hr/>

[1] *ad Att.*, xv, 2.   [2] *ad Att.*, xiv, 15; cf. Rice Holmes, I, 190.

ship, and had been often spoken of as his destined heir. Handsome in the heavy Roman way, gross in habit, inordinate in appetites, through a youth of debt and debauchery he had preserved what Shakespeare makes Brutus call his 'quick spirit.' As a soldier he had not the professional talents of Labienus or Quintus Cicero, but he had something of the 'Caesariana celeritas.' [1] He had a hasty temper, but it was easily appeased, and his humour, good fellowship and zest for life gave him a ready popularity and a genuine power of leadership. Octavius had neither trusted nor liked him. He suspected, as many did, his loyalty to Julius. This magnificent blustering human animal made no appeal to a fastidious youth in delicate health. To him Antony seemed the *faux bonhomme*; he was not a great soldier, he had not the rudiments of culture,[2] though he had a kind of rough eloquence, and no one had hitherto suspected him of statecraft. But now, within sight of his fortieth year,[3] he seemed to have changed his character. As Octavius reviewed what he had been told of his recent doings, he must have reflected that he had played his part with notable moderation and skill. He had kept his hold on the Caesarians without breaking finally with the republicans, and had made himself the first power in the state. He had used Julius's money to buy himself allies, and now he was in Campania recruiting a bodyguard from Julius's old soldiers. Rumour spoke of him as showing the effect of his past in a violent irritability and bouts of neurotic excitement, and of exhibiting a novel anxiety about his personal safety.[4] However that might be, he had so far made no mistakes.

---

[1] Cic., *ad Att.*, xvi, 10.

[2] For his bad Latin, see his letter to Cic., *ad Att.*, xiv, 13 a, and Cic., *Phil.*, xiii, 43. There are many tributes to Octavius's literary fastidiousness, *e.g.*, Aul. Gell., xv, 7; Dio, xlv, 2, 7; Tac., *Ann.*, xiii, 3.

[3] The year of Antony's birth is uncertain; it may have been 83, 82 or 81 b.c. App., v, 8, 33; Gardthausen, ii, 5 *n*.

[4] Cic., *ad Att.*, xv, 20 — 'iste qui umbras timet'; *Phil.*, i, 11, 27.

What he had won he would not readily let go. The one hope was that in the long game a cooler head and a more disciplined mind might outplay this brilliant creature of temperament.

Antony returned to Rome about May 20, with his bodyguard of armed veterans who would also vote in any popular assembly. He had purchased with Octavius's money the alliance of Cicero's son-in-law, the ruffianly Dolabella. At once the city became a hot-bed of rumours. Antony meant to disregard the amnesty to the murderers; he was hoping to make himself dictator; he meant to juggle with the high offices at his pleasure; he was publishing imaginary decrees of Caesar to suit his convenience. The 'liberators' were in a panic, and Cicero despaired of the state. A meeting of the Senate had been called for June 1, but few senators put in an appearance. Antony accordingly chose a simpler and more rapid procedure. He had a plebiscite carried extending the provincial commands of the consuls from two to five years. He secured for himself Macedonia and its legions, and Syria for Dolabella. Brutus and Cassius, to whom these provinces had been assigned by Caesar, were offered instead commissionerships of the corn supply, and, when this insulting offer was rejected, they were allotted the minor governments of Crete and Cyrene. Meantime he got his brother to introduce a new agrarian law to conciliate the veterans.

For Octavius he professed only contempt. He spoke of him slightingly as the 'boy' and sneered at his money-lending ancestry. He refused to hand over Julius's fortune, so that the heir had to pay the legacies out of his own pocket. He blocked his candidature for the tribuneship, by insisting upon a legal objection which had been often disregarded. He granted him an interview in Pompey's old house, but kept him waiting in an anteroom, and in his short talk treated him with studied discourtesy.[1] The young man was stirred to a carefully calculated energy. He had his own band of veterans, and in the streets of Rome he denounced Antony as a traitor to Julius's memory, since he had done nothing to avenge him, and had embezzled the monies which should have gone to the people. He declared that he himself would pay the legacies if it cost him his last penny. With a view to the future he wrote to his friends in the Macedonian legions, telling them of his infamous treatment. The climax came in July when the games were celebrated in honour of Julius's victories. Octavius tried again to introduce the gilded chair and was forbidden by Antony, though this time popular feeling was on his side. On the last day a comet appeared in the heavens, the *sidus Julium*, which the populace took as a sign of Julius's reception among the gods, and which even the calm Octavius welcomed as a happy omen.[2] Antony at last awoke to the facts. This young man had a real following among the more ardent Caesarians, and it would be wise to conciliate him. His bodyguard had already remonstrated with him for his cavalier treatment of Julius's heir. He had now secured by a plebiscite in exchange for Macedonia the command in Cisalpine Gaul,[3] together with the Macedonian legions, and, with this trump card in his hand, he could afford to be generous. He agreed to a formal reconciliation.[4]

The friction with Antony had one good result; it strengthened the position of Octavius with the republi-

---

[1] App., III, 14; Nic., 28; Plut., *Ant.*, 16; Vell., II, 60, 3. Antony had not Caesar's tact, who, when he kept Cicero waiting, made ample apology, *ad Att.*, XIV, I.

[2] Pliny, *N. H.*, II, 93. Malcovati, 63.

[3] The date of the *lex de permutatione provinciarum* is uncertain. Ferrero (III, 85) places it after the conclusion of the games, but it was more likely promulgated in the first half of June. See Levi, *Ottaviano capoparte*, I, 77.

[4] Dio, XLV, 8; Nic., 29; Plut., *Ant.*, 16.

cans. He had the wisdom to keep in close touch with Cicero, and the opinion of Cicero weighed heavily with the conservatives. The old statesman was now in a sad frame of mind, torn between duty and self-interest. He was making plans to return to Greece, and then hesitating to leave his native land. His mood was much that of the famous sentence written after his daughter's death: 'The long ages when I shall be no more are more important in my eyes than the brief span of present life, which indeed seems all too long.' [1] His chief dread was Antony, and his chief hope, in spite of the doubts of Brutus, was now Octavius. He wrote of him to Atticus in June, calling him for the first time Octavianus, and thereby acknowledging Julius's adoption:

> I see clearly that he has brains and spirit, and is as well disposed to our heroes as we could desire. But we must carefully consider the degree of reliance that can be placed on him, taking into account his age, his name, his position as Caesar's heir, and his upbringing. He must be trained, and above all he must be alienated from Antony.... He has an excellent disposition, if it only lasts.[2]

After some months of doubt and waiting, Octavius, aided by the sagacity of Agrippa and Maecenas,[3] had devised a policy, a strategic plan which would permit of much opportunism in tactics. His main purpose was to avenge Julius and to carry on his work, which meant that sooner or later he would find himself in implacable opposition to the republican conservatives. Antony shared in the first part of his purpose; but it was now certain that Antony would not, if he could help it, admit him as an ally, but would labour to make himself *de facto* Julius's heir and successor. To bring Antony to reason two things were needed. He must acquire an armed following of his own, by lavish expenditure and adroit propaganda, for

[1] *ad Att.*, XII, 18.   [2] *Ibid.*, XV, 12.   [3] Nic., 31.

after all his name, his adoption, and his heirship made a strong emotional appeal to the Caesarian veterans. In the second place he must keep on good terms with all who feared and distrusted Antony. To these he must appear as a young man seeking only his legal rights, an admirer of Julius but also imbued with a sober republican sentiment. He must continue to speak the 'liberators' fair whatever he felt about them in his heart. His rôle must be that of a mild Caesarian, but a stout anti-Antonian. Gaius Marcellus, the husband of his sister Octavia, was a valuable *trait d'union*, and so was Cicero.

Antony was nervous about this silent, self-contained young man. It was true that Octavius had supported his claim to Cisalpine Gaul as against Decimus Brutus, but, since the latter was one of the principal assassins, he was bound to do so or lose caste with every Caesarian. But he feared his growing popularity with the extreme among the veterans. He was beginning also to lose his temper. Cicero came to Rome at the end of August, and delivered in the Senate the speech known as the First Philippic, which was a dignified criticism of his recent doings and did much to rally the conservatives. Antony showed his nervousness by a preposterous charge against Octavius of attempted murder, for which he could produce no evidence. The young man ridiculed the accusation, and presently all Rome joined in the laughter.[1]

Yet Antony's position might well have seemed impregnable. He had ousted Decimus Brutus from Cisalpine Gaul and next year would also have Celtic Gaul. His friend Dolabella would have Syria, and, if Decimus received Macedonia, it would be without the legions. Brutus and Cassius were disconsidered wanderers. Most of the provincial governors, who had armies at their com-

---

[1] Cicero believed the story and approved, but the wish was father to the thought. *ad Fam.*, xii, 23. It is rejected by Nic., 30, App., iii, 39, and Plut., *Ant.*, 16.

mand, were Caesarians, and likely to be his friends —
Plancus in Celtic Gaul, Asinius Pollio in Further Spain,
and Lepidus who would presently have Hither Spain and
the Narbonese. Things were moving towards a crisis, and
the vital matter was the control of armies. His first business was to get one of his own. He had already his Campanian levies of veterans and condottieri, and four of the
Macedonian legions assigned to him were on the sea. On
October 9 he set out for Brundisium to meet them. His
wife Fulvia went with him; she had once been the wife of
the gangster Clodius, and was one of those terrible women
produced now and then by the Roman stock, unsexed,
implacable, filled with an insane lust of power. She and
his brother Lucius, a feebler version of himself, were now
his chief advisers.

It behoved Octavius to act at once. His reconciliation with Antony had been shattered by the bogus as-
sassination charge, and the two now stood in the public
eye as declared enemies. He sent agents to negotiate
with the Macedonian legions and distribute leaflets setting forth his case, and he himself made a tour of the
colonies of old soldiers in Campania, summoning them
in Julius's name to re-enlist, and offering each man a
bounty of twenty pounds sterling. He must have either
retrieved some of the ready money which Antony had
embezzled, or disposed of some of the real estate for cash,
for it does not appear that he entrenched upon his own or
his mother's private fortune; from now onwards he never
seems to have suffered from financial embarrassment.
He raised three thousand troops, afterwards organized in
two legions. It was a bold step, for he had no legal military command, and no mandate from Senate or people,
and appropriately it is the first deed recorded in the *Res
Gestae*, that summary of the main events in his life: 'At
the age of nineteen years, on my own authority and at my

own cost, I raised the army by means of which I liberated
the republic from the oppression of a tyrannical faction.'
The army, the same army with which he was to triumph
at Actium.[1] He had taken the first step in his campaign
of vengeance.

Antony was less fortunate. At Suessa he purged his
levies by executing a number of soldiers whose loyalty
he distrusted. At Brundisium he found that only three
legions had arrived, the II, and IV and the Martian, and
that Octavius's propaganda had done its work among
them. They were in a difficult temper, angry with Antony
for his apparent supineness as Julius's avenger, and con-
trasting his meagre bounty with the largesse of Octavius.
Antony proceeded to put to death several officers and
some three hundred men, and for a moment seemed to
have quelled the mutiny. He selected a bodyguard with
which he pushed on to Rome, picking up on the way the
Lark.[2] that famous unit of the Gallic wars, and bidding
his other legions follow by the coast road to Ariminum,
which was the way to Cisalpine Gaul.

Octavius had now to face a delicate problem. He had
got an army of a kind, but what was he to do with it? His
strength was far inferior to Antony's, unless he could win
over the Macedonian legions to his side. His power lay
with the Roman populace and the veterans who worshipped the memory of Julius, and with a considerable part
of the bourgeoisie and aristocracy which distrusted Antony. But he was trying to drive two ill-mated horses in
the same harness. The first stood for vengeance on the
murderers, the second either adored the 'liberators' or
shrank from civil war. In his opposition to Antony he
must not alienate those who, while well disposed to

---

[1] See Hardy's ed. of *Mon. Anc.*, 27.

[2] It is not clear where Antony found *Alaudae*; perhaps they were the veterans whom
he had re-enlisted in his journey through Italy in May. For this legion see Suet., *Div.
Jul.*, 24, and Pauly-Wissowa, I, 1295, XII, 1208.

Julius's heir, were on Antony's side against the 'liberators': in cultivating the Caesarians he must somehow keep the confidence of the classes who saw in him a conservative force not inimical to a restored republic. What must be his next step? Should he remain in Campania with his levies, or should he march to Rome and put his fortune to the test?

It was a difficult decision for a young man of nineteen, but Octavius did not hesitate. He bombarded Cicero with letters asking for advice, but his resolution was already fixed. In this decision he showed his capacity for extreme boldness, as in his relations with Cicero he revealed his gift for patient diplomacy. Cicero himself was in a divided mind. He was in favour on the whole of the move to Rome, for Octavius seemed the only defence against Antony, and he had promised to act through the Senate. But the old man was troubled. Octavius was begging him to come to the capital, and save the republic as he had done once before — a shrewd piece of flattery which did not fail of its mark; but he was afraid of Antony, and did not wish to leave the sea-coast and the means of escape abroad, and he could not be quite certain about the young man's policy. He poured out his troubles to Atticus.[1] Octavius was a mere boy. He would oppose Antony, but was it for the sake of the Republic or for himself? The one thing plain was that a new war was imminent, and he longed for Brutus and Cassius, now exiles beyond the sea.

To Rome Octavius went on November 10 with his three thousand, and at once found himself on precarious ground. At the temple of Castor he held a public meeting, where a tribune savagely attacked Antony; he followed in the same vein, dwelling on Julius's great deeds and the indignities he had himself suffered at Antony's hands. The

[1] *ad Att.*, xvi, 8, 9.

speech was one of his few blunders, for it pleased nobody.
His soldiers, many of whom had served with Antony,
jibbed at the attack on their old leader, and Octavius was
forced to disband those who wished to go home, and to
pay further bounties to those who remained. The conservatives, already scared by the youth's audacity, were
offended by his eulogy of Caesar and all that it implied,
and by the ominous words about 'attaining the honours
of my father.' Cicero liked it least of all. In the last
letter to Atticus which we possess, he exclaims, 'What a
speech!' [1] But he found himself now forced by private
reasons of finance to come to Rome, and, with a courage
the more admirable because of his natural timidity, the
old man girded his loins for his last battle.[2]

Octavius could not remain in Rome, for Antony with
his bodyguard and the Lark was at its gates. He was on
more treacherous ground than ever, for he was beginning
to lose the confidence of the Caesarians, and the conservatives did not take him seriously. He and Agrippa — for
he had no other adviser except half-hearted relatives like
Philippus and Marcellus — two young men not yet
twenty, were defying the most noted soldier of the age,
who could dispose of formidable armies and who appealed
to the same popular emotion as they did themselves. At
the same time they were courting the alliance of an aristocracy whose politics they detested and who were laugh-
ing at them as children playing at war. Antony, too, was
busy with slanders, sneering at Octavius's humble birth,
and spreading tales of unmentionable vices.[3] Octavius
was playing the only game permitted him, but when he

---

[1] *ad Att.*, XVI, 15; cf. Tyrrell, VI, XVIII, *n.*

[2] He arrived on Dec. 9. I follow Rice Holmes (I, 204) in his interpretation of *ad Fam.*,
XI, 5.

[3] Cic., *Phil.*, III, VI, 15; VIII, 21; Suet., *Div. Aug.*, 68. The youth of Octavius was a
target for scandalous tales, which carry their own refutation, for it is difficult to see
how a young man in poor health, with desperate problems daily confronting him, could
have had the time or the inclination for excesses.

left Rome for Etruria, where by a lavish further expenditure he collected further recruits, he must have seen little
light in his path.

Suddenly the situation changed. Antony entered the
capital about November 20, in full military panoply, having left most of his troops at Tibur, but bringing a bodyguard sufficient to overawe the citizens. He was in a vile
temper, and issued an edict abusing Octavius and summoning a meeting of the Senate for the 24th. That day
he did not appear; Cicero says he was drunk, but the
natural explanation is the news which he had from Tibur.
For the Martian legion, remembering its old kindness for
Octavius and swayed by his propaganda, had disobeyed
orders and turned off the coast road to Ariminum, and
was now at Alba Longa. Antony hastened thither, and
was met by closed gates and a shower of arrows from the
walls. He attended the postponed meeting of the Senate
on the 28th, where he hustled through a number of
decrees and allotted certain vacant provinces to his own
supporters. Then he hurried to Tibur, where he had word
that the IV legion had followed the example of the Martian. With his new recruits, the Lark, and the II legion,
he started for Ariminum, leaving his brother Lucius to
bring on the remaining Macedonian legion, the XXXV,
which had now arrived at Brundisium.[1] He had already
ordered Decimus Brutus to hand over Cisalpine Gaul.
Decimus replied that he held his province at the commands of the Senate and the People but, realizing that he
could not meet Antony in the open field, and must wait
upon help from Rome, marched south, and about the
middle of December shut himself up in Mutina (Modena)
and prepared to stand a siege.

Octavius had become the sole hope of the republicans,
a more stalwart hope, for he had got himself a considerable

[1] See Rice Holmes, I, 201–02.

army — two legions of Campanian veterans, one of
Etrurian recruits, the IV and the Martian. Moreover, he
had been in treaty with Decimus Brutus, following his
habit of leaving no possible ally unconciliated.[1] He discreetly acquiesced in the election of one of the principal
assassins, the 'envious Casca,' as tribune. The 'liberators'
ceased to jeer at his youth, and now saw in him a saviour,
the republic's sole champion. Cicero when he reached
Rome found himself the civilian leader in the absence of
both consuls, and Cicero had now decided that Julius's
heir must be trusted.

So, while Octavius slowly marched northward on the
track of Antony, many fateful things happened in Rome.
Dread of a new civil war lay on all parties, even on Antony, who was busy manœuvring for position, and in-
triguing with the governors of the western provinces,
Lepidus, Plancus and Pollio, and who had no desire for
an immediate clash of arms. Only Octavius and Cicero
were determined on what they believed to be inevitable.
Cicero, indeed, had cast all literary preoccupations behind
him, and was now eager to ride the storm. In the words
of Ferrero, 'the audacious figure of the old orator stood
amidst the universal vacillation like a huge erratic boulder
in the midst of a plain.'[2] He had become in his own eyes
the guide towards that state which he had drawn in his
de Republica. His Second Philippic against Antony had
been published, and he was busy corresponding with the
western proconsuls on whose decision he saw that the
issue must ultimately depend. On December 20 he delivered his Third Philippic, a moderate speech in which he
proposed votes of confidence in Decimus and Octavius,
and carried a resolution providing for a meeting of the
Senate on January 1, under the new consuls Hirtius and
Pansa, to annul Antony's disposition of the provinces.

[1] Dio, XLV, 15.   [2] III, 129.

In the Fourth Philippic, spoken on that day to the people, he flung down to Antony the gage of battle.

Cicero was now clearly pledged to Octavius's support. He had addressed him publicly as 'Caesar.' January 1 came and the Senate met under the protection of armed guards. There was a long debate in which Antony's more moderate friends urged that before declaring him a public enemy an embassy should be sent to negotiate. Cicero replied in that masterpiece of invective known as the Fifth Philippic, in which he inveighed against Antony and pinned his faith to Octavius. 'What god,' he asked, 'has given to the Roman people this god-like youth?' He compared his exploits with those of the young Pompey. He took upon himself to guarantee his good faith:

> I know intimately the young man's every feeling. Nothing is dearer to him than the free state, nothing has more weight with him than your influence, nothing is more desired by him than the good opinion of virtuous men, nothing more delightful to him than true glory.... I venture even to pledge my word that Gaius Caesar will always be as loyal a citizen as he is today, and as our most fervent wishes and prayers desire.'[1]

The Senate stuck to the embassy proposal but agreed to continue military preparations, and appointed one of the new consuls to take supreme command of the army. Honours were decreed for Octavius; he was given the rank of senator; the state would pay the bounties he had promised to the two Macedonian legions which had joined him; he was to be entitled to stand for the consulship ten years before he attained the statutory age; a gilded statue was to be set up in his honour;[2] he was joined with the two consuls in command of the army, with the 'imperium' of a pro-praetor. His position was now regularized,

[1] *Phil.*, v, 16, 43, 50, 51.
[2] An honour granted in the past three centuries only to Sulla, Pompey and Julius. Vell., II, 61.

though, since he had the consuls as colleagues, he had not
the chief authority for which he had hoped. On January 7
he assumed the fasces, the symbol of his command.[1] He
had already been offered them by his troops, but had
prudently declined, preferring to wait for the Senate's
grant.[2]

II

The first months of the year 43 B.C. were full of feeble
manœuvring for position. The Senate, in spite of Cicero,
was unwilling to declare Antony an enemy of the state and
so formally embark upon war. Antony, though he could
beyond doubt have crushed Decimus had he acted at
once, was anxious to strengthen his forces and make certain of the western proconsuls, so he was very willing to
protract negotiations; Mutina he must have believed that
he could take whenever he pleased. He replied to the
senatorian embassy by announcing his willingness to
give up Cisalpine Gaul, if he were given Celtic Gaul with
six legions till the end of the year 39, if his veterans were
rewarded, all his decrees confirmed, and no question raised
about the monies he had taken from the state treasury.
When this reply was received, the Senate, under the compulsion of Cicero, decreed on February 2 a state of war.
But the Antonians managed to protract proceedings, and
Pansa, the other consul, did not march till March 19.

Octavius during these weeks had grave cause for anxi-

---

[1] *C. I. L.*, x, 8375.

[2] App., III, 48. January 7 was to Octavius the 'dies accepti imperii' *Mon. Anc.*, I,
3–5; *C. I. L.*, XII, 433. The exact meaning of *imperium* and its different connotations
have involved scholars in disputes in which the legal merges with the metaphysical. It
has been urged that he inherited *Imperator* as a praenomen from Julius, and used it as
soon as he accepted his adoption. (Momms., *Staatsr.*, II, 2, 767, based upon Dio, LII,
40–41; cf. Suet., *Div. Jul.*, 76.) For different views see *C. A. H.*, IX, 728; Greenidge,
op. cit., 337 *n.*; and McFayden, *Hist. of Title Imperator* (1920). I think it improbable
that Octavius accepted the praenomen at the start, for, if so, Cicero would have mentioned it.

ety. His colleague Hirtius was a sick man, and wholly supine. He was not too certain of the loyalty of his own command. While Antony was jeering at his youth,[1] he was also writing to him privately, warning him that Cicero would play him false, and that no anti-Caesarian could ever be his friend.[2] On this latter point Octavius had much confirmatory evidence. Their negotiations with Antony showed how half-hearted the conservatives were in the cause in which he had become their ally. Cicero's burning Philippics were proof of his detestation of Antony, but remarks of his were now being circulated which showed his lukewarmness towards Octavius. Moreover, the news from overseas was putting a new complexion on affairs. Brutus and Cassius had been assigned Macedonia and Syria; the former province Brutus had occupied and had got himself a formidable army, while Cassius was on his way to do the same thing with Syria, and he had been entrusted with the punishment of Dolabella, who had murdered the governor of Asia. With these new senatorial armies in the East the conservatives might soon be in a position to dispense with himself. Further, though Lepidus spoke with an uncertain voice, Plancus in Celtic Gaul seemed to be firmly on the Senate's side. There was every reason to fear that presently he, who had been only accepted as a weapon, would be discarded. Octavius never showed more notably his amazing self-command than in this difficult time. He took no hasty step; he realized that his first business was to clip Antony's wings and make himself formidable. So he behaved as a dutiful servant of the state, waiting on orders, and occupied his too ample leisure in improving his literary and oratorical style.[3]

But the march northward of Pansa towards the close

---

[1] Cic., *Phil.*, XIII, 11.
[2] The letter is preserved in the Thirteenth Philippic.
[3] Suet., *Div. Aug.*, 84.

of March put an end to the time of waiting. Decimus in
Mutina informed Octavius by carrier pigeons [1] that his
garrison was starving, and, unless at once relieved, must
surrender. We need not linger over the details of the slip-
shod campaign which followed. Mutina, on the Aemilian
Way, was about equidistant from Parma in the west and
Bononia (Bologna) in the east, towns now in Antony's
hands. Hirtius lay eleven miles east of Bononia, with
Octavius some nine miles off on his right flank. Ventidius
Bassus, the praetor, a supporter of Antony, was enrolling
three legions of veterans, and Antony awaited their
arrival. But the news of Pansa's march northward on
March 19 stirred him to action, for he was in danger of
being outflanked and surrounded. He left Bononia, and
drew his lines closer to Mutina, placing at the same time
two legions, the II and the XXXV, at Forum Gallorum
in the swampy country between the two towns, in order
to hold up Pansa's approach. His mistake lay in permit-
ting the latter with his raw recruits to debouch unhin-
dered from the Apennine passes. For on April 14 Pansa
reached Bononia. He moved at once to join Hirtius, and
on the 15th fell in with Antony's ambuscade at Forum
Gallorum. It was a fight principally between Antony's
veterans and the Martian, and at first the former's superior numbers told. But Hirtius from nearer Mutina
moved east in support, and, as Antony's troops retired in
undisciplined triumph, he attacked them with twenty veteran cohorts, while Octavius defended the camp. Antony
was checked, and fell back in the direction of Mutina;
Pansa was fatally wounded; he and Hirtius and Octavius
were hailed as Imperatores by their troops. A week later,
on April 21, Antony again offered battle, for his opponents were threatening to raise the blockade. Decimus
sallied from Mutina, while Octavius routed two of An-

[1] Pliny, *N. H.*, x, 110.

tony's legions and drove them back to their camp, into which Hirtius penetrated and died on the ramparts. Antony, decisively beaten and in grave peril, took the Lark and the remnants of his other legions, and fled by the Aemilian Way to Transalpine Gaul. On the 22nd, Pansa died of his wounds at Bononia. Decimus's starving garrison was too weak to pursue, and the men of Octavius had been roughly handled, so Antony, now joined by Ventidius Bassus and his new legions, was left unmolested. He showed again the old Caesarian 'celeritas,' and by the middle of May he was beyond the mountains and safe in Forum Julii (Fréjus).[1]

The two consuls were dead — 'good men,' Cicero wrote, 'but no more.' To the Senate, Forum Gallorum and Mutina seemed final victories, and it summoned confidence to disclose its true prepossessions. Antony was at last declared a public enemy. Decimus was made the hero of the northern battles and voted a triumph. Sextus Pompeius, Pompey's son, was summoned from Marseilles to be head of the navy and warden of the coasts of Italy. Brutus and Cassius were confirmed in their provinces, and given an over-riding command in the empire east of the Adriatic. The Senate believed itself triumphant. It was confident of the loyalty of the western governors, Lepidus and Plancus and Pollio, and with their help, leaving Octavius out of account, it could number over twenty legions against Antony's handful, while Brutus and Cassius held the East with seventeen. The Republic on the old lines seemed already restored.

To Octavius, waiting at Bononia while Decimus toiled painfully across the mountains on Antony's track, it was very clear that presently he would be set aside. An epi-

---

[1] The action at Forum Gallorum has been reconstructed by Rice Holmes, I, 51–54, basing himself on App., III, 66, 67; the scattered references in Cicero (ad Fam., x, 30, 33; Phil., xiv); Suet., Div. Aug., 10, and Dio, xlvi, 37. About Mutina we know almost nothing.

gram of Cicero's came to his ears, that he was to be 'lauded, applauded and discarded,' [1] and the discarding seemed to have begun. He was ordered to hand over Pansa's legions, and his own IV and the Martian, to Decimus Brutus. He was not mentioned in the vote of thanks to the army. He was given no place on the commission appointed to revise Antony's decrees. He was refused a triumph and even an ovation. The conservatives were circulating all manner of rumours about him, such as that at Mutina he had shown the white feather, and was responsible for Pansa's death. Moreover, the Senate was attempting to treat with his troops behind their general's back. It was all very well for Cicero to write of the young Caesar's 'wonderful natural strain of virtue,' [2] but the old man was clearly his friend only so long as he was content to be his tool.

Octavius, casting up his accounts, realized that he had now achieved one-half of his purpose. Out of the scrambling Mutina campaign he alone had won benefits. He had made himself sufficiently formidable for Antony to treat him with respect. He held Cisalpine Gaul and led the only army in Italy. Nothing stood between him and Rome. If Julius was to be avenged, if he was to have a hand in remaking the empire, the time had come to sever the unnatural alliance with the republicans and make peace with Antony. So he declined to hand over his legions to Decimus, and he refused to join in Antony's pursuit. He sat still and waited. One thing he had yet to get before he broke with the Senate. To meet Antony on equal terms, he must be consul and legally head of the state. Therefore for a month or two he continued to negotiate, using as his medium the half-distraught Cicero.

The key of the situation lay with the western proconsuls and their armies, Lepidus in the Narbonese,

---

[1] Cic., *ad Fam.*, XI, 20.   [2] *ad Brut.*, I, 3.

Plancus in Celtic Gaul, and Pollio in Spain. The Senate believed them to be loyal to its interests; Antony was convinced that he could certainly win over the first and probably the other two, and that was why he was now north of the Alps. These three we shall meet again in this narrative. No one of them was a commanding character. Lepidus, 'that weathercock of a man,' [1] now Pontifex Maximus by Antony's favour, was vain, unstable, self-indulgent, a lesser Antony. Plancus was a selfish time-server, 'afflicted with a chronic disease of treachery,' [2] whose only creditable achievement was the founding of Lyons. Pollio, a more reputable figure, was *petit maître* rather than soldier. Octavius believed that they would be clay in Antony's hands, and his forecast was right. On the 29th of May Lepidus came over to Antony's side. Plancus, who was joined by Decimus Brutus, made at first some show of resistance, and all summer there was marching and counter-marching beyond the Alps. But neither Antony nor Octavius had any doubt about the ultimate issue. Most of the troops were Caesarians, and would force their commanders to join the Caesarian side as soon as its leaders had made their peace.

The news of the defection of Lepidus caused the Senate to declare him a public enemy, and to commission Octavius to protect Italy. The latter, while busy negotiating with Antony through the medium of Lepidus, did not forget the situation in Rome. About the middle of July he sent an embassy from his troops thither to settle certain points about the bounties and to request the consulship for their general. The latter question had been already raised by Cicero, but the Senate took refuge in the technical difficulty; both consuls being dead and a praetor not being able to create a higher authority than his own,

---

[1] 'homo ventosissimus,' a phrase of Decimus Brutus. Cic., *ad Fam.*, XI, 9.
[2] 'morbo proditor,' Vell., II, 83.

it would be necessary to wait till the new year, when, as the phrase went, the auspices would revert to the Conscript Fathers. This was the answer given to the deputation from the legions, who were also refused the bounties which they had claimed.

To the mind of Octavius the moment had come for swift action. The Senate had shown itself patently hostile to him, and he could not afford to be put off by a technicality which in the past had been disregarded.[1] With his eight legions he crossed the Rubicon, like his great-uncle before him, and marched on Rome. Resistance collapsed; the three legions there, two of which had come from Africa, declared for him; after assuring himself of the safety of his mother and sister, he entered the city and found himself its master. The Senate hastened to do his will. The urban praetor nominated two proconsuls to hold the election, and on August 19, along with his cousin, Quintus Pedius, he was duly elected consul. Twelve vultures, as in the case of Romulus, obligingly attended his first taking of the auspices. From the public treasury he paid the promised bounties to his troops. The law necessary to confirm his adoption, hitherto blocked by Antony, was passed, the amnesty of March, 44 B.C., was rescinded, and a special court was established to outlaw the murderers of Julius. Cicero left Rome, never to return. His nerve was broken, and he wrote a pathetic last word to Octavius thanking him for his leave of absence, and trusting that it meant forgiveness for the past and indulgence for the future.[2]

Octavius was now consul at a younger age than Pompey, twenty-four years before the statutory date. With eleven legions he was master of Rome and of all Italy. He had on his side not only Caesarian loyalty, but the sympathy of many of the middle classes who saw in him the

[1] e.g. in 49 B.C.   [2] Preserved by Nonius, 436; see Tyrrell, VI, 354.

sole alternative to Antony. For the moment he was
secure; some day he must fight Brutus and Cassius, but
they were far off and had still to combine their armies,
and when that day came he hoped to have Antony by his
side. He had made himself so formidable that the latter
must accept him on equal terms, and between them they
would achieve his first purpose, the avenging of Julius.
What lay beyond that was still on the knees of the gods;
in these difficult times one must live by the day. Three
striplings — Octavius and Agrippa were just nineteen and
Maecenas a few years older — had to their credit an extraordinary achievement, and the chief actor had been
Octavius himself. He had patiently unriddled a situation
of extreme complexity, feeling his way with a precocious
prudence, trimming his sails to catch every favouring
wind, but never forgetful of his ultimate port. He had
sunk his pride and made himself the servant of his enemies, till through them he had won purchase with his
natural allies. He had compelled those who were most
ready to betray him to be his unwitting tools. He had
won a repute for a balanced sagacity, so that men forgot
his youth. He had shown at once an uncanny self-restraint
and a supreme self-confidence; in the happy phrase of
Aulus Gellius he was 'lifted high on the consciousness of
himself.' [1] Above all, he had won the Caesarian glamour,
which for the Rome of that day was what the Napoleonic
legend was in the nineteenth century for France. His
name was now by Roman custom Gaius Julius Caesar
Octavianus. More important, to the legions and to the
people he was Caesar.

[1] 'conscientia sua subnixus.'

CAESAR OCTAVIANUS

BOOK TWO

I. THE TRIUMVIRATE: PHILIPPI

(43–42 B.C.)

> My fate cries out,
> And makes each petty artery in this body
> As hardy as the Nemean lion's nerve.
> Still am I called!
>
> *Hamlet.*

I

OCTAVIAN moved north in September, nominally to oppose Antony as well as to do justice on the luckless Decimus. He waited in Cisalpine Gaul, while Antony and
Lepidus, now joined by the troops of Plancus and Pollio,
came south to meet him. The meeting, prepared for by
much correspondence, took place on an island in a tribu-
tary of the Po, between Bononia and Mutina, at the close
of October or the beginning of November. For two days
the three conferred, and terms of settlement were agreed
upon. Octavian surrendered his consulship, which went to
Antony's creature, the ex-muleteer Ventidius Bassus; Lepidus and Plancus were to be consuls for the year 42; for
the rest of the year, and for five years following, Lepidus,
Antony and Octavian were to be appointed triumvirs for
reconstituting the Republic, with overriding executive and
legislative powers, a dictatorship without the name.
Brutus and Cassius held the East, but the western empire
was apportioned between the three. Antony took Cisalpine and Celtic Gaul, Lepidus the Narbonese and Spain,
while to Octavian fell Africa and the islands, the least easy

command, since Sextus Pompeius held the seas. The soldiers approved the pact, for it meant the narrowing of
the possibilities, or at any rate the area, of civil war. They
were further conciliated by the promise of large grants of
good Italian land, and by the announcement of the
betrothal of Octavian to Claudia, Antony's step-daughter
and Fulvia's child. The Caesarians were at last united.

The allies marched upon Rome and the triumvirate was
proclaimed. Appian has preserved the terms of the proclamation.[1] Vengeance upon the murderers of Julius was
alleged as the chief motive, but before the arch-assassins,
Brutus and Cassius, could be followed overseas, it was
necessary to make Italy safe for the triumvirs. Also, to
furnish a war-chest and to pay bounties to the troops,
money must be raised, since the state treasury was empty.
That meant a proscription on Sulla's lines. A small preliminary list of the proscribed was drawn up in the north,
on which appeared Cicero's name. Then came a long list
of three hundred senators and two thousand knights —
rich men whose money was wanted, dangerous and uncertain men, private enemies of this or that triumvir.
Shakespeare has pictured the ghoulish chaffering:

> ANT. These many, then, shall die: their names are
> pricked.
> OCT. Your brother too must die: consent you, Lepidus?
> LEP. I do consent —
> OCT.　　　　　　　　　Prick him down, Antony.
> LEP. Upon condition Publius shall not live,
> 　　　Who is your sister's son, Mark Antony.
> ANT. He shall not live; look, with a spot I damn him.[2]

Then till the close of the year the four horsemen of the
Apocalypse rode abroad in the land. Some of the pro-
scribed escaped overseas to Brutus and Cassius and
Sextus Pompeius. Some were saved by the fidelity of their

[1] IV, 6.　　　　　[2] *Julius Caesar*, Act IV.

slaves and kinsfolk. Some were begged off by gentle-
women like Octavia. But blood ran like water, and
Pedius, the other consul, died of the horror of it. The
triumvirs achieved their purpose. They could now cross
the sea with a maimed and silent land behind them, and
they had amassed from confiscations enough to furnish
the sinews of war.

Among the first to die was Cicero. He had little estate,
only debts, but Antony could not forgive the lash of the
Philippics. Plutarch has told the tale of that winter afternoon in the wood by the sea-shore when the old man
stretched out his frail neck to the centurion's sword, and
of that later day in Rome when the head was fixed by
Antony's order above the Rostra, and 'the Romans shud-
dered, for they seemed to see there, not the face of Cicero
but the image of Antony's soul.' [1] He met his death in
the high Roman fashion — the only misfortune of his life,
says Livy, which he faced like a man. The verdict is
scarcely fair; juster is the comment of the same historian
that he was so great a figure that it would require a
Cicero to praise him adequately. In the wild years when
the Roman Republic fell, the thinker and the scholar
does not fill the eye in the same way as the forthright man
of action, and Cicero is dim in the vast shadow of Julius.
His weaknesses are clear for a child to read, his innocent
vanity, his lack of realism, his sentimentality about dead
things, his morbid sensitiveness, his imperfect judgment
of character, his frequent fits of timidity. The big head,
the thin neck, the mobile mouth of the orator could not
dominate men like the eagle face of Julius. He failed and
perished because he was Cicero. The man of letters in a
crisis, who looks round a question, cannot have the single-
hearted force of him who sees the instant need. Yet it is
to be remembered that he could conquer his natural tim-

[1] Plut., *Cic.*, 47, 48.

orousness and act on occasion with supreme audacity, a
far greater achievement than the swashbuckling valour of
an Antony. And let it be remembered, too, that it was
Cicero's creed which ultimately triumphed. His dream
came true. His humanism and his humanity made him
the prophet of a gentler world. The man to whom St.
Augustine owed the first step in his conversion,[1] who was
to St. Ambrose a model and to St. Jerome 'rex oratorum,'
the scholar whose work was the mainspring of the Renais-
sance, has had an abiding influence on the world. While
others enlarged the limits of the Roman empire, he 'advanced the boundaries of the Latin genius.'[2]

The proscription of the triumvirs is the darkest stain
upon Octavian's record. So dark, that ancient writers,
looking on the beneficent rule of Augustus, were driven
to assume what psychologists call 'dissociated personal-
ities' — youth debauched, pitiless and self-centred, which
by some miracle was changed by success into a pattern
of virtue. Others have attributed the transformation to
sheer satiety with evil.[3] Human nature has a love for
violent drama and undue simplification, which sober history cannot accept. It must not be forgotten that Octavian lived under a fierce light, and that in a civil war the
wildest gossip is believed. When, after the fall of the
Julio-Claudian house, historians need no longer be cir-
cumspect, ancient tattle was resurrected. It may fairly
be said that most of the scandals about Octavian's youth
should be taken as the malice of Antony's faction,[4] reproduced in later generations for political ends. But one fact
remains which no apologist has adequately excused,[5] his

---

[1] 'Ille vero liber (Cicero's *Hortensius*) mutavit affectum meum, et ad te ipsum,
Domine, mutavit preces meas et vota ac desideria mea fecit alia.' *Confess.*, III, 4.

[2] Julius's own tribute. Cic., *ad Brut.*, 72; Plin., *N. H.*, VII, 117.

[3] 'Lassam crudelitatem,' Seneca, *de clem.*, I, 9.

[4] *e.g.*, Suet., *Div. Aug.*, 68, 69.

[5] Attempts will be found in Vell., II, 61, and Dio, XLVII, 7.

responsibility for a campaign of brutal murder. A fissure in his nature, a miraculous change of heart, are too facile explanations. The proscription was in keeping with a character which had in it strange depths of good and evil, and which, though it broadened and mellowed with the years, remained in essence the same.

In Octavian the emotional side was slow to develop, but from the start the rational was all-powerful. He had always a capacity for affection, even deep affection, but its area was strictly circumscribed. He had this love for his mother Atia, who died at the beginning of the triumvirate; for Julius, in whose case it was joined with a profound intellectual reverence; for Agrippa and Maecenas, where it had something of the *camaraderie* of youth engaged in the same adventure. In later years it was extended to certain members of his family. For these few it was a strong emotion; the rest of the world he regarded at first with suspicion, and never, even when success came, with more than a tepid benevolence. But on the intellectual side he had certain purposes held with a serious passion. The first was to finish the task of re-shaping the empire which his great-uncle had begun. A second was to be himself the chief agent in that work. We need not credit him at the age of nineteen with even the rudiments of the policy which made the principate. What he possessed from the start were certain guiding ideas derived from Julius, a passion for order, a realism about facts, and a belief that he possessed a capacity for reconstruction. So in his intricate course he moved by the light of three principles. One was emotional — the avenging of Julius, a motive into which there entered something of the Roman 'pietas.' A second was intellectual, a determination to bring order out of chaos, a polity out of banditry. This purpose he held with the rigidity of a devotee. The state should be re-made at whatever cost, and only violence could curb violence. To this task he brought both the stony-heartedness of self-absorbed youth, and the moral opportunism of the fanatic. His view was that of Horace Walpole: 'No great country was ever saved by good men, because good men will not go the lengths that may be necessary.'

There was a third purpose, in which the emotional and the rational were blended. He had a strong vein of super-stition, unlike the cool scepticism of Julius, and he was avid of omens. He believed himself destined for a high mission, to which personal happiness, friendship, ease, common morality must all be sacrificed. Like Napoleon he followed his star. The conviction gave his youth that confidence which a Calvinist gets from the sense that his every step is divinely ordained. 'Italiam non sponte sequor' — the cry of Aeneas was always his assurance and consolation.

To a mind thus constituted the proscription was war-ranted both by public and personal necessities. Brutus and Cassius, with the armies of the East, had still to be accounted for. The Senate and the republicans had re-vealed their bitter enmity. Their fangs must be drawn, and their estates mulcted. 'Since we intend,' ran the triumvirs' proclamation to the Roman people, 'to conduct this war at a distance on your behalf, it does not seem to us to be safe either for us or for you to leave the rest of our enemies here behind us, since they would take advantage of our absence and lie in wait for the accidents of war. Nor do we think that, in the present emergency, we ought to be slow to act from any consideration for them, but rather we must put them one and all out of the way.' Brutal, but not without warrant from common sense. It was undoubtedly what the republicans would have done to the Caesarians, had they been uppermost. As for Octavian himself he was still on a razor edge. He was facing implacable foes. Assassins waited for him at every street corner. He had painfully built up his purchase with Antony; if by a half-hearted policy he should weaken the alliance, and the alliance failed, he himself would be the first victim. To insist upon clemency in the circumstances would not only have required quixotic courage, but would have demanded the surrender of every hope he had cherished since boyhood, and the sacrifice of the toil of eighteen desperate months. On the facts Octavian's conduct can be understood, if it cannot be defended.

We must judge it, too, in the light of the moral standards of his day. The past century had been a reign of terror, for Rome had seen nine separate civil wars, four deliberate massacres, and a long series of political murders from the Gracchi to Julius. The life-and-death struggle with Hannibal, with incidents in it which were no better than human sacrifices,[1] had permanently debased the Roman temper and left in it a core of hard inhumanity. Cicero might found law upon the natural love of man for man,[2] but the Roman jurist would have had a long search for that commodity. Even Virgil, the prophet of a better world, permits Aeneas, the ideal figure which to some extent personified the later Augustus, to suffer prisoners in bonds to be immolated on Pallas's funeral pyre. To the Roman of the day the triumvirs' doings cannot have seemed more barbarous than other events in comparatively recent history, than the Gracchan slaughterings, or Sulla's proscription, or the public butchery of seven thousand Samnites, or the six thousand gladiators of Spartacus crucified along the road to Capua.

Of the three men responsible Octavian alone showed some glimmerings of mercy. He had at the start opposed

[1] Livy, xxii, 57, 6.

[2] 'natura propensi sumus ad diligendos homines, quod fundamentum iuris est.' de Leg., i, 43.

the proscription, but when it was agreed upon he bargained as closely as his colleagues, and he was inflexible in carrying out its main purpose, on the ground that that kind of thing must be done effectively or not at all.[1] But it is clear that, outside that purpose, he alone of the triumvirs tried to mitigate the hideous business. His cruelty was politic, not temperamental. In the beautiful story of Vispullo and Turia it was Octavian who removed the husband's name from the list of the doomed.[2]

It is his consent to Cicero's death that has most smirched his repute with posterity. But between him and Cicero there was no kindness. The young man had learned from the elder much that he was one day to put into practice, but the link was of the head, not of the heart. Forty years later, when he found a grandson reading a book of the old philosopher, he spoke of the author as a good man who loved his country,[3] but it is fantastic to see in that tribute penitence for his share in his death. To Octavian, Cicero must have been always the head and front of offence. He had been notoriously ungrateful to Julius who had befriended him; he had exulted hysterically at the Ides of March, and had made gods and heroes of the assassins; he was the brain of the faction which sought to revive the derelict Republic. He had been willing to use Octavian as a tool, but had made no secret of his intention to discard him when he had served his purpose. Was it unnatural that Octavian should do the same by Cicero?

II

The year 42 B.C. opened anxiously for the triumvirs. They had made a peace of death in Italy, but outside Italy

[1] Suet., *Div. Aug.*, 27.
[2] App., IV, 16; Val. Max., VI, 72; *C. I. L.*, VI, 1527; Dessau, 8393.
[3] Macrob., *Saturn.*, II, 4, 18; Plut., *Cic.*, 49.

formidable forces were massing against them. Pompey's son Sextus had maintained himself after Munda in the western seas, and had drawn to himself a great following of old Pompeians. Antony had negotiated with him, but could not pay the five millions sterling which he demanded as the value of his father's property; the Senate had promised him everything and made him admiral-in-chief; the triumvirs had put him on the list of the proscribed. Sextus retaliated by seizing Sicily and Sardinia, and making these islands a cave of Adullam for exiled republicans, and threatening the sea-borne supplies of Rome. The pirate had become an independent potentate. In the East the situation was still more menacing. Cassius was in control of Asia, and busy levying troops and amassing treasure. He had scared Dolabella into suicide, and had got together a formidable fleet, part of which was used to immobilize Cleopatra in Egypt, and part, under Statius, Murcus and Gnaeus Domitius Ahenobarbus, to watch the Adriatic. Brutus relinquished his province of Macedonia, and in the early spring met Cassius at Smyrna and settled a strategical plan. They believed that Sextus Pompeius would keep the triumvirs busy in Italy, and that their first task was to strengthen their grip on the East. They plundered the cities of Asia, patched up a peace with Orodes of Parthia, and in September crossed the Hellespont and took up a position west of Philippi, astride the Via Egnatia and within reach of their fleet at Neapolis. They controlled the sea and the richest part of the empire, and they believed that they could hold the triumvirs to a stalemate till hunger or sedition broke down their armies.

Antony had a difficult part to play, for he had to keep facing both ways. He sent Gaius Norbanus and Decidius Saxa with eight legions across the Adriatic, while he got together the twenty legions which were to be his main expeditionary force for the East. But difficulties of transport and the constant threat from the sea delayed him, and it was not till well on in the summer that the ships could sail. Octavian meantime had his own troubles. On January 1 the Senate had deified Julius, so now — for what it might be worth — he was 'divi filius,' the son of a god. He was instructed to take order with Sextus Pompeius, but the expedition which he sent against him under Salvidienus Rufus was a fiasco. Then his health failed him; it had never been good, and it had been weakened by the excitements of the past two years. But when Antony summoned him and his fleet to his aid at Brundisium he dared not refuse. If Brutus and Cassius were to be crushed, Antony could not be allowed to have all the glory; if they won, he could do nothing in Italy to stave off the irretrievable ruin.

Norbanus and Decidius, marching along the Egnatian Way, secured Amphipolis, passed beyond Philippi, and occupied the passes of the hills. There in late September they came into touch with the advancing republicans. But the latter by a flank move compelled the triumvirs' advanced guard to fall back on Amphipolis, and themselves took up at Philippi a strong position on high ground defended on the north by mountains and on the south by a sea-marsh. Antony, fearing for Amphipolis, hurried along the Egnatian Way, and Octavian, whom ill-health had delayed at Dyrrachium, forced himself to join him.

Philippi, though a decisive event in the world's history, is without military interest as a battle. The armies were nearly equal in infantry, each nineteen legions, and the better quality and training of the Caesarians was balanced by the republican superiority in cavalry. The aim of Brutus and Cassius, with the fleet and the rich East to support them, was to let the enemy break his strength on an impregnable fortress, while that of Antony was to bring matters to a decision at once, since he could not afford to wait. During the first days of October, a season of wind and rain, he offered battle many times but without result. Then he decided to try to cut the enemy's communications with Neapolis, and began to construct by night a causeway across the sea-marsh. The campaign had become a struggle of engineers, like so many of Julius's. Cassius, who commanded on the enemy's left, started counter-works, and battle was joined apparently more by accident than design. The troops of Brutus on the right routed Octavian and broke into his camp, but Antony's fierce assault carried the day in his section and drove Cassius from his entrenchments. Cassius, ignorant of Brutus's success and believing his own capture inevitable, fell on his sword, and the news of his death forced Brutus to retire from the ground he had won. For a fortnight he held his position, but he could not restrain the impatience of his troops and was forced to take the offensive. The triumvirs were quick to seize the chance, for news had come that Murcus and Ahenobarbus had destroyed the transports carrying their reinforcements. The fighting began in the late afternoon of October 23, and in a short time the triumvirs had broken the three lines of the enemy, and, while Octavian stormed the camp, Antony pursued the fugitives into the hills. Brutus with four legions retreated in good order, but next morning, finding escape impossible, he induced a freedman to slay him.[1]

With Brutus perished the republican cause, for he alone of its leaders had the moral authority which can dignify stagnation and reaction. It is a strange accident which

[1] The authorities for Philippi are App., IV, 108 *sqq.*; Dio, XLVII, 41 *sqq.*; Vell., II, 70; Plut., *Ant.*, 22; *Brut.*, 41 *sqq.* For the troops engaged see Rice Holmes, I, 217. The date of the second battle is fixed by the latest found fragments of the *Fasti* of Praeneste. The battle has been reconstructed by Rice Holmes, I, 84–88, and Ferrero, III, 201–07; cf. also Kromayer, *Schlachten-Atlas, Roms.*, Abt., IV. There is a careful study of the preliminary movements by P. Collart in *Bull. de C. hell.*, LIII (1929) 351–64.

has given him so great a name in history, for the man himself was inconsiderable. Of the two chief enemies of Julius, Cassius was the more vigorous and resolute in action, but he was a type common in history, the ambitious condottiere who can readily adapt a principle to self-interest. Brutus was a rarer species, who both impressed and puzzled his contemporaries. Julius out of friendship for his mother Servilia was his constant patron, and seems to have regarded him with a half-amused respect as an interesting relic; it was his policy, too, as it was Napoleon's, to be polite to the old nobility. The famous comment on him, 'Quicquid vult valde vult,'[1] is as much a criticism of his limited outlook as of his intensity of purpose. Cicero wrangled with him and flattered him, but does not seem to have greatly liked him. Brutus had a solemn condescending manner, a hard face, a pedantic style in speech and writing, and a stiff ungracious character. He was capable of extreme harshness, as he showed in his treatment of the Asian cities before Philippi, and he was to the last degree avaricious. There was little principle about him when his investments were in question, and he extorted forty-eight per cent from one wretched Cypriote community.[2] His philosophy of life was not profound, and he died abjuring his creed.[3] He was an egotist and a formalist, yet he won an extraordinary prestige, for to his contemporaries he seemed the living embodiment of certain ancient virtues which had gone out of the world. To adopt Sydney Smith's phrase about Francis Horner, he had the Roman equivalent of the Ten Commandments written on his countenance and about him an air of inaccessible respectability. History has by one of its freaks perpetuated this repute, and he remains the 'noblest Roman' when in truth he was a com-

[1] Cic., *ad Att.*, xiv, 1; cf. Tyrrell, v, 249.
[2] Cic., *ad Att.*, v, 21; vi, 1, 2.   [3] Dio, xlvi, 49.

monplace example of aristocratic virtues and vices. Cicero was in a far truer sense the last republican.

The half-educated Antony had an admiration for acquirements and qualities which he did not share, and was prepared to treat the dead regicide with honour. Octavian is said to have been harsh to the prisoners, and especially to have insulted Brutus's remains. The stories do not hang together,[1] but one thing is plain; Octavian could not away with Brutus, disliking both the individual and the type. He detested the man who had been Julius's protégé and also his murderer. As for the type, he was as intolerant of it as his great-uncle had been of Cato. It seemed to him, in Cicero's phrase, a mere desert island, 'shore and sky and utter desolation.'

[1] They will be found in Suet., *Div. Aug.*, 13; App., IV, 135; Plut., *Ant.*, 22; *Brut.*, 53; but see *Mon. Anc.*, I, 13–15; and Ulpian, *Dig.*, XLVIII, 24.

II. EAST AND WEST

(42–37 B.C.)

I have some rights of memory in this kingdom,
Which now to claim my vantage doth invite me.

Hamlet.

I

PHILIPPI saw the end of the army of the Republic. Its leaders were now refugees or condottieri. Murcus carried some of them to Sextus Pompeius; some joined Aheno-barbus, who with seventy ships took to piracy in the Adriatic; some fell on their swords, some were executed, many were pardoned. The subordinate officers were for the most part admitted to grace, including the son of an Apulian freedman, a youth of twenty-three, one Quintus Horatius Flaccus, who had left his college classes at Athens to follow Brutus.

The first task before Antony and Octavian was to reduce their swollen army, the forty-seven legions made up of their own forces and the surrendering enemy. The second was to pacify the disbanded with bounties and land. The third was to get funds into the depleted treasury, for gigantic liabilities loomed ahead. The fourth was to crush the last elements of disaffection — Sextus Pompeius in the West, the republican oddments in the East — and to re-establish the authority of Rome among the eastern protected princes. In this task there was no time to spare, for it was Julius's delay after Pharsalus which had led to Thapsus and Munda. Lastly there must be some readjustment among the triumvirs, for Lepidus had proved a failure. As consul he had been under the thumb of the terrible Fulvia, and he was strongly suspected of being in treaty with Sextus Pompeius. In any case he had never been more than a cipher, important only for the legions which he brought into the pool.

> a slight, unmeritable man
> Meet to be sent on errands.

The disbandment of the troops was soon accomplished. A military colony was founded at Philippi, the precursor of a vast colonizing activity in the West. Eleven legions, which were willing to continue their term of service, were retained under arms; six went to Antony, and Octavian sent him two of his five in exchange for two that had been left in Cisalpine Gaul. Then came a re-division of the provinces. Cisalpine Gaul dropped out of the provincial category and became part of Italy. Antony retained Celtic Gaul, and took over the Narbonese from Lepidus; Octavian was given Africa and Spain, with the dubious addition of Sicily and Sardinia which were now in the hands of Sextus Pompeius. There was to be a later readjustment if Lepidus proved less treacherous than was suspected.[1]

It was an unequal division, for Antony had not only the lion's share of the spoil but the easier task for the future. He was the true hero of Philippi, and to him the soldiers looked as their commander. Octavian, though he had done creditably in the second battle, had been a sick man during most of the campaign, and was now so feeble that he could only make short daily journeys, and looked so ill that news of his death was already being whispered in Rome. His malady seems to have been a

[1] For an examination of the conflicting statements of Dio and Appian, see Rice Holmes, I, 218–19.

nervous stomachic disorder to which he was always subject, and which became acute in times of stress. How could this ailing youth compete in the eyes of the legions with the magnificent Antony, overflowing with the zest of life and in the prime of his bodily strength? The latter had all the cards in his hand. He had the pick of the victorious expeditionary force. There was in the Gauls a second great army, eleven legions under Fufius Calenus and thirteen under Ventidius Bassus, Asinius Pollio and Plancus, and these generals were his creatures.

Moreover, he had the more grateful task. He had to restore order among the petty princes of the East, but that was no difficult business for Roman arms. He had to raise money in the only region where money could be had. He had the control of that treasure-house of old civilizations to which Roman eyes had long been turning. In the East, too, lay the only practical extension of the empire. He had inherited Julius's plans for a Parthian campaign, and this grandiose dream was always at the back of his mind. The view that Antony chose the East because of a sensual craving for its luxury does not set with the character of the man. He chose it because it was the *beau rôle*, the natural weapon for ambition and the true reward of a conqueror.

Far different was Octavian's part. With slender forces he had to face the formidable Sextus, and in all likelihood others, for he cannot have believed that Antony's satellites would readily take orders from him. He had to restore the reign of law in a distracted and impoverished Italy. With no funds except those with which Antony could provide him, he had to undertake a huge business of soldier-settlement, and find half a million acres of good land in Italy — a thing which involved either disappointing the veterans or embittering the forcibly dispossessed. He had a faint popularity with the legions, but he was cordially disliked by most other classes, who preferred Antony's cheerful brutality to Octavian's cold and condescending rigour. This pallid, dyspeptic young man undertook a task which might well have daunted the most stalwart.

According to Appian his selection was determined by his health,[1] but the explanation is manifestly absurd. The East was a far easier sphere of duty for an invalid than the turbulent West. Octavian took what he was given, for he had no choice. But as his litter jolted along the Egnatian Way, he may have seen light at the end of his path. It is clear that from the beginning he had instincts which were later to develop into principles of government. A proof is his hankering from the start after the office of tribune; he realized what lay in the tribunician power. He saw that if he could succeed in his seemingly hopeless task, and pacify Italy and win her to his side, he would have achieved something far greater than any resounding Eastern triumph. Unlike Julius, he believed that in Italy lay the imperial centre of gravity, and that only on the Italian race could a new empire be built: [2]

Sit Romana potens Itala virtute propago.

So, while Antony smiled at the fool's errand on which he had despatched his colleague, thereby precluding him from further rivalry, that colleague was not wholly malcontent. He had been given the chance of securing what was to be the future foundation of his power.

II

Travelling slowly and painfully, with many halts for rest, Octavian reached Rome early in the year 41. He found Antony's brother Lucius, the consul, fresh from

[1] v, 3.
[2] See on this point S. Dimarzo, 'Augusto e l' Italia' in *N. Ant.* (1932), 312.

celebrating a triumph for some trivial success in Gaul, and
Antony's wife Fulvia in control of the government with
Lepidus as her slave. He exhibited his written compact
with Antony, but for the rest left politics alone, for he was
called to an urgent task. Italy was in chaos. The settlement of soldiers had been going on for a year, and the
results were disastrous. Old tenants had been evicted,
and the roads were thronged with vagabondage; all land-
owners were in fear, and many were bankrupt; deputa-
tions from every town and city were thronging to Rome
to protest against spoliation. He had the clamorous legions which he had brought with him still to satisfy, and
there were hordes of veterans in Italy to whom he had
made promises which awaited fulfilment. With an anxious
heart he appointed commissioners and surveyors, and set
about the business of land distribution.

It was his first big administrative task, performed
against time and under enormous difficulties, and he
showed his quality in it, as he had already proved his talents in the tangled diplomatic game. Where state domains were available the business was simple, but there
was little free state land. But there were wide municipal
territories, and nineteen Italian towns were selected and
a third of their estates marked out for settlement. There
were also further confiscations of property owned by
recalcitrant republicans. Existing owners or tenants,
against whom no political charges lay, were to be compensated, but they had to wait for their money, since as
yet Octavian had no funds. Hard cases were innumer-
able, and his enemies made the most of them. Humble
folk suffered heavily. Horace, escaped from Philippi,
found that his father's little estate had vanished, and had
to earn his bread in the lower ranks of the civil service.
Virgil's small property near Mantua was threatened, but
was for the moment saved by the aid of his patrons,

Asinius Pollio and Cornelius Gallus, and somewhat prematurely he blessed Octavian as the god who had intervened.[1] In Umbria two other poets, Tibullus and Propertius, found their families beggared. Octavian was on delicate ground. He had to keep faith with the soldiers and to retain their allegiance, but not less he had to win the confidence of the civilian classes, on whom depended the rebuilding of the state. He dared not spoil the weapon for which he would soon have further need, but also he dared not wreck the ultimate purpose for which that weapon was to be used.

On the whole he succeeded in balancing his duties. The soldiers were not estranged, and civilian grievances did not become so clamorous that Lucius and Fulvia could use them against him. He was clement whenever he could be clement with safety, and he began to pardon the proscribed.[2] If he could not pay for all the land which he commandeered, he endeavoured to meet hard cases.[3] His mind was easy, too, about the economic consequences. The huge conglomerations of land were being broken up, and most of the soldiers to whom the allotments were made were country folk drawn originally from the farms. Such were the legions he had himself recruited in Italy — in Campania and in the north: such were the troops levied by Ventidius Bassus and Decimus Brutus, by Hirtius and Pansa. It was a clear gain that there should be several hundred thousand men with little holdings carved out of Italian soil.

His success alarmed Fulvia and Lucius. They saw him winning popularity in Italy, while Antony was far away. Ample opportunities for mischief lay to their hand. They claimed to be the voice of hardly-treated civilians. They

---

[1] *Ecl.*, 1, 6–10. [2] Dessau, 8393.

[3] It is clear, I think, that we cannot take the claim in *Mon. Anc.*, 1, 16–19, that he paid for all land taken, to refer to the colonization after Philippi.

maintained that Octavian had favoured his own legions at the expense of Antony's, and that the right of allotting land belonged to Lucius, who, as consul, claimed powers which clashed with those of the triumvir. The motive of Lucius, under the guise of fraternal loyalty, was plain ambition, that of Fulvia perhaps the jealousy of a distracted wife, who sought by violent means to win back an errant husband. The situation was complicated by something very like famine in Rome, since the fleets of Sextus and Ahenobarbus played havoc with the corn supply. Octavian was in a dilemma. He was compelled to make concessions to property owners, especially of the senatorial class, and every concession threatened mutiny among the troops. Moreover, Antony's legates in the West proved hostile, and refused to permit the passage through Gaul of the legions he sent to Spain. It was one of the most critical moments in his career. He tried to bring Fulvia and Lucius to reason, protesting his loyalty to his agreement with Antony, and offering to submit every matter of controversy to the arbitration of the Senate. But they would have none of it, and set themselves to organize a fighting force, Fulvia occupying Praeneste, and, girt with a sword, issuing orders like an army commander.

This appeal to arms was a fortunate thing for Octavian, since it drove his own legions to take up his quarrel. They forced a meeting at Gabii which Octavian alone attended, Lucius and Fulvia declining to appear before what they called a 'parliament in puttees.'[1] They relied on Antony's legates in Italy and Gaul, Calenus, Ventidius Bassus, Plancus and Pollio. But these proved broken reeds, for they did not know what were Antony's real desires. A clash was inevitable, and Octavian moved swiftly. He sent a legion to Brundisium to prevent the descent of

[1] 'senatus caligatus.'

Ahenobarbus from the sea; he left Lepidus with two legions to garrison Rome; he recalled the troops destined for Spain under Salvidienus Rufus; and he gave Agrippa, as his first command, a flying force to harry Lucius. The latter flung himself into the old hill town of Perusia (Perugia) which was believed to be impregnable, and waited to be relieved by his brother's legates. But these legates were running no risks, and relief did not come. All autumn and winter the place was closely beleaguered, much on the plan which Julius had followed at Alesia, and by the end of February in the year 40 B.C. Lucius was compelled to surrender. Octavian was merciful to the Antonian leaders, as he was bound to be, and Lucius and Fulvia were permitted to leave scot-free, to be of no further account till their death. But the town was burned, apparently by accident, and the republican remnants of the garrison and the senatorian refugees were put to death. To Octavian it was the last stage in the avenging of Julius's murder, and the *coup de grâce* of the moribund conservative cause. He saw no reason to be merciful towards irreconcilables.[1]

The fall of Perusia left Octavian in control of Italy. A rising in Campania, led by Tiberius Claudius Nero, was easily put down, and Nero and his wife Livia fled to Sicily. The two legions of Plancus came over to the conqueror. Pollio retired northward, and Bassus hung around Brundisium. Calenus in Gaul opportunely died, and Octavian, hastening thither, took over his eleven legions, which he put in charge of Salvidienus Rufus.

---

[1] The Perusian war is full of uncertainties. Octavian appears to have had four veteran legions with him, besides the six under Salvidienus. Lucius had the six which he raised as consul, and counted upon eleven in Cisalpine Gaul, which were of no use to him. Agrippa seems to have been mainly responsible for the tactics of the siege; but see Reinhold, *M. Agrippa*, 18–20. The authorities are Suet., *Div. Aug.*, 14; App., v, 24 *sqq.*; Dio, XLVIII, 12 *sqq.*; Vell., II, 74. The story of the human sacrifices ('arae Perusinae') reported by Suetonius and Dio and by Seneca (*de clem.*, I, 11), is demonstrably false; cf. J. S. Reid, 'Human Sacrifices in Rome,' *J. R. S.*, II (1912), 41–44.

He could not pacify Lepidus with the African province and six of the Gallic legions. The two dangers which remained were Sextus and Antony, whose alliance he feared, for, though he had now forty legions more or less under him, these two held the sea and could devastate the coast of Italy. His first move was towards Sextus. He had already been twice betrothed — in his early youth to a daughter of Julius's colleague, Servilius Isauricus, and at the age of twenty to Claudia, Antony's step-daughter. Neither marriage had been consummated, and now, through the diplomacy of Maecenas, he espoused Scribonia, a much-married lady, the sister of Scribonius Libo, whose daughter was Sextus's wife. It was purely a marriage of convenience, and the elderly and unattractive wife soon fades out of history. She is remembered only as the mother of his daughter Julia.

Meanwhile what of Antony, who held the key of the problem? Since Philippi, so far as Rome was concerned, he had gone beyond the horizon, and only stray rumours of his doings reached the capital. He had a considerable task before him which he faced with his old energy, while at the back of his head was the dream of a Parthian con-quest which had been the ambition of his great master, and which he believed could alone right the economic dis-equilibrium of the empire. He made a royal progress through the province of Asia, Syria and Palestine, receiv-ing the honours of a god, collecting vast sums as tribute which he paid away as soon as he received them, reward-ing those who had opposed the republicans and punishing those who had aided them, and settling the succession in the client-kingdoms. In Bithynia he met Herod of Judaea, who impressed him with his ability, and whom, though he had befriended Cassius, he set up as tetrarch. There was another client-monarch, Cleopatra of Egypt, who had been a friend of Julius. Her the triumvir summoned to meet him at Tarsus in Cilicia in the late summer of 41 B.C.

Antony is one of the prime instances in history of divided natures. His face, which, if we may judge from his coins, was for all its strength disharmonic and misshapen, was an index to his character. His features stammered, as sometimes his tongue did. He had the Roman gifts of courage in adversity and resource in difficulties; when the east wind blew he was a man and a soldier. He had a real talent for administration, and much of his reconstruction of the East was to endure. But there was no balance in his soul. When the sun shone on him he was apt to sink into sloth and self-indulgence. His customary geniality could change with his moods into sheer brutality. His vanity was inordinate, and he had all the weaknesses of a vain man. In Rome, that hotbed of gossip, his enemies perverted his every act, and his inactivity during the Perusian war was set down to drunkenness and debauchery, when all the time he was busied with affairs of imperial import. Slander has followed him into history, for Plutarch is uniformly hostile, and Dio, who seems to have used the memoirs of Augustus, is naturally unsympathetic, though traces may be found in Appian of the impartiality of the lost work of Pollio.

As for Cleopatra, the scandal-monger has had a clear field. She was the only human being, except Hannibal, who ever put fear on Rome, and she has come down to us as a priestess of lawless love, a supreme seducer of virtue, a sexual degenerate, a nymphomaniac, a mistress of all the unholy arts of the East. There is reason to revise that view. She was no Oriental, being by descent half Greek and half Macedonian, with not a drop of Egyptian blood. So far from being love's plaything, she was from beginning to end the *politique*, pursuing the game of high ambition with a masterly coolness. She may have been in love with Julius, but it is unlikely that any other man ever had her heart. She was highly educated, and her fight was not only for her kingdom of Egypt but for a certain type of Hellenic culture of which she believed herself to be the last champion. With every charm of the woman, she had the tenacity of will and the courage of the strongest man. Above all, she had an abounding magnetic vitality. The quality of her high-coloured ancestors flowered in this ultimate child of their race into something like witchcraft. More feminine than other women, she had more steel and fire than any man, so that like Viola in *Twelfth Night*, she was all the brothers as well as all the daughters of her father's house.

She staged her arrival with consummate art. Plutarch — and after him Shakespeare incomparably — has described her voyage in her galley up the Cydnus, the scented bride-sails and the flutes, the attendant Loves and Nymphs and Graces. She was twenty-nine, which Balzac thought a woman's most dangerous age, not beautiful in the common sense but with a face which no man could forget, and a wooing voice which cast a spell on all who heard it. Antony had seen her as a girl of fourteen, when he was a young cavalry officer with Gabirius in Egypt, and he must have often met her when she was in Rome as Julius's mistress. But now came a revelation. He had the intellectual vanity of the half-educated and he posed as a philhellene, and her coming seemed like a re-enactment of an old divine legend, the birth of Aphrodite from the foam. Hitherto he had taken his pleasure lavishly and coarsely among women, but this woman, all air and fire, was of a different kind from fleshy Roman beauties and Syrian dancing-girls. His imagination and his intellect were ravished by her, for he had the wit to recognize her audacious spirit. He docilely followed her to Alexandria.

There in the winter, while Perusia was starving, she
played an adroit game. She was a genuine Egyptian
patriot, and, so far as our evidence goes, showed notable
talent in her administration of the land. She was endeared
to the native Egyptian people, for she spoke their tongue,
was respectful to their gods, and had about herself a
divine aura as a reincarnation of Isis. She desired to make
her country the richest and most cultivated on earth,
and for that she must have the support of the Roman
legions. The bait was the conquest of Parthia, which
to Antony seemed vital to Rome and for which the wealth
of Egypt would provide the funds. Therefore her task
was to make herself indispensable to Antony, and during
the winter of 41–40 B.C. she wove her enchantments. She
was his boon companion, his partner in fantastic adven-
tures, but she did not forget her purpose. She fostered
his ambitions but gave him nothing, neither funds from
her treasury nor her love, till she was certain that he
would pay her price.

News from Italy slowly filtered eastward. It did not
reach Antony till he had torn himself from Cleopatra
and gone north into Syria at the word of a Parthian invasion. There he found that the client-kingdoms were
in chaos, and the enemy armies led by Roman deserters.
His first business must be to get more troops, and, as this
dawned on him, he had tidings of Perusia. With Lucius
and Fulvia he had no sympathy, for they had prejudiced
his cause by their folly and lost him the good-will of the
Caesarian veterans. But Octavian's seizure of Gaul was
another matter, for it was to the legions there that he
looked for reinforcements in the coming campaign. He
was prepared to be loyal to Octavian, but Octavian in
turn must be loyal to him. He crossed to Athens, where
he found Lucius and Fulvia and heard their tale of woe.
It moved him little, but envoys from Sextus were also

there. If Octavian was playing him false order must be
taken with him. Pollio was in north Italy and Ventidius
was hanging around Brundisium, and Ahenobarbus with
his pirate fleet was on his side. These, with Sextus, enabled him to argue with Octavian, and if the young man
would not hear reason he would join with Sextus to
punish him. Accordingly with Sextus and Ahenobarbus
he sailed for Italy.

He found Brundisium closed against him by Octavian's
garrison, who would have no dealings with Ahenobarbus
as one of Julius's murderers. He blockaded the town, and
seized Sipontum which lay on the coast to the northward,
while Sextus expelled the small force of Octavian from
Sardinia and threatened southern Italy. Agrippa recovered Sipontum and Octavian confronted Antony at
Brundisium. But the soldiers on both sides were averse
to war; and Antony, with the entanglements of the East
in mind, had no wish to coerce them. The death of Fulvia
made things easier. He sent Ahenobarbus to govern
Bithynia and induced Sextus to return to Sicily. Octavian
was no less complaisant, and in the first days of October,
40 B.C., with the help of Maecenas and Pollio, peace was
patched up between the triumvirs at Brundisium. There
was a new division of the empire, Octavian being allotted
all the West except for Lepidus in Africa, and Antony all
lands from the Ionian sea to the Euphrates. Octavian was
given a free hand against Sextus unless he could make
peace with him, and Antony was to have five of the Gallic
legions for Parthia, and an equal right with Octavian to
recruit in Italy. Salvidienus Rufus, who had been appointed to succeed Calenus, had proved a traitor, as
Antony revealed, and on his exposure had committed
suicide, and Octavian saw the transfer of his legions without regret, for he cannot have been sure of their loyalty.

The new friendship was cemented by Antony's marriage to Octavian's sister Octavia, the widow of Gaius Marcellus, and one of the few attractive figures among the Roman women of the time. Beautiful and wise, she was of 'too holy, cold and stiff conversation' to hold for long the flamboyant Antony. The triumvirs paid a visit to Rome, but their ovation was marred by the discontent of the city mob, starved by the failure of the corn supply. It was very necessary to destroy or come to terms with Sextus and his fleet. The latter plan was the first tried. There was an abortive interview at Puteoli, and finally in the early spring of 39 B.C. an arrangement was reached at Misenum at the southern point of the bay of Baiae, when Sextus agreed on terms to withdraw his men from Italy and let the corn-ships alone. There were elaborate festivities on board the fleets and in Rome, and Sextus's daughter was betrothed to Octavia's son by Marcellus. Antony departed eastward, and Octavian hurried to Gaul to instal Agrippa as governor of that province. That fine soldier was at last fairly set on the *cursus honorum*. He had been urban praetor in 40 B.C., and was consul designate for the year 38 B.C.

Octavian, now in his twenty-fourth year, had surmounted another of the enormous hazards of his youth. He had peace with Antony, at any rate for a time, and in that breathing-space he might put order into Italy. His character, now that the watery sun of fortune was making a faint warmth about him, was slowly mellowing. He was still liable to sudden sicknesses, but he had left behind him the chronic anaemia and indigestion which had crippled his adolescence. He no longer stood alone; the companions of his youth had become in the full sense his coadjutors, for the genius of Agrippa for war and of Maecenas for diplomacy was now plainly revealed; he had the loyalty of the bulk of the armies, in whose eyes he wore Julius's mantie, and of the great mass of ordinary citizens, who

were beginning to look to him as the only refuge of the
law-abiding. There seemed to be in him a stability and a
plain good sense which were not in Antony, and still less
in the trivial Lepidus. It was Octavian, not the conservatives, who might be looked to to bring back the old
good days.

Historians have pictured him as at this time universally
detested, an ogre of cold cruelty, jealous, morose, and
implacable, who ruled only by fear, spending his days
between public terrorism and private debauches. There
is no evidence for such a view. The character of Augustus
did not miraculously spring full-bodied into being; it was
already developing in Octavian. He had had to forswear
his youth and play a hard, close-lipped game, and he was
to bear the scars of it till his death. He had as yet little
of that untranslatable thing called 'blanditia,' an easy,
forthcoming civility. But he was slowly unbuttoning himself, and, having been long compelled to live for the day,
he was beginning to see at last a prospect and a horizon.
He was devising a strategy as well as a tactics of power.
The picture of him as an orgiast is simply inconceivable.[1]
For revelries he had neither the health nor the time, since
with a weakly body he was forced to 'toil terribly.' Such
tales had been rife on his first coming to Rome, but Cicero
had described him then as a bright example of old-world
chastity,[2] and the orator would never have dared to incur
public ridicule if his repute had been notoriously otherwise. The morals of Octavian were not higher than those
of his age, but assuredly they were no worse. It is too
often forgotten that the charge of sexual vice was 'common form' in Rome, and did not imply any foundation in
fact. Abuse of an opponent's morals was an accepted

[1] The authorities for the charges are Suet., *Div. Aug.*, 70; Dio, LVI, 43; Seneca, *de clem.*,
I, 10. Ferrero, who has a taste for garish colours, accepts them implicitly (III, 247).

[2] *Phil.*, III, 15.

oratorical practice, which need not be taken seriously.[1] It was like the 'flyting' among the Scottish *makars*, partly a literary convention, partly a tradition with its roots in old religion, like the abuse levelled against a general at his triumph to avert from success the jealousy of the gods. We find Cicero corresponding in the friendliest terms with men like Piso and Vatinius whom shortly before he had pilloried as enemies of mankind.

A proof that Octavian was growing in public favour is Virgil's Fourth Eclogue, which was composed not later than the year 39 B.C. It is a paean over the pact of Brundisium and the new hope of peace. Whether the child who is to be born to inaugurate the Golden Age be the son of Pollio, or of Antony and Octavia, or of Octavian and Scribonia,[2] Octavian is the centre of the picture. The fastidious puritanism of Virgil would never have brought into his high translunary dreams a man regarded generally as a monster of wickedness. A new hope was slowly coming to birth in the Roman world. The old things were passing away; politics, once Rome's chief preoccupation, had disappeared in the clash of arms; the grandees no longer flaunted their wealth in exotic entertainments, for most were dead or bankrupt. With the bad had gone the good; the temples were falling into ruin; [3] the people were starving; the religion of the state, to which Scaevola and Cicero had clung,[4] was disintegrating, and the new creeds from Greece had given Rome nothing in its place. But after years of materialism and misery men were beginning

---

[1] Most of the lesser Latin authors whose works have accidentally survived were eager to relieve their dull pages by retailing ancient scandal, like the stories of Trajan's addiction to wine and boys, and the blameless Nerva's 'Vinolentia.'

[2] The first is the view of Ferrero (iii. 237); the second of *C. A. H.* (x, 69); the third, to which I incline, is fully discussed in *The Messianic Eclogue of Virgil* by Mayor, etc. (1907). See also J. Carcopino, *Virgile et la mystrèe de la IVᵉ Église* (1930), and Rose, *Handbook of Lat. Literature*, 242 *n*.

[3] Augustus had to restore no less than eighty-two. *Mon. Anc.*, IV, 17.

[4] Cf. Augustine, *Civ. Dei.*, IV, 27.

to look into their souls, and with that inquisition came a
sense of sin, a new reverence and a new hope. The mind of
the age was being solemnized; we see the disillusionment
in the men of letters, in Sallust, in Livy's great preface to
his history, in the early verses of Horace,[1] and in Virgil
we find the breaking of light. Salvation could not come
from the high austerities of Lucretius, or the cosmic reconciliation of the Stoics, or the antiquarian ingenuity of
syncretists like Varro. It lay in a return to the old sim-
plicities. Happy the man 'qui potuit rerum cognoscere
causas,' but happier he 'deos qui novit agrestes.'

III

Sextus was not done with. He had legitimate grievances, for in the Peloponnese, which was to have been one
of his provinces, he was prevented by Antony from collecting the revenue. But his prime complaint was that
he was not recognized as an equal by the triumvirs, and
he presently resumed his depredations on the cornships
and the Italian coast. It was a menace which Octavian
was bound to face, for there could be no peace in Italy
with this pirate controlling the sea. War was inevitable,
and Octavian appealed to Antony for help and counsel.
Antony came to Brundisium, but, finding that Octavian
had been delayed, he returned forthwith to Greece, con-
tenting himself with the meaningless advice to his colleague to respect the Misenum pact. This Sextus had
already broken, and Octavian was compelled to prepare
for a campaign, hurrying troops from Gaul, establishing
naval depots at Brundisium and Puteoli, and building
ships to supplement his exiguous navy. He published the
terms of the treaty of Misenum to prove his good faith,
and, since the hollow alliance with Sextus was now at an

[1] *e.g.*, *Epod.*, xvi.

end, he divorced Scribonia on the very day of Julia's birth.

The divorce was a matter of politics, but it had another motive. A new element had come into his life which was a sign of his recovered youth. He had fallen deeply in love. This was not the 'honourable affection' — Mommsen's delightful phrase [1] — with which Julius had regarded his consorts, but a passion which endured to his dying day. The lady was Livia, a daughter of Livius Drusus, the stout anti-Caesarian who had died after Philippi. She was born of the ancient nobility, was beautiful, virtuous and devouringly ambitious, and she was only nineteen.[2] She had been married very young to another aristocrat, Tiberius Claudius Nero, whom Cicero had once sought to espouse to Tullia, and, when scarcely more than a child, had borne him a son who was to be the emperor Tiberius, while a second son, Drusus, was born only three days before her marriage to Octavian on January 17, 38 B.C. She and her husband had been in Perusia during its siege, and had escaped to Sextus in Sicily. They speedily wearied of Sextus's ways, and moved to Sparta, whence they came back to Italy when things became more settled. Octavian probably met Livia on his return from Gaul towards the close of September, 39 B.C. He fell violently in love, and shaved his beard to improve his looks.[3] The wooing prospered and the husband proved complaisant; Livia went to live in Octavian's house, and the wedding ceremony was performed under a special license from the pontiffs.[4]

This marriage, based upon love, had profound political consequences. It brought Octavian into close contact with the *haute noblesse* of Rome and the remnants of the

---

[1] 'eine ehrliche Zuneigung.'

[2] 'genere, probitate, forma Romanarum eminentissima,' Vell., II, 75.

[3] Dio, XLVIII, 34.

[4] The whole question of dates is discussed, and certain traditional scandals refuted, by J. Carcopino, 'Le mariage d'Octave et de Livie,' *Rev. Hist.*, CLXI (1929) 325–36.

senatorial party. It solidified the alliance which he had always desired between the less truculent conservatives and the Caesarian military democracy. It was a conciliatory manifesto, a call to a new alignment of political creeds. On the personal side, it gave him a wife who for fifty years was his wise counsellor and steadfast helpmate; but it also brought into his circle the strain of the Claudii, brilliant, unaccountable, tainted with some deep congenital madness, one of the ablest and most tragically fated of the greater families of Rome.[1]

The campaign against Sextus started badly, for it was like the legendary fight between wolf and shark, fought by opponents whose strength lay in different elements. Also Octavian had none of his great-uncle's mastery of war, and he had the wisdom to know it. He had not Agrippa's power of seeing a campaign as a whole and working on a large strategic plan — the highest form of military talent; nor had he Antony's gift for the leadership of men and his tactical skill in an actual engagement. His gifts were wholly those of the civilian. Fortunately Sextus was no better endowed, being the eternal condottiere, who could win battles but not a war.

The long and critical campaign which began in 38 B.C. has little importance either for the military or the political student. It was an awkward obstacle which had to be surmounted, the penultimate menace which Octavian had to face in his stride towards power. Our only authorities, Dio and Appian, manifestly did not understand what they were writing about, so it is impossible to reconstruct the details with any certainty. Menas, the freedman of Sextus who held Sardinia, brought the island and three legions over to Octavian. The latter appointed him and Calvisius Sabinus, the ex-consul, as his two admirals, and

[1] Livia was herself of the Claudii, for her father, M. Livius Drusus Claudianus, was a Claudian who had been adopted into the Gens Livia.

prepared to attack Sicily, while his land forces were stationed at Rhegium. Sextus was not caught napping. At
Cumae there was an indecisive action, but Octavian was
too slow and cautious: he was checked in the Straits by
Sextus's ships, and next day a storm completed his disaster. He lost half his fleet, and Sextus was left to crow
triumphantly in sea-green robes, and to proclaim himself
the son of Neptune. Happily the pirate was as poor a
general as the triumvir, and made no attempt to follow
up his victory.

The year 38 B.C. therefore had a dark close. For 37 B.C.
Octavian made more ample preparations. He summoned
from Gaul the consul-elect, Agrippa, and put him in supreme command. Agrippa had just won notable successes
against the Germanic tribes, and, first of Roman generals
since Julius, had carried the eagles beyond the Rhine; but,
with characteristic good breeding, he refused a triumph at
a moment when Rome was on short commons and Sextus
was unbeaten. He had still to learn the art of naval war,
but his acute mind told him that the first task was to provide a safe harbour as a base and a training-ground. Accordingly he joined the shallow Lucrine lake in the bay of
Baiae with the deeper lake Avernus, and dug a broad
channel connecting them with the sea. Also Octavian
sent Maecenas to Antony in Greece to beg for help. The
help was given. In the early spring Antony arrived at
Tarentum with a powerful fleet, accompanied by Octavia,
whose persuasions overcame the not unnatural suspicions
of her brother. It was agreed to renew the triumvirate for
another period of five years.[1] Antony was to give his colleague one hundred and twenty ships, while Octavian in

---

[1] It is not clear how far this arrangement received legal confirmation. There had
been a *lex* to establish the first triumvirate, and there seems to have been a plebiscite,
obtained by the legally minded Octavian, to confirm the second. But Appian and Dio
contradict each other and the former contradicts himself. The subject is fully discussed by W. Kolbe, *Hermes*, XLIX, 274 *sqq.*

turn was to furnish twenty thousand legionaries for the Parthian war. Octavia and her child remained with Octavian, and Antony set his face eastward.

He had now virtually handed over to his colleague the ordering of the West, while he himself took the East in fee. His general plan of settlement there was to bolster up client-monarchs, often on insecure thrones. But his chief preoccupation was the threat from Parthia, that strange power, largely Scythian in stock, which had been one of Alexander's satrapies, but which had long ago expelled the Seleucides, and established its own Arsacid dynasty. The Roman renegade Labienus had, as we have seen, invaded and occupied Syria, and after the truce of Brundisium, Antony had sent his lieutenant Ventidius to deal with him. Ventidius was successful: he defeated and killed Labienus in 39 B.C. and next year did the same by Pacorus, the son of the Parthian king Orodes. At the same time an invasion of Macedonia by the Illyrian Parthini was repelled first by Censorinus and then by Pollio. But Parthia had been checked, not defeated, Antony could not fully trust Ventidius, and he was compelled to make a hurried journey eastward to support Herod against his rival Antigonus. After his meeting with Octavian at Tarentum he returned to Syria to prepare in earnest for a major Parthian campaign.

For three winters he had lived happily with Octavia at Athens. If Cleopatra's wit and daring had been a revelation to him of what a woman could be, Octavia showed him the charm of simple goodness. She was as highly educated as the Egyptian queen, and infinitely more restful. He became a decorous husband, and took up the study of philosophy. But the old Adam was still strong in him, and he had outbursts of *folie des grandeurs*, when he permitted some of his eastern subjects to worship him as the god Dionysus. Had Octavia's child been a son things might have gone otherwise, but by the autumn of 37 B.C. he had grown weary of respectability. He had been loyal to Octavian, more loyal than Octavian had been to him, and his discontent with his colleague was extended to his colleague's sister. He was tired of Octavia's 'modest eyes and still conclusion,' and was beginning to bethink himself of a headier vintage. But chiefly he thought of the new posture of affairs. He realized that the task which he had laid on Octavian, and which he had believed would crush him, had in truth made his fortune. He had unwittingly surrendered to him the control of Rome and the western world. The disconsidered underling was in danger of becoming his master. The balance could only be redressed by a resounding triumph in the East, and his eyes returned to Parthia. He had only twenty-four legions, though more were due from Octavian, but his main need was money. This could be got only from Cleopatra, whom for nearly four years he had neglected. The recollection of her usefulness was perhaps as potent with him as the memory of her charms; if in his retrospect he fell in love with her person he was also assuredly in love with her fortune. He summoned the queen of Egypt to meet him in Antioch, and thereby entered upon the last tragic stage of his career.

III. THE BREACH WITH ANTONY: ACTIUM

(37–30 B.C.)

'Nous avons perdu le monde, et le monde, nous; que vous en semble, Tristan ami?'

'Amie, quand je vous ai avec moi, que me fault-il dont? Se tous li mondes estoit orendroit avec nous, je ne verrois fors vous seule.'

Le Roman de Tristan.

More than two thousand years it is since she
Was beautiful. . . .

Now she is but a story that is told
Beside the fire! No man can ever be
The friend of that poor queen!

JAMES STEPHENS.

I

THROUGH seven difficult years Octavian had slowly built up a position which, based at first only on a name and a sentiment, was now solidly founded on popular goodwill. He had contrived the alliance which he had had in view from the start between those who cherished the memory and some of the dreams of Julius, and those who would perpetuate the spirit and most of the forms of the Republic. Rome thirsted for peace, and the pact with Sextus at Misenum had been forced on the triumvirs by public opinion. It was clear that this settlement could not stand, and that there would be no peace until Sextus was crushed, since his ambitions and grievances would remain a perpetual irritant, and he formed a rallying point for all that was most intransigent in Roman conservatism. Therefore two major tasks lay before Octavian, now in his twenty-sixth year. First, he must drive Sextus from the seas and draw his fangs for ever. Second, there must come some day a trial of strength with Antony. There could not be two masters of the empire with irreconcilable temperaments and divergent purposes.

The campaign against Sextus can be briefly recounted, for it was only a distasteful duty which had to be performed, and revealed nothing about Octavian except that he was no great master of war. The operations of 37 B.C. were mainly preparatory, concerned with the creation by Agrippa of Portus Julius, the new naval base, shipbuilding to supplement Octavian's small fleet — a new type of heavy, high-decked warship suitable for boarding [1] — and the training of the crews in seamanship. The campaign of 36 B.C. began on July 1,[2] the date being fixed by Octavian for the month called after his adopted father. The plan, in which we may detect Agrippa's hand, was for a converging attack on Sicily — Octavian from Puteoli, Statilius Taurus from Tarentum, and Lepidus from Africa with sixteen legions and a force of cavalry. Sextus was outnumbered, but he made the most of his position, stationing himself at Messana to command the Straits, while he left the defence of Lilybaeum and the West to his lieutenant Plinius Rufus. The elements fought on his side. On the third of the month came a violent storm which sent Taurus limping back to Tarentum, while Octavian, with whom was Agrippa, lost half his squadron off Sorrento. Lepidus alone managed to land in Sicily and blockade Lilybaeum.

Though the season for seafaring was not far from its

---

[1] Agrippa also invented a new type of grappling iron, and a collapsible wooden tower.
[2] This is Appian's date (v, 97); Dio puts the beginning of the campaign in the spring.

close, Octavian dared not wait. Rome was in a ferment, the repute of Sextus had risen high, and Maecenas was sent back to quiet the populace. Octavian refitted in haste his damaged navy, hurried round the colonies to recruit more veterans, and by the middle of August was ready again for sea. His new position was nearer Sicily, at Vibo, while Taurus lay at Scylacium, thirty miles to the east across the neck of land. Sextus, to whom Menas had re-deserted, watched from Messana the possible landing-places on the north shore of the island. The new plan was for Agrippa to keep him busy while Octavian and Taurus landed at Tauromenium on the east shore, joined hands with Lepidus, and came in on Messana from the south. At first things went well. Agrippa won a slight naval success at Mylae and occupied several coast towns. But Octavian's landing came to grief. Sextus's cavalry attacked him by land, and Sextus's fleet beat him at sea. For a moment it would seem that Octavian despaired, and begged a friend to put him to the sword. By the skin of his teeth he escaped with one companion to the mainland of Italy, where he joined his lieutenant Messalla Corvinus. He had left his legions under Cornificius marooned in Sicily, he did not trust Lepidus, and he had no word of Agrippa.

It was a dark hour, but dawn was near. Agrippa captured Tyndaris, a key position, and Cornificius joined him after a hazardous march over the skirts of Etna. Sextus was doomed, for on all sides the enemy legions were closing in on Messana. He tried his fate at sea, and on September 3 came the decisive battle off Mylae, when Agrippa's dreadnoughts with their superior grappling power overcame the lighter Pompeian craft. Only seventeen of the latter escaped to Messana. Thither Sextus fled, but for him it could be no refuge, and in civilian dress with his few remaining ships he retreated to Antony in the

East. Octavian had surmounted the penultimate hazard of his youth.

One lesser task remained — to deal with Lepidus and the swollen army of Sicily. Lepidus, the world's weather-cock, had a grievance against his fellow triumvir, which, as it seemed to his trivial mind, fate had now given him a chance of avenging. He was the general on the spot who received the surrender of Messana, and was enabled to add its garrison to his own forces. Strong in the command of twenty-two legions he attempted to dictate to Octavian, demanding Sicily in addition to his own province of Africa. There was some justice in his complaint, but he was the type of man who, having no fixity of purpose or dignity of character, invites cavalier treatment. His own troops preferred to follow Octavian, and he was compelled to throw himself at the conqueror's feet. He was allowed to remain Pontifex Maximus, and he retired into private life enriched by the loot of his triumvirate. The legions were a more serious matter, and Octavian had to deal with one or two ugly mutinies, which he quieted by disbanding twenty thousand men, by the awarding of bounties to those who remained with the colours, by the establish-ment of colonies, and by honours to commissioned and non-commissioned officers. To Agrippa, the architect of victory, was given a golden crown decorated with the beaks of ships, to be worn on all triumphal occasions, an honour new in the Roman world.[1]

II

At the age of twenty-seven Octavian had attained a power which none but Alexander and Julius had held before in history. Under his command were forty-three legions, a cloud of cavalry and six hundred ships of war.

[1] On this 'corona classica' see Reinhold, *op. cit.*, 42–43.

He had for his area of government the whole western empire — Italy, Illyria, Africa, the Gauls and Spain. He had behind him the enthusiasm of the Caesarian veterans and the sympathy of the Roman mob. The middle classes had largely lost their former Pompeian sentiment owing to the doings of Sextus, and had been gratified by the restoration of many thousands of runaway slaves from the vanquished fleets.[1] By his marriage with Livia he had entered the inner circle of the nobility, and the most stubborn of aristocrats had come to see in him the only hope of a restored order and peace. The old Republic had gone for good, but in this young man there was something of the ancient Roman virtue. He had reverence for tradition and would not take the office of Pontifex Maximus arbitrarily even from the discredited Lepidus. He gave many proofs that he loved the former ways and that in any reconstruction the focus would be Rome and Italy. The master of the armies of the West was no mere military demagogue, but one who, though Julius's heir, was patently feeling his way to the restoration of many things which Julius had scorned or neglected. Here was a bridge-builder who would not forget the need for abutments in sound tradition. All classes in the nation were coming round to him, and republicans like Statilius Taurus and Messalla Corvinus now stood staunchly by his side. Moreover, there was about him a strange atmosphere of divine favour. He had come safely through countless hazards and triumphed against incalculable odds. The western world had accepted Octavian's own belief in his star.

Senate and People combined to shower honours upon him, but this remarkable young man showed no special desire for honours. He received an ovation for his defeat of Sextus; a triumph was impossible, since the campaign had been domestic police-work and not foreign conquest.

---

[1] 30,000 according to *Mon. Anc.*, v, 1-3.

He had the usual statues and triumphal arches, and the right, which Julius had had, to wear at all times a laurel wreath. More notable was his own act when, before his entry into Rome, on November 13, he assembled the people outside the city bounds and told them what had been achieved.[1] That was the behaviour of one who regarded himself as a magistrate and not as a tyrant.

What precisely his status *de jure* was it is hard to say. He was a triumvir, but the extension of the triumvirate was of doubtful legality. He had assumed for several years the praenomen of Imperator, but this was in the nature of an inherited family title and had no constitutional significance.[2] He held his authority by general agreement as *de facto* tutor, curator, constable of the state. But one privilege was granted him of high significance — the sacrosanctity enjoyed by the tribunes — a privilege extended two years later to Livia and Octavia. This was not the full powers of a tribune — these did not come until six years later — but it involved personal inviolability and the right of sitting with the tribunes in the Senate. With a sure instinct he had always hankered after the tribunician authority, which gave him not only a much-needed personal protection, but a foothold in the only body from which he might expect serious opposition.[3]

For four years Octavian set himself the laborious task of making Italy habitable for honest men. He was hard put to it for money, since Sicily had long ago been bled white, and Antony was drawing the revenues of the opu-

---

[1] Dio, XLIX, 15.

[2] See on this point *C. A. H.*, x, 122 *n.* He had been already hailed four times as Imperator by the armies in the ordinary way — in 43, 40, 38 and 36 B.C.

[3] The grant did not carry the political powers of the tribuneship, 'auxilii latio,' 'coercitio' and 'intercessio.' Appian (v, 132, 548), who is followed by Orosius (VI, 18, 34), assumes the grant in 36 B.C. of the full 'tribunicia potestas' for life, but Dio (XLIX, 15, 5–6) makes it clear that the tribunician power was progressively acquired by Octavian, as it had been by Julius. See *Mon. Anc.* (ed. Hardy), 42; Rice Holmes, I, 221–22; Niccolini, *Il tribunato della Plebe* (1932), 159 *sqq.*

lent East. Yet he managed to reduce taxation, and to
remit the arrears of the contributions imposed originally
by the triumvirs. He restored to the old magistrates certain of the powers usurped by the triumvirate, and he settled his disbanded troops without further confiscations.
By building new temples and repairing old ones he provided relief work for the Roman unemployed. He laboured to suppress brigandage throughout Italy and
crimes of violence in Rome, and for the purpose established a police force on the Egyptian model. Agrippa as
aedile in 33 B.C. (he was now a rich man, having married
the daughter of Atticus, Cicero's friend) reconstructed
the Roman water supply and drainage system.[1] Nor did
domestic reforms divert Octavian from the task of guarding his frontiers. Statilius Taurus was sent to restore
order in the African provinces, and Messalla to bring the
Salassi in the Val d'Aosta to reason. In person he conducted a campaign against the Iapydes among the Croa-
tian hills and forests, where he won a high repute for personal bravery.[2] He besieged and captured Siscia, the chief
town of the Pannonians at the junction of the Kolpa and
the Save, and next year, with Agrippa, carried the war
into Dalmatia. By the year 33 B.C. he had, with a most
modest expenditure of men and money, brought the whole
coast of the eastern Adriatic under the Roman peace.[3]

But his principal task, which makes these years of
supreme importance in history, was to enable Italy to find
her soul. He had established his title to his material inheritance as the heir of Julius; he had still to decide what he
could accept from the bequest of thought and dream.

[1] For details see Reinhold, *op. cit.*, 47–52.

[2] Pliny, *N. H.*, VII, 148; Suet., *Div. Aug.*, 20.

[3] The authorities for the campaigns are App., *Illyr.*, 13, 15–28, and Dio, XLIX, 34 *sqq.*
For the Alpine campaign see E. Pais, *Dalle Guerre Puniche a Augusto* (1918), pt. II.,
375–413; for the Illyrian war see N. Vuliç in *L'Acropole* (1932), VII, 155 *sqq.*; Swoboda,
Octavian und Illyricum (1932); and G. Veith, *Die Feldzüge des . . . Octavianus in Illyrien*
(1914).

What the bequest was we can only guess; it is not easy to read behind the blurred palimpsest the original script of that supreme mind; but certain features seem clear. Like Alexander, Julius conceived of a world-empire of which Rome should be the shrine and the heart, but without predominance. That empire would be an oecumene, a unity of civilization, its citizenship would be extended to all found worthy, and Roman law made its common law. A standing army, which should also be a school of citizenship, and a centralized bureaucracy would provide order and just government. The forms of the Roman city-state might to some degree be preserved as antiquarian curiosities, but Julius had the contempt of the realistic mind for shells from which the life had departed. He stood not for Rome or Italy, but for a new imperial culture, which would draw what was best not only from the Latin tradition, but from Greece, from the East, even from the wilder lands of the West and North. At the head of this economy must be one man, a monarch by whatever name he might be called, sole chief of the army and of the bureaucracy, the ultimate fount of power. Such a kingship it is probable that Julius would have made hereditary,[1] as the simplest way of ensuring a peaceable succession, and, merely as a practical expedient, he would have surrounded it with something of the half-divine glamour of the eastern thrones; but he meant it to be not a satrapy of slaves but a commonwealth of free spirits.[2] He sought to retain the Latin simplicity and hard good sense and to marry them with the colour and art of more imaginative peoples. His monarchy would have been both Roman and Hellenistic, and such diverse commentators as Mommsen and Eduard Meyer are alike justified. But it would have been a monarchy and not a republic;

[1] At his death he had perhaps reached no decision on the point. Cf. Plut., *Brut.*, 7.
[2] This is a natural deduction from Cic., *ad Fam*, XII, 17.

and we of today, with the history of the later empire in our mind, and with our experience of the brittleness and inelasticity of republican forms, may well pay tribute to the acumen of the boldest of all architects of empire.

Some of this Octavian unhesitatingly rejected as impracticable. The kingship, for instance; Julius might have compassed it, but nothing save supreme genius could force it on a reluctant Rome. Besides, it was Antony's game, and he could only succeed as Antony's anti-type. Some of it he accepted and set himself to work out in his own terms — the single army, the centralized government. Some things he disliked, such as the contempt for the old republican forms; he held that it was bad policy to innovate too rashly, and he was sufficient of the bourgeois — unlike Julius, who was the essential aristocrat — to have a lingering admiration for the old houses and the old ways. But especially he differed from the theory of a flat, unfeatured imperial citizenship, an empire equal in all its parts. Rome must remain the directing mind and Italy the power-house. The logic of the statesman as well as the sentiment of the provincial forced him to this view, for he must have a fulcrum from which to work. We shall see how, when opportunity was given him, he faced his wider tasks; in the meantime, while his authority was not yet beyond question, he turned his mind to the problem of Italy — a proof of where his heart lay.

Italy needed both a material and a spiritual regeneration. She was wearied by the long years when she had been the cockpit of war, and she had all but lost hope and faith. Octavian set himself two duties especially — to revive her ancient religion, and to restore profit and amenity to rural life. It was a favourable moment, for misfortune had abated the grandiosity of the Roman temper, and there was a widespread reaction towards simplicity. Men's minds were returning to homely things. Horace, now by grace of Maecenas a member of the leisured classes, exchanged the bitterness of his early satires for the more mellow and cheerful outlook of his second book; Varro put the economy and practice of agriculture into a manual; and Virgil in his *Georgics* produced the epic of rural Italy. The well-managed soldier-settlements had made countless small farms out of the big estates, and the independent small farmer, the yeoman, the strongest stock in the land, had his numbers multiplied.[1] The rural population was greatly enlarged, and rural life was given a new dignity as the one enduring thing in a world of change. There was still no deep fissure between town and country, for the well-to-do citizen had his country farm, and every Italian market-place was within sight and hearing of the fields. The new emphasis on the preciousness of the Italian soil affected both rustic and townsman.

This rural revival involved a mode of life and a religion. Octavian was not only devout in restoring the urban temples; he revived many old rites and ceremonies, forbade the practice of certain eastern cults, and expelled from Rome Greek and Asiatic magicians. He sought to bring back the 'religion of Numa,' a religion of usage and sentiment rather than of creed, for the world was sick of the dust of philosophical debate. It was a religion attached to things and places, to homely and familiar 'stocks and stones,' full of small, friendly rites and kindly mysteries — altars gay with flowers and sweet with green herbs, stumpy wooden images of Ceres and Bacchus garlanded with blossom, a multitude of little household gods more like brownies than deities. There were wilder festivals, too, when the madness of spring and the new moon crept into the rites, and grave ceremonial occasions, like birth and death and the assumption of manhood. In every

[1] For the true status of the Italian yeoman see Tenney Frank, *Aspects of Social Behaviour in Ancient Rome*, ch. III.

incident of the year religion played its part, for the rural
Italian was a crude Platonist who found divinity in the
humblest objects of common use. But it was an ordered
and a bracing life, whether lived in a simple country farm
or in a grandee's villa, a life close to nature, where each
season brought its duties and its comforts — the freshness
of spring, the aromatic heats of summer, the mellow content of autumn, the tonic winters when the hail beat on
the shutters, and the household within, and even the
images of the dead, were snug in the glow of the hearth-fire.

In this task Octavian had august colleagues. Virgil,
introduced by Pollio to Maecenas, was now in the full
sunlight of public favour, and the cause of the Italian land
was dear to one who had himself known the bitterness of
exile. The *Georgics*, the 'best poem of the best poet,' as
Dryden called it, is partly 'laudes Italiae,' a fervent panegyric on the homeland, but it is also a guide to the new
men just adventuring on the soil, to 'show them the way
which they do not know.' Horace, too, country-bred and
now himself a squire, pointed the same moral with a
sharper pen, for he was as much moralist as poet. He is
not only the panegyrist of country simplicity, but a caustic
voice reminding Romans of their duties to the gods.[1] Both
men saw in Octavian the herald of a nobler world and
interpreted his thoughts to the Roman people and to
himself.

III

Meanwhile Antony had been following his own course
in the East as an independent and somewhat hostile potentate. When he left Italy in the autumn of 37 B.C. it
was to enter upon his long-contemplated Parthian campaign. For this he needed money, and he could get it from

[1] *e.g.*, *Sat.*, II, 2, 103.

no other source than Egypt. Cleopatra could provide few troops, since she had only palace guards, but she had a well-filled treasury. She had no interest in the Parthian war, but she was faithful to the main policy of her life, the restoration of Egypt to the position which it had held under the first Ptolemies, and to attain this end and secure Antony's help she must pay his price. She met him at Antioch in the early spring of 35 B.C., and in the revulsion from Octavia he fell wholly under her spell. Now at last he became the devout lover. He acknowledged the twins, Alexander the Sun and Cleopatra the Moon, whom she had borne him, and he handed over to her Cyprus, part of Syria, and other old possessions of Egypt as a first instalment of his bargain. He did not yet publicly marry her, but their close alliance was now advertised to the world.[1]

Antony did not adopt the plan of campaign which eighteen years before had been the ruin of Crassus. He could not afford to be drawn into a lengthy war, with the situation in Italy so hazardous and perplexed. He had the plans of Julius before him, the essence of which was an assault upon the Parthian capital, Ecbatana, by way of Armenia as an advanced base, and accordingly he assembled his ten legions and ten thousand horse at Zeugma on the Euphrates, and turned northward along the right bank of that river. But the plan, which Julius had designed for a lengthy campaign and ample forces, failed when it was put into execution in a hurry with inadequate troops. On the high plateau of Erzerum he was joined by his reserves, and reviewed an army of something over one hundred

[1] The date of Antony's formal marriage to Cleopatra by Egyptian rites is disputed, since the ancient authorities are vague. Kromayer (*Hermes*, XXIX, 582–84), Ferrero (IV, 264), and *C. A. H.* (x, 66) place it in the beginning of 35 B.C., while Gardthausen (*N. J. cl. Alt.*, XXXIX., 1917, 161 *sqq.*) argues for 32 B.C., after the divorce of Octavia, and Rice Holmes (I, 227–31) seems inclined to the same view, based upon the general probabilities and the evidence of Plutarch, Eutropius, Eusebius, and the coins.

thousand men. His first objective was the Median capital, Phraaspa, which he reached about the middle of
August and to which he promptly laid siege. But, having
divided his forces, the Parthians were able to destroy
part of them, his intelligence service was defective, his
Armenian allies failed him, and, since a winter siege was
out of the question, he was compelled to retreat. He
wisely chose the difficult route through the mountains of
Tabriz, and after twenty-seven arduous days, in which he
showed all his old fortitude and resource, he brought his
eagles across the Araxes. By the end of the year he had
his remnant safe in Syria with a loss of over twenty thousand men. He reported a victory to Rome, which was only
half believed. The first attempt at the conquest of Parthia
had failed disastrously.

Cleopatra had met him during his return journey with
supplies of food and clothing, and the rest of the winter
was spent with her at Alexandria. Early in the spring of
35 B.C., Octavia, hearing of his difficulties, felt it to be her
duty to join him, but a curt message from him bade her
return at once to Rome. Faithful to her conception of a
wife's part, she stayed on in Athens in spite of Octavian's
disapproval, taking care of Fulvia's children as well as of
her own two daughters. Meantime in Alexandria the two
elderly lovers — Antony was at least forty-six and Cleopatra ten years younger — were bringing their purposes
into harmony. The queen of Egypt was not ill-pleased by
the Parthian failure, since a resounding success would
have made Antony independent of her and revived his
prestige in Rome, and she desired that he should be forced
to look to her alone for the fulfilment of his hopes. His
design of grandiose eastern conquest slowly faded out of
the air. He meant, no doubt, to enter Armenia again in
the summer of 35 B.C., but the refugee Sextus Pompeius
made trouble in Asia before he was hunted down and

slain, an achievement which damaged Antony's popularity among the Pompeians in Rome. It was not until 34 B.C. that he overran Armenia and made it a Roman province — a barren conquest which brought him no special repute. Meantime in Alexandria Cleopatra was moulding him to the shape of an eastern satrap.

What was now Antony's purpose, for, though he was becoming wax in a woman's hands, the rôle of lover alone could not content him? Cleopatra from her girlhood, with the clear sight of one whose passions were always subservient to her ambitions, had realized that, unless something of the old empire of the Ptolemies could be restored, Egypt must die. That restoration could only be accomplished with the aid of the Roman legions, and to the master of these legions she offered the bribe not only of her person but of an opulent and glittering eastern throne. Antony for long repelled the temptation. He was well aware how hard it would be to make Roman soldiers the tools of such a plan; they were men of the West, whose ultimate hope was for allotments of Italian land. But fate was constraining him to follow Cleopatra. His Parthian failure had robbed him of the prestige of a conqueror. Octavian had played his game so adroitly that he had won the greater part of Italy to his side. In many ways the young man had disregarded the interests of his fellow triumvir; he had disgraced Lepidus on his own responsibility; he had not shared with Antony the provinces recovered from Sextus; he had not sent him the agreed Italian contingents; the compact of Tarentum had been shattered. The West was failing Antony, so he must turn perforce to the East. There was also his love for Cleopatra, the passion of a middle-aged *roué* for something higher than mere comely flesh, for an alert intelligence and an unconquerable spirit. It is likely, too, that years of gross living had somewhat blunted his mind. He was become more of a passive creature, apt for flamboyant dreams rather than the hard Roman realism.[1]

He had made his election, and in the autumn of 34 B.C. there were strange doings in Alexandria. Antony celebrated a triumph for his Armenian campaign — a direct insult to Rome.[2] It was Cleopatra's hour. She sat on a high throne of gold, assuming the place of the Roman Jupiter Optimus Maximus, to receive the gift of captives. Still more magnificent was the next ceremonial, when she sat beside him robed as Isis, with a little lower their three children, Ptolemy, Cleopatra and Alexander, and the young Caesarion. Antony addressed the people, declaring that Caesarion was the legitimate son of Julius, and hailing him as King of Kings and his mother as Queen of Kings. Then followed what is known as the Donations of Alexandria, by which Alexander was given Armenia and all the lands east of the Euphrates; Ptolemy, Syria and Cilicia and the overlordship of Asia; and the little Cleopatra, Cyrenaica and Libya. The triumvir himself remained plain Mark Antony, but this was for Roman consumption; to the eastern world he was Dionysus-Osiris, the consort of the goddess-queen of Egypt. But the fact that he had taken upon himself the making of kings is a clue to his true ambition. He virtually proclaimed himself Roman emperor and Cleopatra his empress, a fulfilment of the prophecy that when she had cast down Rome to the dust she would raise it again to heaven, unite East and West, and inaugurate the Age of Gold.[3]

Antony had played Octavian's game. The latter had his own grievances against him; the unauthorised occupation of Egypt, the execution of Sextus, which had deeply offended Roman sentiment, his treatment of Octavia, his

---

[1] This was Seneca's view — 'a great man turned to un-Roman ways by his love of drink and Cleopatra.' *Ep.*, 83, 25.

[2] Cf. Bouché-Leclerq, *Hist. des Lagides*, II, 274.

[3] Cf. *C. A. H.*, x, 80–83, and the authorities there cited.

distribution to aliens of Roman lands. But what rankled most deeply was his dishonouring of the memory of Julius by his acknowledgment of Caesarion. There was an old tenderness for Antony in Roman society, and many senators were his partisans. But there was no tenderness for Cleopatra. That a woman and an eastern should presume to direct Roman armies and rule Roman lands cut Rome's pride to the quick. Moreover there was a lurking dread of that spectre which had long haunted the western mind, domination by the East, and the transference of world-power from the Tiber to the Nile. The passionate lines of the poets show how lively was this fear.[1] Octavian saw that his policy must be to foster it by every propagandist art. Antony was building a fleet; the last struggle could not be long delayed.

The pace of events quickened during the year 33 B.C., the year of Octavian's second consulship. He had been steadily increasing his repute by his success in the frontier wars, and by his domestic reforms, and in that year he received from the Senate the signal honour of an authority to create new patrician families in order to fill the priesthood — a proof of his acceptance by the conservatives.[2] He was busy winding up his minor campaigns, and mustering his strength for the final arbitrament. Meantime Antony, after marching to the Araxes and making futile pacts with the king of Media, was concentrating his forces at Ephesus, where Cleopatra joined him with a war-chest of some four million sterling. To Octavian's protests he returned insulting replies. He had the boldness to send a deputation to Rome demanding the Senate's approval of his Egyptian doings. The consuls for 32 B.C. were Antonians, Gaius Sosius and Domitius Aheno-

---

[1] See especially Virg., *Aen.*, VIII, 685–88, 705–06; Hor., *Epod.*, IX, 2; and Ovid, *Met.*, 15, 826.

[2] Dio, XLIX, 43.

barbus, and they suppressed this dispatch. But to the Senate they communicated the news that Antony regarded the triumvirate as having expired on the last day of 33 B.C. and did not wish it renewed. He hoped, no doubt, to compel Octavian to assent, and leave him with no legal support for his extra-ordinary powers.[1]

But the dispute had now gone deeper than legalities. Sinister tales were coming from Egypt. Early in 32 B.C. Octavian attacked Antony in the Senate, and the consul Sosius replied with vehemence, and would have moved a motion against him had not a tribune interposed his veto. Presently the two consuls fled to Antony, and Octavian announced that all who so desired might do likewise, with the result that about one-third of the Senate left for the East. This proof of Antonian feeling in Rome convinced him that his wise course was to direct the public enmity against Cleopatra rather than against Antony. Plancus, aforetime Antony's henchman, arrived from Egypt to change sides, and furnished him with ample material for such propaganda. Cleopatra had a bodyguard of Roman soldiers; Antony walked by her side among her eunuchs; he wore Egyptian robes and arms, and played a part in religious mummeries hateful to the Roman spirit. Then in May came the news that Antony had divorced Octavia[2] and had been publicly wedded to the Egyptian queen. There was a violent revulsion in Roman sentiment, the former tenderness for Antony died away, and fear of this witch of the East, shamelessly traduced by Octavian's agents, hag-rode the popular mind. Plancus brought news, too, of a will of Antony's deposited with the Vestal Virgins, and this Octavian seized and published — the only instance in which he violated a religious

[1] The date of the expiration of the second term of the triumvirate has ever since Mommsen been the subject of much learned argument, which is examined by Rice Holmes, II, 231-45.

[2] Livy, *Epit.*, 132; Plut., *Ant.*, 57; Dio, L, 3.

custom. It affirmed the legitimacy of Caesarion, gave huge legacies to Cleopatra's children, and provided that his body should be buried beside her at Alexandria in the royal mausoleum.[1] The natural assumption was that Antony meant to transfer the capital of the empire to Egypt. Popular fury forced the Senate's hand. He was divested of his imperium and deposed from the consulship for 31 B.C. to which he had been elected. In the late autumn, in solemn ceremonial accompanied by the Conscript Fathers, Octavian, as fetial priest, proclaimed war before the temple of Bellona. But against Cleopatra alone; for it was necessary to mass the public resentment against the foreigner, and Octavian already, in 36 B.C., had announced the end of the civil wars.[2] The issue was not between Octavian and Antony, but between Rome and the queen of Egypt, between the West and the East.[3]

It has been the fashion of historians to describe Octavian's position at this moment as precarious, but in truth he had already the master-hand. First, for his constitutional status. He was still nominally triumvir, with a doubtful legal sanction, but he wisely did not rely upon any such authority. It was a time of revolution, when nice legal distinctions are meaningless, and the commander of the legions fell back upon a power which had always been implicit in the Republic, that of curator and constable of the state. In the early autumn — perhaps on the advice of Maecenas — he resolved upon a bold step, and summoned the whole western world, senators, troops and civilians, to swear allegiance to him and acclaim him its leader against Antony. The business was elaborately

---

[1] Suet., *Div. Aug.*, 17; Plut., *Ant.*, 55. Rostovtzeff (*Soc. and Econ. Hist. of Rom. Empire*, 29) considers this will to have been a forgery; but his view is in defiance of the ancient authorities and — it seems to me — of the probabilities of the case.

[2] Dio, L, 6. Suetonius (*Div. Aug.*, 17) says that Antony was declared a public enemy.

[3] 'omnigenumque deum monstra et latrator Anubis | contra Neptunum et Venerem contraque Minervam | tela tenent.' Virg., *Aen.*, VIII, 698–700.

organized, but the oath was voluntary; Bononia as an old client-city of Antony's was exempted, but even Antony's own colonists subscribed.[1] This was an unprecedented act, but it was in consonance with Roman tradition, and in conjunction with his third consulship in 31 B.C. it brigaded behind him both Senate and People. But it had also vital importance for the future, since it meant not only the fusion of the Caesarian and the republican parties, but the institution of a new political machinery, a form of one-man supremacy which had no relation to the oriental type of kingship. The triumvirate was wiped out, and Octavian was given a 'facultas imperandi,' a right of command without limitation of function or time. It was Rome's answer to Antony's un-Roman doings. The wheel had come full circle. Against a military usurpation was now arraigned the old spirit of republican Rome. It was the beginning of that 'civilitas,' that deference to public opinion and to republican tradition, which was to characterize his empire.[2]

It was also a proof of the dawning of that 'auctoritas,' that personal authority, which, far more than any legal or constitutional device, was the true secret of his later power. In twelve years this young man had won a singular prestige. He had inherited the glamour of Julius, and out of it had made a new thing. He had interpreted his heritage as a duty to serve the people — *noblesse oblige*; but he had also construed it as a duty to fear nothing — *noblesse ne se laisse pas intimider*. He had been marvellously patient and discreet, and he had been miraculously

---

[1] 'juravit in mea verba tota Italia sponte sua...' *Mon. Anc.*, v, 3–6; Dio, L, 6; Suet., *Div. Aug.*, 17. For different views on this point see Caspari, *C. Q.*, v (1911), 220 *sqq.*, and Rice Holmes, II, 247–51.

[2] Cf. Suetonius of Augustus, 'clementiae civilitatisque ejus multa et magna documenta sunt' (*Div. Aug.*, 51), and of Claudius, 'in semet augendo parcus atque civilis' (*Div. Claud.*, 12); also Tertullian (*Apol.*, 14), 'hoc imperium, cujus ministri estis, civile non tyrannicum.' On the importance of the oath see Levi, *Ottaviano capoparte*, II, 177 *sqq.*

bold. Antony might annex the trappings of Hellenistic monarchy, but Octavian had borrowed from it something profounder, which was a new thing in Rome — a conception of the king as saviour and father. From Homer's Agamemnon, 'the shepherd of his people,' the conception descends through Greek history, through Plato and the Orators and the Hellenistic kings, and then through Augustus to the Byzantine emperors — the vision of a monarch whose primary attribute should be loving-kindness flowering in good deeds.[1]

If Octavian's position was now impregnable in prestige, it was also by far the stronger from the military point of view. Antony had greater financial resources, for Octavian was poor and had to resort to unpopular fresh taxation, but in all other respects he was outmatched by his adversary. Octavian had a loyal and compact army, and in his commander-in-chief, Agrippa, the best soldier of the age. Antony had around him a coterie of Roman refugees, hopelessly divided in their views, and he had the embarrassing company of Cleopatra. He had a following of client-kings,[2] who at the best were half-hearted and were in terror of defying Rome. He had behind him Greece and Macedonia and Thrace, Egypt and Cyrene, and the Aegean islands, but Octavian in the West had a better nursery of men. In vain Antony had tried by his propaganda to seduce the loyalty of Italy. He had a fleet of some five hundred ships of the line, most of them new and heavy vessels,[3] and he had nineteen Roman legions — a total of over sixty thousand men — and some eighty thousand Asiatic horse and foot. To meet him Octavian did not mobilize his whole strength — not more than

---

[1] φιλανθρωπία revealed in εὐεργεσίαι. The king is φίλος, εὐεργέτης, σωτήρ. Demosthenes, de Corona, 43, and Stobaeus, Florilegium (ed. Gaisford), II, 314.

[2] For the list see Plut., Ant., 61.

[3] They had from six to nine benches of rowers — floating citadels or towns, says Florus (Epit., II, 21).

eighty thousand foot and twelve thousand cavalry, and
perhaps four hundred ships, for he did not overrate his
enemy. Antony's plan of campaign was to stand on the
defensive in Greece, since he believed that Octavian dared
not delay but must be forced to attack at a disadvantage.
It has been a mystery to many why he left the initiative
to his enemy, when by an invasion of Italy in 32 B.C. he
might have caught Octavian in a difficult hour. But Antony had no choice. He could not take Cleopatra with
him across the Adriatic, and Cleopatra would not suffer
him to go without her. Also his base was Asia Minor and
he had to string out his forces for the defence of Egypt.
To concentrate army and fleet and lead them to Italy in
32 B.C., would have been a task beyond the power of
Julius himself.[1]

IV

In the campaign of Actium the main features are clear,
but many of the details are obscure, and explanations
must be conjectural. Like Aegospotami and Pharsalus
and Philippi, it was a decisive event in history, but, like
these actions, its military interest is small. The traveller
who takes boat from Corfu for the Ambracian gulf, and
surveys its shining reaches backed by tawny hills and the
blue Aetolian mountains, will get no fresh enlightenment
from his survey. The riddle of Actium is not in the details
of the fighting but in the minds of the combatants.

By the late autumn of 32 B.C. Antony's forces lay along
the west coast of Greece from Corcyra (Corfu) to Methone
at the extreme south-west point of the Peloponnese.
The larger part of his army was in winter quarters at
Actium, the southern peninsula at the entrance to the
Ambracian gulf, and in the gulf itself was the main

---

[1] This question has been fully discussed by Kromayer, *Hermes*, xxxiii, 60 *sqq.*

strength of his fleet. He and Cleopatra made their headquarters at Patrae, at the mouth of the gulf of Corinth.
Supplies could only come by the Egyptian ships, and this
explains why the northern coast and the Via Egnatia were
surrendered, and with them the best communications
with Macedonia and the East. Contingents at Leucas and
Methone were necessary to protect the route from Egypt.

This fact determined Octavian's initial strategy. He
concentrated his forces at Brundisium and Tarentum,
and early in 31 B.C. crossed to Greece; why Antony made
no effort to prevent him is one of the minor mysteries of
the campaign. Maecenas was left in charge in Rome, and
Octavian took with him all the senators and knights who
might have made trouble in Italy. In order to cover his
landing, his admiral, Agrippa, attacked the Egyptian
corn-convoy in the south, took Methone, and slew its commander, Bogudes of Mauretania. Octavian safely reached
Epirus, and marched swiftly southward in the hope of surprising Antony in the Ambracian gulf. But the latter,
alarmed by Agrippa's doings, had hastened to the gulf,
where he found the entry safely blocked by his ships, and
had fortified a strong position on the Actian peninsula.
Octavian, foiled in his attempt at a surprise, took up position at Mikilitsi in the hills on the north side, near where
the city of Nicopolis was afterwards built, and connected
his camp by walls and entrenchments with his harbour in
the bay of Comarus. When his reserves had arrived Antony endeavoured to force a battle, crossed the strait, and
encamped his army two miles south of Octavian, while
he sent his cavalry in a broad sweep to the north to cut
off his enemy's water supply. But he found blockade impossible, for he could not hold a line five miles long, his
cavalry manœuvre failed, and he was compelled to fall
back to Actium. He was now the blockaded instead of
the blockader, for Agrippa had worked havoc with his

sea communications. He had captured first Leucas and then Patrae, and there was no more corn from Egypt.

The hot summer dragged on, and every day Antony's position became more comfortless. Octavian's legions and crews were in healthy quarters, but Antony's were weak from malaria and on famine rations. The latter was compelled to bring food from eastern Greece, over the mountain tracks of Aetolia.[1] Worse still, desertions became frequent, and executions of suspects did not mend matters. Amyntas took over to Octavian two thousand Galatian horse;[2] Domitius Ahenobarbus, now sick unto death, followed suit; so did Dellius, whom rumour alleged to be Cleopatra's lover. His forces were rapidly getting out of hand, and all summer disputes raged in his councils. Cleopatra had as little love for this campaign as she had had for the Parthian war, for, if Antony defeated Octavian and entered Rome in triumph, he would pass out of her orbit; but she was no fool, and it is hard to believe in the treachery with which Josephus credits her,[3] or Ferrero's story of her malign mastery.[4] Canidius Crassus would have abandoned the ships, lured Octavian into Macedonia, and fought the final battle on land — an impossible plan in the then condition of Antony's troops. Cleopatra wished to use the fleet and fight a way out; if they succeeded, good and well; if not, she and Antony could at least escape to Egypt, refit their armies, and defend the East against Octavian.[5] Her advice was followed, and in the last days of August Antony completed his preparations. A deserter had informed Octavian of the general plan, though not of certain secret details, and he made his dispositions accordingly.

At first he hoped to avoid a battle. He proposed to let

---

[1] Plutarch's grandfather was one of the pressed carriers.
[2] Hor., *Epod.*, IX, 17–18.   [3] *in Ap.*, II, 5.   [4] IV, 90 *sqq.*
[5] Plut., *Ant.*, 63; Dio, L, 15; cf. Kromayer, *Hermes*, XXXIV, 29 *sqq.*

the Antonian fleet clear the straits and then overhaul it, believing that the sight of Antony fleeing for Egypt would lead to wholesale desertions. But Agrippa urged that a fight was inevitable, since it was unlikely that his lighter vessels would be able to overtake Antony's monsters under a full spread of canvas. The position had been reversed since the campaign against Sextus, and Octavian had given up his heavy dreadnoughts for smaller and more manageable craft.[1] The last days of August were stormy, but the morning of September 2 dawned clear and fine, with the usual light breeze blowing from the sea. In summer on these coasts the wind changes in the afternoon, and blows with some force from the north-west. Of this Antony meant to take advantage; it might enable him to separate Octavian's fleet from its land base, and, if he failed, it would speed his own retreat. He burned all the ships he did not need, and in the remainder embarked about half his army, while to Cleopatra's detachment he entrusted his treasure-chests. He himself commanded his right wing, and Sosius the left, while Cleopatra was in rear of his centre.

Early on the second Octavian put to sea, himself taking charge of his right squadrons, while Agrippa, who was also in general command, had the left wing and faced Antony. He took up position a little less than a mile from the entrance of the channel and rested on his oars. Shortly before midday Antony's fleet emerged, and the two waited until the wind shifted. When that moment came the forces joined battle. What followed is not clear, except that Antony and Agrippa were hotly engaged, and that the latter's lighter craft handled Antony's dreadnoughts much as Drake in the English Channel dealt with the leviathans of the Spanish Armada. On both wings the fight was going badly for Antony, and on both he was in

[1] Reinhold, *op. cit.*, 55–56.

danger of being outflanked. Desertions and surrenders seem to have begun in his centre, when suddenly he left his flagship in a galley and joined Cleopatra, who had hoisted sail. Who first gave the signal is uncertain, but the plan had been agreed upon beforehand as the last resort in case of defeat. When Antony's fleet saw its commander in flight with the Egyptian ships, its power of resistance broke. Some vessels got back to harbour, and the rest surrendered or were destroyed. Octavian, surprised by this unexpected and crowning mercy, waited all night at sea, rescuing men from the burning hulls, and in the morning returned to the gulf to discover the situation there. He found that the opposition was melting fast. The fleet was gone, but for some days the army under Canidius held its ground, though the desertion of its general had broken its spirit. Presently Canidius fled to Antony in Egypt, and the legions surrendered to Octavian, some being disbanded and sent to Italy, while the rest were incorporated in his own army.[1]

Antony's defeat was irretrievable. His own army, Rome, and all the western world had turned against him. His client-kings and Cleopatra herself were ready to forsake him. After Actium the Greek cities at once surrendered, except Corinth, which was taken by Agrippa. Octavian wintered in Athens, and in January, 30 B.C., at Agrippa's request, crossed in wild weather to Brundisium and settled the trouble with the disbanded soldiers and the dispossessed landowners by promising them payment out of the treasure of Egypt. His next task was to secure that treasure and wind up accounts with Antony and Egypt's queen. The purple sails of Cleopatra's flagship

[1] The authorities for Actium are Dio, LI, *sqq.*; Plut., *Ant.*, 65 *sqq.*; Vell., II, 84; Florus, II, 21; Orosius, VI, 19; Servius on Virg., *Aen.*, VIII. The best modern reconstruction is that of Kromayer, *Hermes*, XXXIV. See also *C. A. H.*, X, 103–05; Rice Holmes, I, 153–58, 259; Gardthausen, II, 196 *sqq.* Important recent studies are those of W. W. Tarn, *J. R. S.*, XXI (1931), 173–99 and M. A. Levi, *Athenaeum*, X (1932), 1–21.

brought Antony safely to the East, but there he found that his last hope had gone. His legions in Cyrene repudiated him and joined Octavian's legate, Cornelius Gallus. At Alexandria he fell into a profound melancholy, and listened idly to Cleopatra's gallant schemes for seizing the silver mines of Spain or sailing far into the sunrise and founding a new Indian empire. The virtue had gone out of him. He sent envoys to Octavian to sue for terms, but Octavian returned no answer. Then in July, when the latter's cavalry were near, he made one desperate effort in defence. His troops deserted him, and, when he had the false news that Cleopatra was dead, he fell on his sword and, mortally wounded, begged to be taken to the royal mausoleum where she was secluded. There he died in her arms, to the infinite relief of his conqueror. Octavian had wiped him out of his scheme of things, and now he had opportunely removed himself from the world.

The last act of the drama was a grim one, culminating in one supreme hour of romance. Octavian had replied smoothly to Cleopatra's entreaties, for he wished to preserve her alive to grace his triumph. It would be a final proof to Rome that the peril from the East had gone. There was little chivalry in the Roman temper. When he met her in Alexandria she tried to move him by impassioned appeals to the memory of Julius, but he listened with downcast eyes and said nothing. He was not amenable to the pathetic. He had had her conveyed to the Palace and kept under strict guard. She now knew her fate and met it like a queen. Octavian put to death the two boys, Caesarion aged sixteen, and Antyllus, Antony's son by Fulvia, who was two years younger. It was his last act of politic cruelty — politic, because while they lived they endangered the foundations of his power. She realized that to her he would be not less pitiless. An asp, the divine emissary of the Sun-god, was brought to her in a basket of green figs, and when Octavian, warned by her letter, hastened to her chamber, he found her lying dead — robed and crowned — with her waiting women, Charmion and Iras, by her side. He was content, for she had solved for him a difficult problem. He allowed her to be buried beside Antony, and gave the faithful maids a splendid funeral.[1]

V

The death of Antony, when 'not cowardly' he put off his helmet, has been made a moment of high drama by the genius of Shakespeare. But his true farewell to life was when he went aboard Cleopatra's galley. The picture of him sitting in the stern, his head sunk on his breast, a refugee with a foreign woman, reveals the downfall of his character and his hopes. For a little while he was execrated in Rome; his statues were overthrown, and his name was blotted from the records; Virgil may have drawn from him the robber Cacus of the *Aeneid*.[2] But Rome could not long cherish enmity against one so human and in many ways so characteristically Roman. Augustus restored him to the Fasti, and three later emperors were proud to share his blood. His character, like his face, had no symmetry. He had remarkable talents, but they were ill co-ordinated, and his tempestuous soul was in perpetual disequilibrium. Each of his virtues — and they were many — was nullified by some rampant vice. With the steady resolution and the cool, steeled courage of Octavian his flamboyant and spasmodic qualities could not compete. In him he

---

[1] Later writers, like Suetonius (*Div., Aug.*, 17), Plutarch (*Ant.*, 86) and Dio (LI, 14), are inclined to doubt the story of how Cleopatra died, but the earlier writers like Horace (*Od.*, I, 37, 26–27) and Velleius (II, 87) accepted it; cf. *C. A. H.*, x, 110 *n*. Ferrero (IV, 114) is more than usually fantastic. The best account of the deaths of Antony and Cleopatra will be found in Bouché-Leclerq, *Hist. des Lagides*, II, 315–44.

[2] See R. S. Conway, *Makers of Europe* (1931), 74.

found his eternal anti-type, and the soothsayer in Shakespeare's play warned him truly:

> Thy demon — that's thy spirit which keeps thee — is
> Noble, courageous, high, unmatchable,
> Where Caesar's is not; but near him thy angel
> Becomes a fear, as being o'erpowered.

He is the classic instance of the second-rate man who is offered a first-rate destiny, and who, in stumbling after it, loses his way in the world.

Cleopatra has long ago passed beyond the libels with which her reputation was blackened by a terrified Rome — even the maledictions of great poets, whose hate confers an unwelcome immortality. Charmion's tribute, 'a lass unparalleled,' is the world's verdict. She stands with Helen of Troy as one of the two women whose influence over the hearts of men has become a legend and a symbol. But the common picture of her as a martyr of love, a mortal Aphrodite, does scant justice to her powers of mind. To Egypt she was a wise and capable ruler, and in Egypt for long her memory was cherished. A Coptic bishop of the seventh century could speak of her as the most illustrious of her sex, 'great in herself and in her achievements.' She was a notable woman of business, she inaugurated and directed industries, and she organized the supplies for Antony's army and fleet. If she wrote a book on cosmetics, she is also credited with works on coinage and weights and measures. She was a friend of Philosophers, like Philostratus the Platonist and Nicolaus the Peripatetic. She had a courage so clear and fine that no man or woman ever made her afraid. In the downfall of Antony's fortunes she did not despair, but struggled on to the end, and welcomed death only when all was over. With much earthy dross in her, she was yet pre-eminently a creature of 'fire and air.'

It is easy to dismiss the false Cleopatra, but the true

one can only be conjectured, for the material for a reasoned verdict is lost. Could we know what Julius thought of her we should be in a better case, for it is likely that Julius inspired much of her policy, and was the only man who ever captured her mind as well as her heart. Her main purpose is clear. She was the heir of Alexander, and, as we have seen, sought to rebuild the monarchy of Egypt with the help of Rome. But there was more in her than mere dynastic ambition, for she had 'immortal longings.' She was the prophetess of an ancient culture which she believed to be doomed without her aid. From Julius she may have learned the ideal of an empire which should be a true fellowship of humanity, and in which all the old cultural bequests would be harmonized. Her months in Rome had convinced her of the hardness and narrowness of the Roman temper, and her association with Antony and his friends did not abate her dislike of its grossness. She was in revolt against the Roman philistinism which would crush under its chariot wheels a multitude of ancient and beautiful things, and constrict into a mercantile uniformity the infinite variousness of the world she loved. The virtues of the Italian temper were hidden from her, and she saw only its vulgarity. She stood for Hellenism and for something else — something which only Julius had understood — strange and wonderful things descended from primeval monarchies in the Asian and African spaces, secret lore for which Latin had no idiom:

> Imperishable fire under the boughs
> Of chrysoberyl and beryl and chrysolite,
> And chrysoprase and ruby and sardonyx.

If such was her creed history can pass judgment on her failure. Hers was a bastard Hellenism, and her conception of world-empire was a whimsy. The grave beauty of the great age of Greece had gone from the world, and the gem-like flame of its spirit had been replaced by the fires of baser altars. The Hellenistic had ousted the Hellenic. The simplicity and *ascēsis* of an elder Greece were to be sought in Italy rather than in Egypt, with its garish, superheated court, its pedantic universities and its servile peoples. Alexandria had little to teach Rome. The enduring bequest of the East was to spring half a century later, not from the effete successors of the old monarchies, but from the bare Palestinian hills. As for the dream of the habitable earth peaceful under a universal empire, the dream of Alexander and Julius and Cleopatra, the motive power to realize it must come from the West, where men could still be both disciplined and free. Behind the cold front of Octavian lay the vision, the will, and the power.

FIRST CITIZEN

BOOK THREE

I. FOUNDATIONS

(30–27 B.C.)

His greatness weigh'd, his will is not his own;
For he himself is subject to his birth:
He may not, as unvalued persons do,
Carve for himself; for on his choice depends
The safety and the health of this whole state.

Hamlet.

I

TO the historian, looking back from the vantage-ground of two thousand years, Actium seems like the undrawing of a curtain and the letting in of daylight on the world. He knows that it meant two centuries of peace, and many more of ordered government and established law. But, to contemporaries, it seemed as if things were still on a razor edge; one great fear had been laid, but others remained. The phrase of the elder Pliny, 'the unthinkable majesty of the Roman peace,' [1] would have sounded to them baseless rhetoric. The world could draw breath for a moment, but its nerves were still quivering. It had lived so long among catastrophes that it scarcely dared to hope. Rome longed dumbly for one thing above all others — not liberty, but law, and that the old law and the familiar grooves. The poets might make high festival:

Nunc est bibendum, nunc pede libero
pulsanda tellus —

but little gaiety mingled with the relief of the ordinary

[1] 'immensa Romanae pacis majestas,' *N. H.*, XXVII, 3.

Roman, who was satiated alike with the fervours of the democrats and the rigidity of the conservatives. He accepted the need for a new scheme of things, but it must be as like as possible to the former things. His hopes were centred on the young man, not yet thirty-four, now moving homeward from the East. On one thing only all were agreed. This man must take the ordering of the world into his hands, and, whatever the future might hold, he must be for the present the repository of power.[1]

Augustus — to anticipate by two years the name by which Octavian is best known in history — spent the closing months of 30 B.C. in settling the affairs of the Near and Middle East. The Donations of Alexandria were annulled, Egypt was annexed, and its wealth passed to Rome. He adjusted some of the relations of the client-kingdoms, but for the most part he allowed Antony's arrangements to stand. Parthia and Armenia he left for the moment alone. He was at Samos when, on the first day of the next year, he entered upon his fifth consulship. Travelling slowly, he reached Brundisium in the early summer, and was compelled to rest for a few days near Naples, where Virgil met him and read to him the completed *Georgics*.[2] That meeting between the conqueror and the poet may have had momentous consequences, if, as we may well believe, the golden lines of the one revived in the other his old Italian enthusiasm. For Augustus during these months was suffering from the relaxed and surfeited mood which always attends success, the listlessness which follows supreme effort. For fifteen years there had been no remission of the strain on body and spirit.

The remainder of this book must be a study of his mind, the way in which he faced and solved an infinity of problems. His moral and material predominance was now

[1] Tac., *Hist.*, I, L; Dio, LXIII, 19; Florus, *Epit.*, II, 14.
[2] Donatus, *Vita Virg.*, II, 40.

assured, but there still remained for him a test of character, the severest of all. He was called by universal consent to a new and immense burden, nothing less than the rebuilding of the world, and he was very weary. He differed from Alexander in thinking the consolidation of an empire a harder task than the winning of it.[1] His health, too, had worsened in these last months, and he was a sick man when he arrived in Italy. All his life he struggled against bodily frailty. He had a weak throat and apparently a poor circulation, for he could not face either extreme heat or cold; much exertion fevered him; his digestion was bad, and he had to live on a strict diet; he was constantly threatened by kidney trouble. He may well have thought that his days would be few on earth, and that it would be foolish to put his hand to a task which he could not complete; he did not guess that, while Alexander had only been given ten years for his work, he would be granted forty-four.[2] For glory in the common sense he cared not at all, and he looked forward with distaste to the honours which Rome had prepared for him. He had little vanity; unlike Julius he did not want a laurel wreath for every-day wear or the red buskins of the Alban kings, though he liked high boots to increase his stature. Moreover, youth and all the dreams and caprices of youth had long ago passed from him; he had none of the engaging boyishness which Julius retained till the last day of his life. The thought of the trumpeting and ceremonial and grandiloquence which awaited him was repellent to his tired spirit; he desired not to be pinnacled and pedestalled, but to sink into the crowd and rest.

More important, he seems for a little to have shirked the task before him. This was not from any distrust of his own abilities, for of these he was always confident. He

[1] Plut., *Mor.*, 207.
[2] Cromwell had only nine; Napoleon, after 18th Brumaire, only fifteen.

knew himself 'par negotiis,' and believed himself 'capax imperii.' But the edge had gone from his spirit, and he shrank from the long, toilsome road in front of him. Would it not be better that, having given the world a formal peace, he should retire, like Sulla, into a private life of ease, and let a restored republic jog along in the old rut? Dio, in his fifty-second book, has set down a lengthy discussion in which Agrippa advised a republican restoration and Maecenas argued for a principate. It is unlikely that these homilies were ever delivered; they were probably academic prelections, echoes of debates in the schools in which the opposing rôles were naturally allotted to the two chief counsellors; [1] but the fact that Dio incorporates them in his history points to a persistent Roman tradition that Augustus did pass through some such period of doubt.[2] We have also the explicit statement of Suetonius,[3] and there is some reason to think that the fourteenth ode of Horace's first book is a plea that the peacemaker should not leave his task half done.[4]

The mood passed, whether owing to the fresh inspiration given by Virgil, or to the arguments of his friends, or to a soldierly unwillingness to leave his post, and Augustus submitted to the inevitable; inevitable, because without his guiding hand the Roman polity would soon slip back into chaos. Long before he arrived in the capital he had cast up his accounts with himself and made his decision. Soberly he assessed the elements of his power. . . . He had the army — twenty-seven legions after his disbandment was complete — that High Command which had been the

---

[1] This fashion, derived from the schools of rhetoric, is common to all the Roman historians, even to the unexpansive Tacitus. Cf. *Ann.*, III, 33–34; XI, 23–24; XIV, 20–21.

[2] There is no evidence that Agrippa ever had the smallest tincture of republican sentiment. See Reinhold, *op. cit.*, 65; P. Meyer, *de Maecenatis oratione a Dione ficta* (1891).

[3] 'De reddenda republica bis cogitavit: primum post oppressum Antonium.' *Div. Aug.*, 28.

[4] This was the view of Franke, *Fasti Horatiani* (1839); cf. Conway, *Makers of Europe*, 54 *sqq.*

basis of the power of Sulla and Pompey and Julius; almost
the only army in the world, and one wholly under his
orders. He held his command not in virtue of the dubious
triumvirate, but by universal consent embodied formally
in the oath sworn by the western world.[1] It was a command, superior and unlimited and specially devised for
an emergency.[2] He had the consulship, the chief magistracy, and most of the powers of a tribune. Between them
these three offices gave him a title to remodel the state.
But behind them, more important than any legal sanction, was his 'auctoritas,' the personal pre-eminence he
had won over the Roman mind.

As he marshalled his thoughts one principle stood out
before all others. He desired success, not victory. The
sole triumph he had sought was over Cleopatra and the
menacing East. He must labour to avoid humiliating any
Roman, or any class, interest, or loyalty in Rome or Italy.
He had a far-sighted ambition and an iron will with which
to achieve it. Suetonius has recorded his confession of
faith: 'May it be my privilege to establish the state firm
and secure and to reap the fruit of my toil, so that I may
be called the author of the best possible government, and
bear with me the hope when I die that the foundations
which I have laid will remain unshaken.'[3] But, joined to
this purpose, was a fastidious judgment about ways
and means. He must divine what men would welcome and
shun what men might resent. He must delicately mould
and adjust the popular will to his own. The very defect
which made him a poor soldier — his disinclination to
hazard everything for the immediate need — was a virtue
in the statesman. He would take no risks with a thing so
brittle as the Roman polity, on which depended the fate

[1] *Mon. Anc.*, VI, 13–16 (cf. Hardy's ed., 151 *sqq.*); Rice Holmes, I, 262–63; Greenidge,
op. cit., 338.

[2] For parallels in Roman history see Hammond, *The Augustan Principate*, 15–17.

[3] *Div. Aug.*, 28. It was the answer to Cicero's appeal to Julius, *pro Marc.*, VIII, 23–25.

of forty-four millions of men. His reforms must proceed
organically, like a process of nature. There must be no
melodramatic short-cuts, no grandiose *coups*. He did not
believe — so runs one of the sayings ascribed to him —
in fishing with a gold hook, the loss of which would out-
weigh the value of any catch. There was another reason
for caution. Julius, his model, had had a long apprentice-
ship in Roman public life and provincial government; he
himself was still a novice, for the triumvirate had not been
an education for the normal statesman.

His first task must be to amend the political machine.
His views had now clarified themselves on this matter.
Monarchy, as Julius conceived it, he wholly rejected.
Julius, again, had been a radical reformer, but a conservative reaction had set in and his own inclinations were in
that direction. But on the necessity of a single personal
authority he agreed with Julius; only he must give it a
legal base and a civilian façade.[1] The question of how,
and by what form of succession, it should be continued,
he left over for the moment as too difficult. He must content himself with the actual machine. Rome desired not
self-government, but good government, and that meant
an ultimate autocracy; but Rome also wanted continuity
with her past, and that meant the preservation of the old
republican forms. How were conservatism and efficiency
to be harmonized? Moreover, in working so complex a
mechanism as the government of the empire he must have
willing coadjutors.

After much thought he found the solution. He would
formally preserve the ancient magistracies, but he would
acquire for himself the powers without the offices.

That is the key to Augustus's reconstruction. To get
rid of the appearance of absolutism he must induce the
grandees, who understood the technique of affairs, to lend

---

[1] I borrow the phrase from L. Homo, *Auguste*, 111.

a hand and sulk no longer in their tents.[1] In this task Livia, with her noble birth, her tact and her supreme good sense, was invaluable. There was in all classes in Rome a deep reverence for the old aristocracy, even among its most envenomed critics. This aristocracy must be enlarged and enriched by new men, as Julius had always designed, but its long-descended core must never be forgotten.[2] That core was now in a humble mood, and he did not despair of winning it to his side. The history of the principate reveals his success. Among his helpers he was to have members of the proudest of Roman houses, the Calpurnian, Cornelian, Valerian, Aemilian and Fabian.

He was convinced that the centre of gravity must be Italy. He was Italian by birth and training and his view was no doubt coloured by sentiment; but it was also a reasoned policy. Italy had only been incorporated in Rome for a few decades, and Italian patriotism was still in the making. He must foster it by reviving old traditions, by encouraging the idiom of local life, and by maintaining the purity of the Latin stock. He was definitely of the western world, and not a *Weltkind* like Julius. Rome must be the Eternal City; the preponderating element in any culture must be Latin. There must be a new Populus Romanus, co-extensive with the Italian race, strong enough to keep its character in a cosmopolitan empire, for only thus could any government have an enduring foundation. Both from sentiment and policy he chose to be on the grand scale parochial.

Of the empire, stretching to the four corners of the globe, his conception was of a gigantic client-state, an asset and also a responsibility. He would give it peace, security, law, self-respect and a decent freedom, but

---

[1] 'Of all societies in the world, those which will always have most difficulty in escaping absolute government will be precisely those societies in which aristocracy is no more, and can no more be.' De Tocqueville, *L'Ancien Régime*, pref., xvi.

[2] Tac., *Ann.*, I, 2.

always it must take second place to Rome. There was no nationalism in those huge impersonal states to set itself up against the Latin pride. To them Rome was a plain benefactor, while economically and, to a lesser degree, politically, they could do Rome service. His view may be put in some words of Lord Acton: 'The combination of different nations in one State is as necessary a condition of civilized life as a combination of men in society. The inferior races are raised by living in political union with races intellectually superior. Exhausted and decaying nations are revived by contact with a younger vitality. Nations in which the elements of organization and the capacity for government have been lost, either through the demoralizing influence of despotism or the disintegrating action of democracy, are restored and educated anew under the discipline of a stronger and less corrupted race. This fertilizing and regenerating process can only be obtained by living under one government. It is in the cauldron of the State that the fusion takes place by which the vigour, the knowledge and the capacity of one portion of mankind will be communicated to another.'[1] Of Italy he thought more nobly, of other lands less hopefully, than Julius; so far as Rome was concerned, the empire would be principally the beneficiary, not the benefactor.

On the details of frontier policy he had not made up his mind, but on the main principle he was clear. Rome wanted no more conquests. The army which he contemplated was not a field force but a permanent garrison to keep order in the different provinces and to be the warden of the marches. When he cast his eye abroad he saw the African frontier from Egypt to the Atlantic more or less secure. He had no fear for Gaul and Spain, for they were merely a matter of internal police. For the rest, the empire's natural boundaries were those of the Mediterra-

[1] *Hist. of Freedom and other Essays*, 290.

nean watershed, but past history had compelled it to press beyond them northward and eastward. This fact must be faced. What was necessary was to trim the frontiers so that they might be most easily defensible, and above all to perfect the frontier communications. It might be wise to let Armenia drop out of the Roman orbit, where it did not properly belong, but so bold a policy had been made difficult by recent events. On one point he was resolved; the Danube must be the north-eastern frontier, for only thus would it be possible to secure that overland route to the Bosporus which was the strategical key to imperial defence. As to the Rhine he was undecided. It might be necessary, as a purely defensive measure, to push eastward into Germany and link up with the Danube by a shorter route.

II

The formal entry into Rome took place on the 13th of August. The Senate had already expanded in a deluge of honours to the conqueror. On the first day of the year all his *acta* had been ratified; triumphal arches were erected in Brundisium and Rome bearing the words 'republica conservata'; [1] his birthday and the day of Actium and of his entry into Alexandria were made sacred days for ever; [2] three triumphs were to be celebrated — for Dalmatia, for Actium and for Egypt; the Vestal Virgins, the Senate and the citizens were to welcome him at the gates; his name was joined with the gods in ceremonial hymns; the temple of Janus was closed for the third time in Rome's history.

Augustus accepted only those honours which he could not avoid, for he lacked the Roman appetite for pageant;

---

[1] *C. I. L.*, VII, 872.

[2] For the Augustan sacred days and the Augustan calendar generally, see the appendix 'Le calendrier d'Auguste' in Gagé's ed. of the *Res Gestae* (Paris, 1935).

notably he refused the civic procession. But the triumphs were obligatory, and they reached a magnificence far beyond that of the triumph of Julius seventeen years before.[1] The tribes of the city offered him a subvention of one thousand pounds weight of gold; this he declined, and instead made a handsome donation to the people out of the Egyptian treasure, besides cancelling all arrears of taxation and paying all his debts. The first day was assigned to the Dalmatian and Pannonian victories; on the second came the Actium celebration and a parade of the beaks of Antony's ships; the third was the day of Egypt, when the children of Antony and Cleopatra walked in the procession, while the image of the dead queen was borne in a litter. After that came games and exhibitions of wild beasts on an unprecedented scale, the dedication of the temple of the deified Julius, and the opening of the new Julian Senate-house. Two points in those splendid ceremonies struck the thoughtful spectator. The image of Cleopatra was carried in the conqueror's triumph, but her statue was allowed to remain where Julius had placed it in the temple of Venus Genetrix. Augustus had no quarrel with the dead.[2] There was a change, too, in the ordering of the procession. The republican custom by which the great officers of state preceded the triumphing general was dropped, and they paraded behind. It was a gentle reminder to Rome of the true position of this modest, constitutionally-minded citizen — the master of Egypt and its wealth, a god incarnate to three-fourths of mankind, the commander of 300,000 veterans, the undisputed ruler of the world.

The ceremonies were a strain on Augustus's precarious health, and he was a sick man during the autumn and most of the winter. This compulsory leisure was fortunate, for it enabled him to plan in detail the next stages.

---

[1] Virg., *Aen.*, VIII, 714–23. [2] Dio, LI, 22.

In his own house on the Palatine, which had once been
the home of Hortensius, and in Maecenas's mansion on
the Esquiline, there were many long hours of talk.
Agrippa was now his neighbour on the Palatine, honours
·had been showered on him which made him the second
man in the state, and by his marriage to Marcella, Octavia's daughter, he had entered the dominant family.
He was more soldier than constitution-maker, better perhaps at action than at thought,[1] but he had a deep central
sagacity which made him useful ballast to the quick-witted
and imaginative Maecenas. These three men in the winter
nights sketched out the first plan of the empire.

The twin principles of the new system were, first, that
the reality of power should remain in the hands of Augustus, and, second, that such a central control should be
given a constitutional façade. This meant that any
scheme must be accepted and ratified by what remained
of the mechanism of the Republic. He had been living on
real, but for the most part irregular, grants of authority;
these must be relinquished and a new dispensation established on a basis of strict legality. His former powers had
enabled him to clear the ground, but something different
was needed before he could build. The new authority
might be extra-ordinary and beyond precedent, but it
must spring from the traditional sources, the Senate and
the People. He was beginning to see what the ultimate
form of the Roman polity must be, but he had no intention of presenting it as a clean-cut and fully articulated
scheme. He would start with the rudiments, and guide
the evolution on the lines he desired. He was a statesman,
not a political theorist.

First for his name, since the head of the state must
have a title. 'Imperator,' to which Julius had inclined,
he unhesitatingly rejected. He used it now as a prae-

---

[1] 'consultis facta conjungens.' Vell., II, 79.

nomen, like his great-uncle, and he added it to his name
as other generals did who had been saluted on the field of
battle. But as a term of daily use it smacked too much of
dictatorship and the sword. There was one word which
had the merit of describing precisely the position he ·
sought to hold, and which had the right kind of traditional connotation, the word 'princeps.' Cicero had used
it of Pericles, who was the ideal statesman to Roman pub-
licists of all parties [1]; and of Pompey, whom he had chosen
as his leader.[2] As adopted by Augustus,[3] it was a popular
appellation, not a term of constitutional art, defining a
status rather than an office. It described not a separate
estate in the realm, but the man on whom the chief executive burden of the state must fall, and it is best translated
'First Citizen' — first citizen and principal servant.[4]
'Princeps' was not an abbreviation of 'princeps senatus,'
the Leader of the House, a dignity which he was about to
receive and which he held until the end of his life, but it
had a flavour of that old republican institution.[5] The
new title, therefore, had every merit. To Caesarians
and reformers it suggested Pericles and the Gracchi and
Julius's dreams, while for the conservatives it was linked
with the speculations of Cicero and the career of Pompey.
It combined diverse loyalties and aroused no antagonisms.

Wiser than Julius, Augustus gave thought to the title
by which he should be familiarly known, for he recognized

---

[1] 'princeps civitatis suae.' de Rep., I, 25.

[2] ad Fam., I, 9; pro Planc., XXXIX, 93. Cf. ad Att., VIII, 2. He had also used it of
Julius, ad Fam., IX, 17. The Greek translation (as in the Fifth Edict of Cyrene) was
ἡγεμών.

[3] He uses it three times in the Res Gestae (Mon. Anc., II, 42–45; V, 44–49; VI, 6–8).

[4] 'President,' which Ferrero favours (IV, 134), is certainly a mistranslation if the word
is used in the modern sense. The conception of 'first servant of the state' is clearly set
out in connection with Trajan by Dio Chrys. (Or., I, 22) and Pliny (Pan., 63–65), 'non
est "princeps supra leges" sed "leges supra principem."'

[5] Dio, LIII, I. For different views on this point see Rice Holmes, I, 263–64. The
Greek translation of the word in connection with the Senate was πρόκριτος, Dio, LVII,
8. Cf. Momms., Staatsr., II, 774, 776 n.

that names have a dangerous potency. His next step
was to decide upon the precise form which his authority
should take. He must have the reality of power, but he
must dress it in a cunning constitutional habit. He knew
well the antiquarian propensities of his countrymen and
their passion for the minutiae of constitutionalism, and
he was prepared to indulge it to the full so far as theory
was concerned, provided that in practice he had the guiding of the state. His concern was less with abstract authority than with function. There was no such thing as a
Roman constitution, for under the Republic the polity
had always been insensibly changing, and if he set out to
restore the Republic in full he would have found no general agreement as to what that Republic meant. His
business, therefore, was to interweave his personal 'auctoritas' with institutions which had still a strong appeal to
the Roman mind, but, since these institutions were not
clean-cut and rigid, he could subtly adapt them in the
interweaving. His task was not that of the lawyer, but
of the practical statesman; the logic which guided him
was not of paper but of facts.

His first step was simple. To begin with at any rate,
he must hold the main office, the consulship, hold it in the
old fashion by annual election. That would give him the
dignity of the traditional head of the Roman state, and
the handicap of colleagueship could be got over by the
selection of the right kind of colleague. But the consulship
alone was not enough. The kernel of his authority lay in
his command of the chief — and, but for the Parthian, the
only — army in the world. How was this command to be
legitimated? Only by the grant of the 'imperium proconsulare,' so that he would be at once consul and proconsul. This was a departure from normal republican
practice, but it was not without precedent, for in 52 B.C.
the double office had been held by Pompey, and Pompey

was still dear to conservative sentiment. Eduard Meyer is right when he claims that Augustus was the heir of Pompey rather than of Julius.[1]

But the imperium of a proconsul was not valid in the city of Rome, and in any case some authority was needed which should bring him more closely into touch with the people and conceal the truth that his ultimate power lay in the command of the army. The popular office of tribune was closed to him as a patrician, but already he had been granted many of the tribune's privileges.[2] Now he must be invested with the others, for the key of his new policy was to acquire the power without the office. Julius had done this in 48 B.C. when he was given a seat on the tribunes' bench in the Senate, and on this point Augustus was ready to follow dutifully his great-uncle's lead. The full powers of a tribune carried rights of inestimable value to the man who sought to govern the state without the appearance of perpetual dictation. He won personal inviolability, the right of summoning the Senate and controlling its debates, of presiding at the elections in the Assemblies, of nominating and commending candidates, of vetoing the act of any magistrate, of interfering in and controlling the administration of justice, of aiding any citizen within the city bounds and a mile beyond. Since the powers were separated from the office, he escaped the impediment of collegiality, under which in old days one tribune could nullify the work of another. He must be at the head of the tribunes and yet beyond their reach.

---

[1] *Caesars Monarchie*, 548; Strabo (XVII, 3, 25) says that the command of the army was specifically granted by the Senate, and the law granting it to Vespasian (*C. I. L.*, VI, 930) speaks of it as having been vested in Augustus, but it is likely that this was due to a confusion of *de jure* and *de facto*. There is no evidence of any grant to Augustus of a military imperium, except that which was implied in the 'imperium proconsulare.' For the 'lex de imperio Vespasiani,' contained in a tablet set up by Rienzi in St. John Lateran and now in the Capitoline Museum, see Dessau, 244, Momms., *Staatsr.*, II, 878, and *C. A. H.*, XI, 404–08.

[2] See p. 95, *supra*.

An acute critic like Tacitus saw in the tribunician power
the real secret of Augustus's predominance.[1] The principate was not a dictatorship or a kingship or a more potent consulship, but a magnified tribuneship. It definitely
linked the Princeps with the popular tradition of the
Gracchi and of Julius, and set him before the world as pre-
eminently the guardian of the plain man's interests. The
military imperium was the actual basis of his authority,
but the tribunician power was at once its popular colouring
and the source of its moral appeal. The *Res Gestae* shows
how highly Augustus valued it.[2] The royal power in the
Middle Ages was the chief defence of popular rights; it
deduced from the Roman empire; is it fantastic to see this
duty as in direct descent from that now assumed by the
empire's founder?

There was another power which he must possess before
he could deal with the hardest part of his problem, the
status of the Senate. He must have some of the rights of
the censor. Without these he could not proceed to recast
the Senate and the aristocracy, which was a necessary step
in his reconstruction. He had no desire to hold the post
of censor, for he had wisely determined to avoid a multi-
plication of personal dignities, but he must have the censorian power. He could carry out measures of reform in
public and private morality through the tribunician
power; but for the taking of a census — neglected since
70 B.C. — and the revision of the Senate and the whole
class system, he must have an *ad hoc* authority. In
28 B.C. he entered upon his sixth consulship with Agrippa
as his colleague, and some time before that date he was
granted by the Senate a special 'potestas censoria,' in
virtue of which he held a census of the people, purged the

---

[1] He calls the tribunician power 'summi fastigii vocabulum,' *Ann.*, III, 56.

[2] *Mon. Anc.*, I, 28–30; II, 21–23; III, 12–17. Ferrero (IV, 242 *n.*) seems to be mistaken
in underrating it.

Senate, which had become unselect and unwieldy, replenished the patriciate from good plebeian stocks, and held the solemn sacrifice of purification on behalf of the people, which Rome had not known for forty-two years.[1]

With a Senate purged and reduced in numbers and a purified aristocracy he was now ready for his great step — the division of the burden of empire between the Senate and himself. He had no need to concern himself greatly with the popular Assemblies. In theory the supreme legislative organ, they had enjoyed a brief revival under the democratic régime of Julius and were still useful on special occasions, but they had become dull inorganic things, without individuality or prestige. But the Senate was a different matter. It was the very heart and soul of the Republic, and had still in the popular eye the glamour of ancient dignity and long descent. Having revived the distinction of its membership by expelling the low-born element introduced by Julius and Antony, he could ally it with himself in the business of government. His intention was to restore all of the Republic that would work; the Republic meant nothing without the Senate, and the Senate would lose caste without the aristocracy. A Senate based upon a winnowed patriciate, a Roman thing and not, as Julius had intended, an imperial hotch-potch, the repository of all that was best in Roman tradition — this was his ideal. To such a body he would assign every duty which it could efficiently perform, but of such efficiency he would be the judge. In the last resort the army gave

---

[1] The increase of the patriciate was done under a special law, the lex Saenia (*Mon. Anc.*, II, I; Dio, LII, 5). There is much dispute as to the grant of the censorian power. Undoubtedly in the absence of censors the consuls did perform censorial functions (cf. E. Herzog, *Röm. Staatsverfassung*, I, 797), and some scholars have assumed that Augustus acted under the censorian power inherent in the consulship (Hardy, ed. of *Mon. Anc.*, 56; Hammond, *op. cit.*, chaps. IV and X). But the Fasti of Venusia (*C. I. L.*, IX, 422) say plainly that Augustus and Agrippa held the census 'censoria potestate,' and it seems reasonable to assume with Mommsen a special grant by the Senate on a point where Augustus wanted all possible constitutional buttressing. This is also the view of *C. A. H.*, X, 123, and Rice Holmes, I, 261–62.

him the casting vote, though he had no desire to parade
this ultimate power. The Senate should reign like a modern constitutional monarch, and it should be permitted to
govern up to the full limit of its capacity.

III

The ground was now prepared for what was to be at
once the restoration and the transformation of the Roman
constitution; but first it was necessary to create a fitting
atmosphere. In his sixth consulship in 28 B.C. Augustus
shared scrupulously both its honours and duties with his
colleague Agrippa. By a single edict he abolished as from
that date all the *acta* of the triumvirs in order to wipe out
the memory of the old absolutism. He increased the distribution of free corn, and made presents of money to
needy senators to enable them to undertake public office.
His aim was to restore the Roman morale by inspiring confidence in his own mildness and decency. Above all he
sought to prove his loyalty to Rome and to kill the rumour
that he had any thought of changing the seat of government.[1] He continued his town-planning schemes and the
restoration of dilapidated temples and the building of new
ones; much of the expense he met out of his own pocket,
and he permitted no harsh expropriation of land. He induced his friends to imitate his gifts to the people. The
discovery of the Carrara quarries enabled him to sheathe
much old brick and cement in marble. Many famous
buildings and public works began to take shape; the
temples of Vesta and Jupiter Capitolinus, and that of
Apollo on the Palatine, where the Sibylline books were
housed; the temple of Mars Ultor, vowed since Philippi;
the replanning of the Field of Mars, with its great mauso-

---

[1] Cf. Hor., *Od.*, III, 3. For this question, which for a generation had disquieted the
Roman mind, see Pascal, 'L'Abbandono di Roma' in *Rend. I. L.*, LVII (1924), 713–24.

leum of the Julian house; while Agrippa finished in marble
the Saepta Julia which Julius had begun in travertine, and
erected the first Pantheon,[1] Statilius Taurus completed
the first amphitheatre and Plancus built the great temple
of Saturn. Here, said the ordinary citizen, as he saw the
builders busy in all quarters, is a Roman in truth and no
déraciné — one who loves Rome and believes in her
eternity.

Augustus might build for all time in marble, but he had
no illusions about the temporary nature of the constitution which he was about to offer to the people. It was a
trial trip, a provisional arrangement strictly limited in
duration, a structure which might have to be profoundly
modified. The fundamental principles, which he was
careful not to emphasize unduly, he did indeed believe to
be essential, but the details were to be largely a matter
of slow evolution and adjustment. He was summoning
Rome to a partnership in a great experiment and taking
her frankly into his confidence — confidently, because
he knew that he possessed supreme advantages. One was
the deep weariness of all classes and their longing for a
settled life. He had given the world peace, and the world
now turned to him for security. A second was his wealth,
his family fortune and the treasures of Egypt, which enabled him to lighten public burdens and cancel public
debts, and inaugurate great works to relieve unemploy-
ment, and restore Roman pride without recourse to new
taxation. A third was the fact that he had no competitor.
There was no figure which for a moment could compare
with his in authority. More important, there was no
political creed passionately held which might be an obstacle to his own. Doctrinaire republicanism had sunk

---

[1] The present structure was rebuilt by Hadrian, presumably on the original lines.
Agrippa's building contained a statue of Venus with earrings made from Cleopatra's
pearls (Pliny, *N. H.*, IX, 121). In the vestibule there were statues of Augustus and
Agrippa (Dio, LIII, 27).

almost out of sight; it had become less a dogma than a lingering sentiment, which he was ready to conciliate since he himself shared it.

One creed might indeed have been a formidable rival — the bequest of Julius — and Augustus might have found his most serious difficulty in his own early loyalties. But the Caesarian legend was already beginning to fade out of the air.[1] The far-sighted policy of Julius had never been well understood in Rome, and even those who grasped it had rarely been adherents. Augustus from the start had discarded much of it, and had given the autocracy, on which it was based, a subtler interpretation. To the conservatives it seemed that the Augustan tradition was in most ways the flat opposite of the Julian. The Caesarians were content, for their great man had been amply avenged and they had never penetrated into the secrets of his audacious mind. Only here and there some disconsidered thinker may have realized that a wonderful vision had passed from the world, and continued in secret to venerate his ineffectual dreams.

[1] A friend of Augustus, like Livy, could ask quite frankly whether it was not a disaster that Julius had ever lived. The reaction is plain in later writers. Even a stout Caesarian like Velleius Paterculus does not regret the Ides of March, and Suetonius, who is appreciative of Augustus, thought the murder of Julius a just act.

II. RESPUBLICA CONSERVATA

(27–23 B.C.)

Les lois, dans la signification la plus étendue, sont les rap-
ports nécessaires qui dérivent de la nature des choses.

MONTESQUIEU, *L'Esprit des Lois.*

Thus do we, of wisdom and of reach,
With windlasses and with assays of bias,
By indirections find directions out.

Hamlet.

I

THE stage was set, and the time had come for that abdica-
tion which must be the prologue to the new era. On the
13th of January 27 B.C.,[1] before a purged Senate, Augustus,
now entering upon his seventh consulship, made the *gran
rifiuto*. Seated in his curule chair, his face still pallid from
his recent illness, this young man, who had spent half of
his thirty-six years in unremitting toil, resigned to the
Roman people all his extra-ordinary prerogatives. He
was consul, he had the honorific title of Princeps, he had
the tribunician power; everything else he returned to its
parent source. He read his speech, for he rarely extemporized and never on grave occasions, and, though we cannot accept the rhetoric with which Dio credits him [2] as
the authentic words of one who loved an austere style, the
purport is clear. 'I shall lead you no longer.... Receive
back your liberty and the Republic; take over the army

---

[1] The date is determined by Ovid, *Fast.*, I, 587.
[2] Dio, LIII, 4.

and the subject provinces, and govern yourselves as has been your wont.'

The senatorial dovecotes were fluttered. Those members to whom the speech came as a surprise were genuinely alarmed, for they feared the return of the old bad times, of rival armies, divided commands, and administrative chaos. But a sufficient number of senators had been taken into the secret to insure that what the Princeps had anticipated would be smoothly effected. Gratefully they welcomed his resignation — and declined it. The powers which he had handed back to them they restored to him in a new form and with a fresh authority.

First they showed their gratitude by another shower of honours. On January 16 the Senate decreed that the doorposts of his house should be decked with laurel, that on his lintel should be placed the civic crown of oak-leaves granted to the soldier who had saved a comrade's life in battle, that the month Sextilis should be called after him, and that on a golden shield in the Senate-house should be inscribed a tribute to his 'valour, clemency, justice and piety.'[1] More important, on the motion of the consular Plancus, that old congenital traitor,[2] he was given a new name. Just as Sulla had been known as the 'Fortunate' and Pompey as the 'Great,' so to all time Octavian should bear the name of 'Augustus,'[3] a term of honour, not a title of office. He would have preferred 'Romulus,' whom Rome had always saluted as the leader who had brought her out of darkness into light;[4] Rome's second founder should have the appellation of her first. But Romulus had been a king, and the most distant monarchical suggestion must be avoided. 'Augustus,' which met with no criticism, was

[1] *Mon. Anc.*, vi, 16–21; *C. I. L.*, ix, 5809; Macrob., *Saturn.*, i, 12; Livy, *Epit.*, 134.

[2] 'morbo traditor,' Vell., ii, 83.

[3] Velleius (ii, 91) and Dio (LIII, 16) imply that the senatusconsult on this point was supplemented by a law of the Assembly.

[4] 'o pater, o genitor, o sanguen dis oriundum, tu produxisti nos intra luminis oras.'

probably the idea of Maecenas, the *éminence grise* in the background, and it was cunningly chosen. Its plain meaning was much that of the modern 'by the grace of God'; it suggested a favourite of Heaven, someone, in Dio's words, 'more than human,' [1] but at the same time a man and no eastern divinity. By its derivation it implied the augural function which Augustus always emphasized, for the 'lituus' is common on his coins. A line of Ennius had made familiar the expression 'augustum augurium' as applied to Romulus, Cicero had spoken of Rome's founder as 'optimus augur,' in 29 B.C. Octavian had celebrated the 'augurium salutis.' The epithet linked the Princeps to old religious usage and to the first king of Rome, whose name could not be assumed. It was a fitting prelude to the new 'inauguratio.' [2]

A saviour had arisen who, having preserved the state from destruction by his emergency powers, had now handed back these powers to the Roman people. The Republic had been restored — or, more properly, conserved, for it had never ceased to exist. The dream of the dead Cicero had come true. [3] There was no question of the Princeps laying down his task; a man does not carefully select a new name, with hankerings after that of the founder of Rome, if he has any thought of retirement. His resignation was a matter of form, a piece of wise eti-

[1] LIII, 16. 'Augustus' was translated in Greek by Σεβαστός, 'venerated,' but in Rome, as explained above, it had a richer and more varied connotation. The word is very rare in Latin until the first century B.C. Cicero uses it thirteen times, chiefly in the *de Legibus*.

[2] Haverfield's ingenious linking up of the name with the use of *Aug* on Mark Antony's coins will be found in *J. R. S.* (1915), v, 249. For the connection of Augustus with Romulus see J. Gagé in *Mél. de l'É. F.* (1930), 130–81. Contemporary Rome was alive to the augural connotation of the name; cf. Ovid, *Fast.*, 1, 603–04, and Virg., *Aen.*, VII, 153, where Servius explains 'augusta moenia regis' as 'augurio consecrata.'

[3] Within the past decade there had been a Ciceronian revival. The *de Legibus* had been published, and copies of the *de Republica* had been multiplied. In September 30 B.C. Cicero's son became Octavian's colleague and 'consul suffectus' and officially announced the death of Antony. Cf. Oltramare, 'La réaction cicéronienne,' in the *Rev. des É. L.* (1932).

quette, in order that Senate and People might feel that with them rested the shaping of the new state. But the nature of the reconstruction had already been privately agreed, and the Senate was only too ready to abide by the counsel of one who was both the most potent and most expert of living statesmen.

He must hold the chief republican magistracy, not only out of deference to tradition, but in order to give him status in Rome and Italy. The annual consulship combined with the tribunician power would make him the executive head in domestic affairs, and the fact that he would have colleagues would enable him to bring eminent senators into the administrative circle. He must continue to command the armies, and for that purpose he must have the proconsular imperium and the governorship of those provinces where the army was stationed. This was a commonsense arrangement if the frontiers were to be secure, and there were good precedents for it in Pompey's career. He could not, of course, govern those provinces in person; that must be done through legates of praetorian rank, for which there was also a Pompeian precedent. The ten richer and more settled provinces were left to the Senate to be administered by ex-consuls and ex-praetors in the old fashion. In only two, Illyria and Africa, was there any likelihood of trouble. Augustus took the frontier territories of the West, North and East — Spain and Lusitania; the Gauls with their Germanic borderland; Syria and Cicilia; Egypt, which for three years had been administered as his private estate, and Cyprus which was closely attached to it.

In all this there was nothing revolutionary, nothing without sound republican parallels. The Princeps had colleagues in his magistracies of equal powers; the proconsular imperium was shared with the Senate, and if it was only in Africa that a senatorial proconsul had troops under his command, that was because they were not needed elsewhere. If the will of the Princeps was in fact prepotent, the reason lay in his fame and his moral ascendancy, and these were things which could not be legislated for. He realized the profound truth that a revolution, if it is to endure, must be in large part a reaction, a return to inbred modes of thought which have been neglected. He was formally justified in his claim in the *Res Gestae*: 'I declined to accept any office inconsistent with the institutions of our ancestors.... I stood before all others in authority, but of actual power I possessed no more than my colleagues in each separate magistracy.' [1]

The same discreet ingenuity was manifest in the other details of the reconstruction. The Senate was exalted in dignity and its sphere of influence enlarged. It had again the control of the ordinary finances, and became the chief legislative body. According to the republican theory the People issued commands and the Senate put these commands into official resolutions. [2] The old conjunction was retained, but the popular Assemblies were now rather forms than realities, though Augustus was scrupulous in retaining the semblance of popular control. They still had the formal business of election to the magistracies, and could be used in special circumstances for legislation to which it was desirable to add a specific popular sanction. [3] But their ancient judicial functions were not restored, and they had lost their prerogatives of making peace and war. There is evidence that Augustus, like

---

[1] *Mon. Anc.*, I, 37–29; VI, 21–23. Some have argued, basing themselves on Ulpian, *Dig.*, I, 16 and Dio, LIII, 32, that Augustus was now invested with an overriding imperium over the senatorial provinces. But I share Professor McFayden's scepticism on this point (*C. P.*, 1921, XVI, 34–37). The influence of Augustus in that sphere under the 27 B.C. arrangement was, I think, due to his general 'auctoritas' and not to a specific grant.

[2] 'senatus censuit populusque jussit,' Cic., *pro Planc.*, XVII, 42.

[3] After Tiberius there were no more technical 'leges,' save one or two under antiquarian emperors like Claudius and Nerva.

Julius, toyed with the idea of giving the Assemblies greater power and making them representative of the whole body of citizens in Italy;[1] but the thing was not feasible, for the actual voters on normal occasions could only be the unrepresentative Roman plebs. But what was lost to the Assemblies was given to the Senate. It became the main law-giver. It was accorded extensive judicial powers; it was entrusted with onerous executive duties; above all it was made the ultimate fount of power, since from it the Princeps drew his mandate, and what it had given it could withhold.[2] The Princeps might bend it to his will, but that was because of his 'auctoritas' and not from any legal privilege. The Senate was more than a modern constitutional monarch, reigning and not governing; it had a substantial amount of governing to its share. It incarnated two main principles; it carried on the traditional aristocracy, and it was wholly Roman, thereby setting Rome before the eyes of the overseas empire as the centre of power. Formally it had greater purchase than it had enjoyed since the days of Sulla; in practice it had weighty, but carefully defined, executive functions. In spite of the consular, proconsular and tribunician authority of the Princeps it was a substance, not a shadow.[3]

A proof that this was the purpose of Augustus is his determination to draw the Senate into administrative work. The great offices of state and the higher military commands were reserved for its members and several new posts were added to the senatorial career. In seeking for an executive for the empire he leaned heavily on the senatorial class. In the instructions written at his death

---

[1] See p. 212, *infra*.

[2] When he fell sick in 23 B.C. Augustus gave his reports and accounts to his fellow consul, and he left them to the Senate at his death.

[3] Velleius sums up the official view of the reconstruction: 'restituta vis legibus, judiciis auctoritas, senatui majestas, imperium magistratuum ad pristinum redactum modum ... prisca illa et antiqua reipublicae forma revocata.' II, 89.

he urged that public business should be entrusted to all who had the ability for it,[1] but *ceteris paribus* he always preferred the old aristocracy. Still more notable evidence is his creation of a cabinet or privy council from the Senate to assist him, even in matters where he had been given supreme authority. This cabinet, afterwards enlarged both in size and length of tenure, consisted of a consul, a praetor, an aedile, a tribune, a quaestor, and fifteen senators chosen by lot, and it held office for six months. It prepared business for the Senate and, being a microcosm of that body, could keep him in touch with the Senate's temper; it appears, too, to have assisted him in his own administrative problems.[2]

Such was the first scheme of reconstruction; a trial scheme, for it was to last for ten years only, after which it was to be renewed or revised. It was a masterly effort to combine the Republic, not in its pristine form but in the shape to which it had been slowly evolving since the Gracchi, with the demands of the new empire. It must be judged by its practical efficiency, which includes its popular acceptability, not by its conformity to antique modes or laws. Two errors must be avoided. The first, on which the charge of duplicity against Augustus has been based, is to assume that the later developments of the principate were foreseen at the start by its founder. The settlement of 27 B.C. was meant to be experimental and alterable under the pressure of facts, for Augustus, like Raleigh, believed that 'councils to which Time hath not been called Time will not ratify.'[3] Dio is a special sinner in this re-

---

[1] Dio, LVI, 33.

[2] This seems clear from the Fifth Edict of Cyrene. These Edicts range in date from 7 to 4 B.C. and were first published by G. Oliverio in *Notizario Archeologico* (1927), IV.

[3] 'Knowing what did actually result from any given act, it is easy to assume that it was part of the conscious purpose of the act, which is not always the case. Even if it is true that the restoration of the Republic was unreal, this is not of itself an adequate proof that Augustus meant it to be unreal or was entirely to blame for its unreality. Indeed it can be shown that to a large degree the unreality was due to causes for which he was not in any way responsible.' March, *Founding of the Rom. Emp.*, 219.

spect. With the development of the principate up to his own time in his mind, he assumed this development to have been the intention of Augustus, and many later historians have followed his assumption. But the prime merit of the settlement was that the centre of gravity was given freedom to shift as the necessities of government demanded. The second error is to imagine that Augustus had in mind a rigid code of political philosophy and law, to which he deceitfully professed to adhere while undermining its principles. His purpose, on the contrary, was a practical compromise. It is equally idle to credit him, as do the later Greek historians, with the political thought of their own age, or, like the Roman jurists, with the rigid legal conceptions of the old Republic. No man ever lived whose habit of mind was less abstract and more pragmatic.

Did he or did he not restore the Republic? The question is really without meaning, though it has occasioned a wealth of misplaced ingenuity.[1] What republic? That of the old simple city-state? But no antiquarian piety could have brought that to life again, for it would have meant the reduction of the Roman people to a manageable size, the abolition of the system which made rank depend on office, a return to the pre-Marian composition of the army, and the restoration of primitive manners and morals. No Roman of any class would have accepted

[1] The different views may be summarized as follows: For the reality of the restoration the ancient authorities are *Mon. Anc.*, VI, 13, and Vell., II, 89, and among the moderns, Ferrero, IV, 135; E. Meyer, *Kleine Schriften*, 441–92; Momms., *Staatsr.*, II, 747 *sqq.*; O. Hirschfeld, *Die kaiserlicher Verwaltungsbeamten*, 470; Marsh, *op. cit.*, 219; Pelham, *Essays*, 31–32; Hammond, *The Augustan Principate*, 4 *sqq.* That the restoration was a farce is the view, among ancient authorities, of Tacitus, *Ann.*, III, 28; Dio, LII, 1; Strabo, XVII, 3, 25; followed, among moderns, by Gardthausen, *N. J. cl. Alt.* (1904), 214–51; Dessau, *Gesch. der röm. Kaiserwelt*, I, 39; Rostovtzeff, *Soc. and Econ. Hist. of Rom. Emp.*, 38–43, and Rice Holmes, II, 180 n. An intermediate position is adopted by Mitteis, *Röm. Privatrecht*, 352; Schönbauer, *Untersuchungen z. röm. Staats- und Wirtschaftsrecht, Zeitschrift der Savigny-Stiftung*, XLVII (1927), 264–318; Kolbe, *Von der Republik zur Monarchie* (1931), 39–65, and P. de Francisci, *Storia del diritto romano*, II, 232 *sqq.*

such a revolution. Does the question concern the restoration of civic liberty? Then let us be careful in our definitions. The Roman 'libertas' was never the Greek 'eleutheria'; it was not freedom unfettered, but freedom from arbitrary rule, and did not involve an atomic self-sufficiency, but could be as well, or better, attained as part of a greater whole; it might be defined, in Clerk Maxwell's words, as 'an abandonment of wilfulness without extinction of will ... whereby, instead of being consciously free and really in subjection to unknown laws, it becomes consciously acting by law, and really free from the interference of unrecognized laws.' 'Principatus' and 'libertas' were counterparts, not contradictories.[1]

Augustus preserved whatever of the republican institutions had still vitality, and adapted them to a new executive purpose. The principate cannot be fully defined by legal categories, though its foundation was deep in ancient law. It was a product of an urgent necessity, an experiment intended to develop, and since it was based upon both the traditions of Rome and upon practical needs it had an organic elasticity, a real power of adaptation. Monarchy in the common sense it was not; but it might be called a limited monarchy if the emphasis be laid rather on the adjective than on the noun. Mommsen's term 'dyarchy'[2] has point in regard to the allocation of administrative duties; but while there was a division of labour there was no division of sovereignty. Or, again, as Oltramare suggests, it may be called in theory a 'triarchy' according to Cicero's formula,[3] a mingling of royal, aristocratic and popular powers. But it is simpler to look upon it neither as monarchy nor as republic, but

[1] Tacitus (*Agric.*, 3) praised Nerva for having 'reunited the principate with liberty,' which shows that he did not regard the two things as incompatible.

[2] Better perhaps 'diarchy,' as Gardthausen suggests (II, 306 *n.*), on the analogy of δίθυρος and δίφθογγος.

[3] *de Rep.*, 69.

as a mixed constitution, a new thing, the development of which must be on the knees of the gods. It began with a balance, but whether the emphasis would shift to Princeps or Senate only time could show.

Of the legal sovereignty in the narrower sense there could be no doubt. It resided, as in republican days, in the Senate and the People. In theory these were supreme; all the powers of the Princeps emanated from them, and what they had granted they could withdraw. This right of resumption was emphasized by the limitation of the grant to ten years. It was a return to the pre-Sullan constitution. His proconsular power, that imperium which was the foundation-stone of his authority, was the restoration of the old unlimited consular power of the earlier Republic. It was still possible to make out an unanswerable case for complete and undivided popular sovereignty. The Princeps was a magistrate in the traditional sense, with an extraordinary jurisdiction established in the republican way after sound republican precedents.

But the legal aspect was not the only, or the most vital, one. In effect Augustus had a status which the laws could not limit, a status won by strong men in all ages despite the forms of a constitution. The dominant fact was his 'auctoritas,' his personal ascendency. He was the master of the ultimate argument in any dispute, the army; and, though his military command came from the Senate and could have been withdrawn by the Senate, there was no alternative between its continuance and anarchy.[1] The cardinal fact of the principate was that the legions throughout the empire, wherever they might be stationed, took the military oath to Augustus and obeyed him as

---

[1] 'Augustus did not found a military tyranny or make the army the chief element in his empire. He did, to be sure, concentrate in his own hands the entire military strength of the state, but he did so as the servant of the state, and with a view to preventing the inroads upon the authority of the state, which occurred under the late Republic.' Hammond, *op. cit.*, 148; cf. Rostovtzeff, *op. cit.*, 40.

their only sovereign. The logic of facts was to make this
high command endure for life, since any change was unthinkable. He was resolved never to let slip those reins of
power, and Rome was not less resolved, and it was therefore certain that time would increase and not diminish his
influence. The old institutions, though Augustus had all
the will in the world to preserve them, were bound to
wither in the shadow of the new. He summoned the
energies of the past to legitimize the future, but these
energies were already half-exhausted. If all his powers
had republican precedents their combination in the hands
of one man was a novelty, in one man of extraordinary
administrative genius. Not all his constitutional probity
and antiquarian zeal could put life into dying things.
The mechanism of the small city-state could not long be
combined with the mechanism required by a vast empire.

The new polity was confirmed in a law by both Senate
and People.[1] There was no dissentient voice. Conservative lawyers like Antistius Labeo might doubt, but they
were silent, as was the slender school of traditionalists,[2]
represented later by men like Thrasea Paetus and Hel-
vidius Priscus. Their creed was a sentiment like eighteenth-century Jacobitism in Britain, with much pride of
ancestry but without hope of posterity. 'Les républicains,'
in the words of Lamennais, 'sont faits pour rendre la ré-
publique impossible.'

II

Most men, having launched a new project of government, would have felt bound to remain at the centre of
things to keep an eye on its working. But so assured was

---

[1] Dio, LIII, 12.

[2] The *Controversiae* of the elder Seneca preserve a few names of irreconcilables, mostly
rhetoricians, like Titus Labienus and Cassius Severus.

Augustus of the merits of his plan and of the compliance of Rome, and so confident in his star, that after seeing to the repair of the Via Flaminia, the Great North Road, he departed on the first of those journeys which made him, except for the restless Hadrian,[1] the chief traveller among the emperors. He realized that in the long run the justification of the principate lay in its practical efficiency, and he was minded to have no mistakes. An imperial civil service, of which Julius had laid the foundations, must be organized, and for that he needed local knowledge. He turned first to what for Rome was the most vital problem, the West.

In the autumn of 27 B.C. he went to Gaul, taking with him his stepson, Tiberius, Livia's son by her first marriage, now a boy of fifteen, and Marcellus, who may have been a year older, the son by her first husband of his sister Octavia, Antony's widow. His purpose was to reorganize the province which had been won by Julius and secured by Agrippa and Messalla, and to this period we may ascribe the new division into the Narbonese in the south, Aquitania in the southwest, Lugdunensis in the centre, and Belgica in the north. Opinion in Rome, if we may believe the poets, anticipated a fresh effort to conquer Britain, but, though he may have advertised this intention as a warning, the aim of Augustus was consolidation, not conquest. He spent the last months of 27 B.C. in the Narbonese, enlarging and beautifying its cities, establishing schools throughout all Gaul for the teaching of Roman law and the Latin tongue, and holding a census for the purpose of taxation.

But with the beginning of 26 B.C. he had to change his plans. Sudden trouble sprang up in various parts of the empire. The tribes on the Macedonian border were again

---

[1] Hadrian spent twelve out of the twenty-one years of his reign in imperial progresses. Augustus visited every province except Sardinia and Africa.

threatening, in spite of the victories of M. Crassus in the preceding year; the Salassi in the Val d'Aosta were at their old business of raiding, and northern Spain was dangerously restless. Spain, the oldest Roman province in the West, and the chief source of the empire's mineral wealth, demanded his first attention. His task was to subdue the Asturians and Cantabrians of the north and west, with the two Roman armies, each three legions strong, stationed in Nearer and Further Spain. The details of the campaigns are obscure. In that of 26 B.C. against the Cantabrians he himself commanded, backed his way to the coast at Santander, and was compelled to supplement field victories by much arduous guerilla warfare. The toil and hardships wrecked his precarious health, and he was forced to retire to Tarraco, leaving the war in 25 B.C. to his lieutenants. Successes of a kind were obtained, but the Iberian mountaineers could only be conquered by a slow process of attrition, and it was not until 19 B.C. and Agrippa's campaign that they were finally subdued. More important than the sword was his policy of town building, the transference of tribes, and the enlistment of tribesmen in legions for foreign service. Military roads acted as bridles for unrest, and new veteran colonies were at once watch-towers and strategic bases.

From the East, too, came disquieting news. One of the main purposes of Augustus's western journey was to examine and adjust the financial system on which he saw that the empire's future must depend. Much of his time in Gaul was devoted to this task; the Spanish campaigns had for their chief motive the safeguarding of the Spanish mines, and the expedition against the Salassi was probably as much an attempt to control the gold production of their Alpine valleys as a matter of frontier defence. But Egypt was the corner-stone of his new economy and any disorders or disasters there were matters of grave concern.

He treated the country as a family estate administered
by his own prefect, and the first occupant of this high
post was his old comrade-in-arms, Cornelius Gallus, the
friend of Pollio and Virgil and himself no mean poet.
Possibly on the suggestion of Gallus, in 25 B.C. an expedition was despatched against the Sabaeans, who occupied
what was the Eldorado of the age, Arabia, with its fabled
wealth of gems and spices and gold. It may have seemed
to Augustus an easy way of filling his treasury, and it
caught the imagination of the Roman poets.[1] But the expedition was badly handled and failed miserably. Instead
of embarking at Berenice it sailed from the northernmost
Egyptian harbour, Arsinoe, and had a six months' march
before it reached the Sabaean capital. There the legions
were compelled to retreat from lack of water and with
difficulty recrossed the Red Sea. It was the first and last
wild-cat scheme of exploitation to which Augustus set
his hand.

More serious was the situation in Egypt itself. Cornelius Gallus in his new post seems to have let his fancy
run riot, and to have been unduly impressed by his own
magnificence. Having quelled a rising in the Thebaid, he
marched south and declared a protectorate over part of
Ethiopia, led perhaps by the old dream of finding the
springs of Nile. Strange rumours began to come out of
Egypt, of wild boastings by the prefect and of statues of
himself with grandiloquent inscriptions set up throughout
the land. He was formally accused at Rome and recalled
by Augustus, who forbade him to set foot in the imperial
provinces. What followed is obscure. The Senate seems
to have been too hasty in interpreting the desires of the
Princeps, and to have decreed the banishment of Gallus
and the confiscation of his estates, thereby driving him to
suicide. Augustus felt deeply this tragic end of his old

[1] Cf. Hor., *Od.*, I, 35; Propertius, III, I.

comrade, not the less since he was also the close friend of Virgil; he shed tears when the news came, and complained bitterly that he was the only man who seemed unable to set limits to his displeasure with his friends.[1]

The Princeps returned to Italy at the close of 25 B.C. with a preoccupied mind. He was still in bad health, and his new machine seemed to have much grit in it. Apart from foreign anxieties, the situation in Rome was not easy. He had left Agrippa, his colleague in the consulship of 27 B.C., in general charge of home affairs. But Agrippa had many other things to do, what with reorganizing the imperial army and navy and building noble public monuments, and a year later Augustus appointed Messalla Corvinus to the post of city prefect. It was an old magistracy, this office of 'praefectus urbi'; but Messalla, who had a stiff republican sentiment, considered it a too daring innovation, and resigned in six days. It was clear to Augustus that he must still walk warily.

But the matter which most exercised his mind was how the principate was to be carried on in the event of his premature death. The frailty of his body had made him think deeply of the future. There was no question of hereditary succession as in a monarchy; the only hope of continuity was that he should train up the man to succeed him, and familiarize Rome with the prospect. If he died suddenly Agrippa would follow him; but if he were granted a reasonable span of life, he naturally desired to have a successor from his own family. He had two eligible young kinsmen, Marcellus, his nephew by blood, and Tiberius, his step-son. Julia, his daughter by Scribonia, was now fourteen, and in 25 B.C. she was given in marriage

---

[1] Suet., *Div. Aug.*, 66; for the relations of Gallus and Virgil see *Ecl.*, VI and X. Gallus may have been the author of the *Ciris*, traditionally ascribed to Virgil; cf. Skrutsch, *Vergil und Gallus* (1905). According to Servius the odd irrelevance of the second half of the fourth book of the *Georgics* is due to the fact that it was intended to close with a laudation of Gallus, but the view has obvious difficulties, for which see W. B. Anderson, *C. Q.* (1933), XXVII.

to Marcellus, who was now home from the wars, Agrippa
taking charge of the ceremony. In 24 B.C., after his return
to Rome, Augustus took formal steps to indicate his views
on the succession question. Marcellus was authorized by
the Senate to sit among the members of praetorian rank
and to stand for the consulship ten years before the legal
age, while Tiberius was permitted a premature candi-
dateship of five years. This meant that the former would
be curule aedile the following year, and the latter quaestor.
These were the same honours as had in 43 B.C. been
granted to the young Octavian.

The year 23 B.C. opened badly. There was an abortive
conspiracy against the life of the Princeps, in which two
eminent senatorians were implicated, one of them, Mu-
rena, the conqueror of the Salassi and the brother-in-law
of Maecenas. Beyond question there were still elements
in Rome of disaffection and thwarted ambition which required curbing with a strong hand. Then there was the
heavy task of working out in detail the new administrative
and financial arrangements for the empire. Agrippa,
whose own house had been burned, was now living with
the Princeps on the Palatine, and was in close and constant attendance on his master. The young Marcellus was
proving a little difficult, for his marriage to Julia and his
precocious dignities were hard for youth to support without arrogance, but fortunately Agrippa, the true coad-
jutor of the Princeps, was too wise a man to take quick
offence. To cap all, Augustus fell gravely ill.[1] The question of the succession revived in an urgent form, for he
was looking death in the face.

He summoned the chief magistrates and senators to his
sick-room, and made them what he believed to be a farewell speech. To his fellow consul, Calpurnius Piso, a re-

---

[1] The malady was probably typhoid fever, for which cold compresses and cold baths
were once considered the proper treatment.

publican of the old rock, he gave the detailed statement of the military and financial position of the empire on which he and Agrippa had been long at work. To Agrippa he handed his signet ring, thereby marking him out as the man whom he recommended to the Senate and People as most fitted to carry on his task. Of Marcellus there was no mention; the reins of power could not be entrusted to an untried lad still in his teens. For a little Rome held her breath. Augustus had kept to the strict constitutional etiquette, indicating his preference but leaving the choice of his successor to the Senate.... But the choice was not required. A Greek physician, the freedman Antonius Musa, by his cold-water treatment had, before midsummer, restored the Princeps to health.

The crisis revealed to Augustus certain defects in his scheme of empire and certain weaknesses in his own position. The annual consulship was not only a personal burden, and because of its collegiality a potential embarrassment, but it limited unduly the offices to which senators might aspire. There was need of drastic reforms in provincial administration, a task in which Agrippa must be his chief agent, and for this purpose he must have a clear overriding authority, even in the senatorial provinces. The succession question might sleep for the moment; Rome would in time grow accustomed to the thought of Marcellus, and meanwhile Agrippa was the man for an emergency. There was much to be done in Rome itself, and a sharper definition was needed of his actual powers; administrative reform was a difficult business enough without complications about *ultra vires*. Republican sentiment, too, must be more delicately conciliated, for only thus could it be speeded towards a dignified death. So he prepared himself for a revision of the constitution. First, to clear the ground, he resigned the consulship on July 1, having arranged that his successor should be L. Sestius

Quirinalis, who, like Piso, was an old republican and had fought by the side of Brutus.[1]

III

In July he met the Senate. He began by affirming his fidelity to the constitution, offering, as a proof, to read his will to show that, with death in prospect, he had named no successor, but had left the choice to the Roman people. The Senate declined to hear it. They declared that they needed no evidence on that point; a temporary shortage of corn in Rome had made them more eager than ever for a strong administrator, and they insisted (the policy having been carefully prearranged) that the time had come when the authority of the Princeps must be more fully defined and enlarged. A senatusconsult, later approved by the Assembly,[2] gave that authority its final legal form.

First came the keystone, the imperium. Having relinquished the annual tenure of the consulship, Augustus had now the imperium only as proconsul, and could not exercise it in Rome or in the provinces allotted to the Senate. This difficulty was got over by the grant of a 'majus imperium,' which was valid over all provinces and also within the city walls.[3] This meant that he had a paramount authority throughout the empire; he enlisted all troops, nominated all officers, and the military oath was taken in his name; he was the sole fountain of honour; he decided on the distribution of public lands and the settlement of veterans; and with him lay the declaration of war and the making of peace. He could interfere in the

---

[1] Horace, the court poet, dedicated an ode to him (1, 4) placed after odes to Maecenas and Augustus, which shows the political significance of the appointment.

[2] Ulpian, *Dig.*, 1, 4, 1.

[3] Dio, LIII, 32. For a different view from that taken above see McFayden, 'The Princeps and the Senatorial Provinces,' *C. P.* (1921), XVI.

government of the senatorial provinces when he thought it necessary.[1] A scheme, paralleled by Pompey's position between 67 and 62 B.C., had been devised for providing that the ultimate command should be held continuously by the same man without peril to the state. Wisely the arrangement was limited to a term of years.

Not less important was the grant of the tribunician power for life — for life, but with an annual renewal, so that all documents could be dated by the years, beginning from 23 B.C., in which he held it. The title now first appears upon his coinage to show the importance which he ascribed to it. It was his supreme link with Rome and its people, and we have already seen what rights it gave him of controlling public affairs. His resignation of the consulship deprived him of certain privileges in regard to the Senate's meetings, and these were specifically restored to him. He was given the consular power of introducing business, the right of convening the Senate, the right of issuing senatorial decrees, and, by means of his privy council, he could settle the agenda for each session.

These prerogatives, an unlimited proconsular imperium and the tribunician power, were the twin foundations of the new version of the principate. He could have had more for the asking, but he judged them enough. They made him in effect all-powerful. He commanded the armies and ruled the overseas empire. He could direct the deliberations of the Senate and the Assembly, and control the election of magistrates. He had a tribune's sacrosanctity. He had the ultimate legislative power. Though not Pontifex Maximus until the death of Lepidus in 13 B.C., he was in virtual charge of all religious matters, and nominated the members of the sacred colleges. He presided over the review of the equestrian order. The

---

[1] Cf. the words in the Fifth Edict of Cyrene, ὅσην φροντίδα ποιούμεθα ἐγώ τε καὶ σύγκλητος.

police, public works, and the corn supply of Rome were
in his hands. Because he could feed the public treasury
from his private funds — his own house was the greatest
banking and mercantile business in Rome — he was on
the way to control the finances of the state. And all these
many and varied powers had been acquired without doing
violence to republican sentiment, and, while their chief
sanction was his personal prestige, they had been solidly
buttressed by regular laws.

In four years the principate had scarcely begun that
process of articulation which was to make it one of the
most complex and yet smooth-running systems of government known to history. But, owing to stress of facts, it
had made a daring advance since 27 B.C. The emphasis
had clearly shifted from the Senate to the Princeps. Two
startling innovations had come into being. The overriding
authority of the Princeps was not now, as it was in Pompey's case, conceived as for an emergency only and therefore terminable; though legally it had a limit attached to
it, it was realized that it must continue at least as long as
Augustus lived, since an alternative was inconceivable.
More important, the supreme command was definitely
separated from the civil government. Augustus was no
longer technically a magistrate; though he had consular,
proconsular and tribunician powers he was neither consul, proconsul nor tribune. Subject to the withdrawal of
his powers by the Senate and People — which was a practical though not a theoretic impossibility — he had the
ultimate say on every question. The day of Byzantine
autocracy was postponed for three hundred years, but,
with all its republican flavouring, the principate had travelled far from the Republic. The state had now a dual
character, in which the ideas of Roman magistracy and
Hellenistic monarchy were subtly blended, and it was

precisely this mixture which was to give it its power over the varied populations of the empire. Augustus had not designed the form it took, but his wise opportunism had permitted a constitution to emerge which had an organic vitality because it fitted the facts. A great scholar has reproached him because he 'willed the impossible and set up the impermanent'; [1] but what he willed was tentative, a thing the feasibility of which was left to the test of time, and the taunt of impermanence is idle in the case of an institution which endured for centuries and is still part of the framework of the modern world.

The revolutionary development of 23 B.C. had no serious critics. The literary evidence for the early empire is tainted, for it comes chiefly from intellectuals and traditionalists; far more important is the proof from epigraphy and archaeology of a widespread contentment with the new design, contentment soon to develop into an almost religious veneration. Tacitus puts into the mouth of Galba words which fairly describe the mood of Rome and Italy: 'Those whom you are to rule are men who cannot endure either complete slavery or complete liberty.' [2] The aristocracy acquiesced in it; under the four years of the principate many had restored their fortunes, and some were back at their old business of feathering their nests at the public expense. Augustus had been scrupulous in giving the highest posts to grandees of all parties. If Agrippa and Statilius Taurus were lowly born, he could point on the other side to Valerii, Cornelii, and Calpurnii and descendants of the proud houses of Aemilius Paullus and Scipio.[3] The middle classes assented, for they had now some hope of peace and commercial security, and they knew that Augustus intended to make full use of the equestrian order. The puritan section of Roman society, and

---

[1] Hirschfeld, *Die kaiserlichen Verwaltungsbeamten*, 468, quoted in *C. A. H.*, x, 181.

[2] *Hist.*, I, 16.

[3] A study of the Fasti shows the preponderance of aristocrats in high office. Cf. Marsh, *The Founding of the Rom. Emp.*, 241–42.

it was not negligible, saw in him a lover of ancient decorum
and piety. The proletariat, scared by the famine and the
floods of the Tiber, looked to him to safeguard their precarious livelihood and their scanty pleasures. What they
longed for was competent government, for they were the
first victims of inefficiency. It is too often forgotten that
the urban mob, and their leaders, the Populares, were
never in the modern sense democrats. The provinces
looked to Augustus as their protector against the evil
days of exploitation by greedy proconsuls. They had no
sentimentality about Senate and People, for they had
known the harsh incompetence of their rule.[1] Youth, too,
saw a more spacious future before it, not only in the
stimulus of the imperial ideal, but in the facts that political office was now open to young men, and that, since public posts were now salaried, there was a career offered to
talent for those of modest means.[2] Strabo, who lived
through it all, set down the verdict of his contemporaries
when he wrote: 'Never had Rome and her allies enjoyed
richer blessings of peace and prosperity than those which
Augustus bestowed upon them from the time when he assumed absolute power.'[3] Later there were to be revolts
against this or that Princeps, but never against the principate.

IV

Having settled the constitution Augustus was now free
to devote himself to the task which he had most at heart,
the drastic reform of imperial administration. He had
little of the lawyer in him and less of the philosopher; his
talent, as he knew well, was not for theory, but for practice; he did not think of the abstract perfection of a system but of its meaning in the life of the human beings
whom it affected. Persons and things were his concern,
not doctrine. But he also understood that a dogma may

[1] Cf. Tac., *Ann.*, I, 2.   [2] Dio, LIII, 15.   [3] VI, 288.

be not less a fact than a tax or a campaign, and he did not neglect public opinion. He had Ateius Capito as his legal adviser, and the adroit and subtle Maecenas as his minister of propaganda, the physician who watched over the soul and spirit of Rome.

But Agrippa remained his chief counsellor and his principal executive officer. The succession had not been settled, but a provisional arrangement had been reached; Marcellus was to be trained for the task and Rome slowly accustomed to the notion, while in an emergency the state could be left in the strong hands of Agrippa. Contemporary Roman gossip, faithfully reproduced by later historians, naturally assumed some jealousy between the stripling so suddenly exalted and the veteran who had borne the heat and burden of the day. The older man may have had his moments of pique for he was not unambitious,[1] but his mission to the East in the autumn of 23 B.C. was not, as the common story went, an enforced exile to prevent friction with Marcellus.[2] The explanation is inconsistent with what we know of the characters of both Agrippa and Augustus. He was despatched to the East with a commission to report, for in that quarter lay the chief anxieties of the Princeps. He went as the vicegerent of Augustus with a secondary proconsular imperium, which gave him authority over all the imperial provinces in that quarter; Syria, which ranked as chief of the imperial provinces, was his special duty, but this he governed by legates, preferring to exercise a general control from Lesbos.[3] At the same time Augustus may have desired, by Agrippa's absence, to let Marcellus stand out more prominently in Rome's eyes. He was his nephew and the husband of his daughter, and, if there

[1] Cf. Vell., II, 79, 'parendi . . ., sed uni, scientissimus, aliis sane imperandi cupidus.' He tried to persuade Horace to celebrate his doings, Od., I, 6.

[2] Vell., II, 93; Dio, LIII, 32; Suet., Div. Aug., 66; Tib., 10; Pliny, N. H., VII, 149.

[3] Josephus understood the position, Ant., xv, 10. The subject is fully discussed by Reinhold, op. cit., 167–75.

was a son, a future Princeps might be in direct descent of his own blood.

That hope was destined to fail, for before the close of the year Marcellus was dead. He caught the same fever which had attacked Augustus, and, though Antonius Musa laboured with his cold-water treatment, he succumbed to the disease — or to the remedy. We know little of this boy of twenty, but the bitter sorrow of Augustus, and of Octavia who henceforth lived in retirement, and the widespread popular grief,[1] suggest that he had all the grace of youth and the promise of manhood. He came of fine stock, for his father was a man of birth and character, and his mother was a saint. His epitaph has been written by Virgil in the noblest lines ever dedicated to an inheritor of unfulfilled renown, when Aeneas in the underworld meets the slender shade with Night fluttering about its brow.[2]

> Heu pietas, heu prisca fides invictaque bello
> dextera! Non illi se quisquam impune tulisset
> obvius armato, seu cum pedes iret in hostem
> seu spumantis equi foderet calcaribus armos.
> Heu, miserande puer, si qua fata aspera rumpas!
> tu Marcellus eris. Manibus date lilia plenis,
> purpureos spargam flores animamque nepotis
> his saltem accumulem donis, et fungar inani
> munere.

[1] Tac., 7 *Ann.*, 1, 3; *C. I. L.*, v, 7376.

[2] *Aen.*, vi, 878–86. The lines are untranslatable, but here is Mackail in prose and Dryden in verse:

'Alas his goodness, alas his antique honour, and right hand invincible in war! none had faced him unscathed in armed shock, whether he met the foe on foot, or ran his spurs into the flanks of his foaming horse. Ah poor boy! if thou mayest break the grim bar of fate, thou shalt be Marcellus. Give me lilies in full hands; let me strew bright blossoms, and these gifts at least let me lavish on my descendant's soul, and do an unavailing service.'

> 'A new Marcellus shall arise in thee!
> Full canisters of fragrant lilies bring!
> Let me with funeral flowers his body strow;
> The gifts which parents to their children owe,
> This unavailing gift at least I may bestow!'

III.   CREATIVE EVOLUTION

(23–2 B.C.)

Et du premier consul déjà, par maint endroit,
Le front de l'empereur brisait le masque étroit.
                VICTOR HUGO, *Les Feuilles d'Automne.*

FROM 23 B.C. onward two duties concern the historian in his study of Augustus's mind. He has the task of the annalist in recording the sequence of events, but he must sometimes halt in his narrative, survey the posture of affairs, and assess its meaning, for, as in the human body, little changes in habit and structure may have a deep organic significance. In this chapter it is his business to examine the twenty years of evolution during which the Augustan principate reached its mature form.

I

Augustus was impatient to get to the task which he conceived to be his prime duty, that of making life secure and tolerable for every class in the empire. He had had to acquire the requisite powers, but that was only the prologue; the heavy labour would lie in using them to work out a new system of administration and law. The programme was vast, and could only be excuted by a strong central government unhampered by periodic changes. He realized, too, that the loss of the old republican freedom must be compensated for by the efficiency of the new authority. If people were forbidden to misgovern themselves they must be satisfied that they were being well governed. A wise paternalism seemed to him an essential concomitant of autocracy.

He went first to Sicily, an island which had drifted into poverty. Once the granary of Rome, it had been ousted from the monopoly of the corn trade by Egypt, Sardinia and Africa, and its land had largely passed from tillage to pasture, huge ranches owned by absentee Roman landlords. His aim was to revive the small mixed farm and the free cultivator. He used public land where it was available, and he bought more, and on it he settled seven colonies, partly of veterans and partly of Italian countrymen, hoping in this way to restore the economic balance and to provide a romanizing nucleus in an island which had never fully acquired the Roman tradition.

In 22 B.C. there was an urgent demand for his return to Rome. Floods and famine had terrified the people, and the mob threatened to burn the Senate-house unless Augustus were forthwith made dictator. He refused the dictatorship, which was needless, but took into his own hands the corn supply, and in a few days relieved the scarcity at his private expense. He refused also the perpetual consulship and censorship which were pressed on him; these were empty names, for he already had the powers. But Rome was getting out of hand, so he summoned Agrippa from the East to act as his regent in the capital. Agrippa during 21 B.C. performed his task to admiration. He restored order, and laid an embargo on Egyptian rites which were becoming an unwholesome fashion in Rome. As a proof that he recognized Agrippa as his colleague in the government, Augustus offered him the hand of his daughter Julia, the widow of Marcellus. Maecenas is said to have advised the match on the ground that Agrippa had now grown so powerful that he must either become the Princeps's son-in-law or be put to death.

There was a sad disparity in years, for Julia was at the most eighteen, while her husband was slightly older than her father; moreover, Agrippa had to divorce Marcella, Octavia's daughter and the mother of his children. This union of an elderly soldier, wholly preoccupied with the cares of the state, and a brilliant, pleasure-loving girl was the first of those marriages of convenience which were to endanger Augustus's family peace.

Rome being again in order, Agrippa spent the next two years in Gaul and Spain. In Gaul he set himself to the work of reorganization which Augustus had begun six years before, improving the road system and after his usual fashion, beautifying the cities. Nemausus (Nîmes) owed the first of its splendid buildings to his enterprise. Then he was called to Spain, where he completed the conquest of the Cantabrians, his first military service since 31 B.C. He reported his success, not to the Senate, but to Augustus, and refused a triumph, for it was his view that the supreme military glory should not accrue to independent generals, but that all victories should be regarded as won by the Princeps.[1]

Meanwhile Augustus had left Sicily for Samos, where he spent the winter of 21–20 B.C. For Greece he did little except separate it from Macedonia and constitute the province of Achaia. The shabby city which had once been Sparta received some slight recognition. Corinth was given certain boons, since it was a Julian colony, but Athens, which had consistently taken the losing side in the civil wars, was left to academic decay. He was no philhellene, as indeed were few of the governing Romans.[2] But when he crossed to Asia he found himself on more congenial soil, for Asiatic Hellenism welcomed him as a

[1] For the constitutional significance of this view see Momms., *Staatsr.*, I, 135; its originator was Julius, in his use of 'legati.'

[2] Dio Chrysostom, in addressing Trajan, speaks of 'Socrates, an old and poor Athenian *of whom you may have heard.' Or.*, III, 1.

sovereign in exact accord with its traditions. He travelled through Asia Minor to Syria, relieving poverty in the cities, adjusting the tribute, laying out roads, instituting public works, rewarding merit and punishing incompetence and misgovernment.

His chief problem was that of the client-kingships, notably Armenia, with which was bound up the security of the eastern frontier. The client-kingship was a useful institution which had already lasted for two centuries, and which enabled Rome to exercise an ultimate control without the burden of day-to-day government. Armenia was a perplexing business. Geographically it belonged to the Parthian sphere of influence, for it was connected, through Media, with the Iranian plateau, and its people were wholly Iranized. If Rome annexed it she would be in effect driving a wedge into Parthia and making her frontier defences more difficult; if she left it alone it would be at Parthia's mercy and would be a dangerous base for attacks on the empire. So, while Judaea, Cappadocia and Commagene retained their old status, Armenia was in a perpetual flux. Artaxes was its king, and Phraates was king of Parthia, and a son of the latter was a hostage in Rome. Artaxes had ruled badly and was opportunely assassinated, but Augustus, instead of making Armenia a Roman province, gave the throne to the late king's brother, Tigranes. He had sent back the son of Phraates to his father on condition that the Roman standards lost by Crassus and Antony were returned, and he had Tiridates, the pretender to the Parthian throne, as a weapon to be used if necessary. He now compelled the Parthian king to fulfil his bargain, and Tiberius in Syria received the standards, and certain prisoners who had almost forgotten their native land. Rome went wild at the news, for Carrhae had long been a thorn in the national memory and Parthia a brooding nightmare. No poet of eminence

refused his tribute,[1] and it became for a generation a
stock theme in Roman literature. There was now peace
with Parthia; Roman sovereignty over Armenia was accepted as the price of it, and Rome had her hands free for
her task in the North and West.

Though the Roman populace would have preferred a
resounding field victory, it was a diplomatic triumph, and
Augustus at the close of his life had not lost his pride in
it.[2] He was well aware that this was no final settlement,
but only a breathing space. Armenia was to remain a
storm centre necessitating periodic campaigns, and Trajan's annexation and Hadrian's withdrawal were no better solutions of the eastern frontier problem. But for the
moment he had an easy mind. He spent the winter of 20
B.C. resting at Samos, where he received embassies from
many lands, even one from distant India, which brought
to the West the first tiger. Early in 19 B.C. he crossed to
Greece, where he was initiated into the Eleusinian mysteries, an odd escapade for one of his character. He met
Virgil in Athens, and the poet crossed with him to Brundisium, where, on September 22, he died at the age of
fifty-one.

The death of Virgil was felt by Augustus as a grievous
personal loss. In temperament the two men had little in
common. The lean poet, rustic in speech and manner,
whose melancholy eyes and worn features are preserved
for us in the Hadrumetum mosaic,[3] was far indeed from
the splendour which confronts us in the Prima Porta statue. But Augustus had the gift of recognizing the value
and significance of much that he imperfectly understood.
He could not penetrate into Virgil's secret world, but he

[1] *e.g.*, Virg., *Aen.*, vii, 604–06; Hor., *Ep.*, i, 12, 18; *Od.*, iv, 15; Propertius, iii, 10, iv, 4,
5, 12, v, 6; Ovid, *Fast.*, v, 567–94.

[2] See *Mon. Anc.*, v, 40–43, 'Parthos trium exercituum Romanorum spolia et signa
reddere mihi supplicesque amicitiam populi Romani petere coegi.'

[3] Found in 1896 at Sousse in Tunisia. See Mackail's ed. of the *Aeneid* (1930), xlvii.

realized that in it there was something which meant much
to the new society which he sought to create. The broken
lines, the strange half-lights, the wistfulness, the aching
'desiderium' which make Virgil unique among Latin poets
must have been hidden from the solid, four-square master
of the world, but he could appreciate the austere exquisite-
ness of an art which had made a new thing of the Latin
tongue. He felt dimly that this man embodied all that was
best in his age, both what he himself could enter into and
what he could only respect from outside. Virgil had given
the world the flute notes as well as the drums; the exulta-
tion of victory and thrill of power, but also the peasant's
frugal days and the gracious magic of the countryside.[1]
All this Augustus understood, but what he most cared for
was that in the epic, which had taken him eleven years to
complete, the poet had written new scriptures for Rome.
Over this work he had watched with eager interest, writing from Spain in 25 B.C. to ask how it was progressing.
It was the saga of his own family, the Julian, who claimed
descent from the curly-headed son of Aeneas. But it was
also the great story of Rome — 'tantae molis erat Ro-
manam condere gentem' — a proud memory and a glow-
ing inspiration. Virgil had been the complete Roman, a
lover of wild nature and the North, but also a devotee of
cities, for after his youth he left Mantua behind him and
lived wholly in Rome and Naples. All Italy, all the empire, was his home. With a sound instinct Augustus forbade the poet's executors to fulfil his wishes and burn the
manuscript, thereby preserving for the world an inestimable treasure. To the Romans Virgil was the preacher
of a nobler creed of morals and the prophet of a larger
destiny, for he gave expression to all that was best in the

[1] An example is in Book VIII of the *Aeneid*, the description of the shield of Aeneas, in
which a beautiful simile is drawn from the Italian peasant mother who has to rise before
dawn.

stock and made the imperial ideal a thing of vision and high poetry. But not less he was the interpreter of humanity in every age, its sufferings and consolations, and therefore the poet not only of the Rome which has gone, but of a spiritual Rome, an Eternal City which can never perish since it is built of man's hopes and dreams.

II

Augustus arrived in Rome in October 19 B.C. There had been trouble there, during Agrippa's absence in Spain, over the consular elections, and he was met in Campania by an anxious deputation of senators and magistrates, glad to welcome the man on whom all classes had come to depend. He refused any kind of triumph and slipped quietly into the city by night. For the next two years he remained in Rome, a period of strenuous labour. Just as his foreign journeys were not mere tours of inspection but crowded with the details of administrative reorganization, so the months spent in the capital were filled with incessant toil. The principate was slowly developing under his hand. In 17 B.C. the ten years' grant of imperium came to an end, and was renewed for another five years. This was a foregone conclusion, but a further step was taken. The co-regency of Agrippa, now home from Spain, was confirmed. To him were granted an imperium over the provinces for the same term as that of the Princeps, and also the tribunician power. In effect the two men were now joint rulers of the empire, with equal powers, but Augustus remained the senior by virtue of his personal 'auctoritas.' The old republican collegiate system had been virtually revived, but instead of two annual consuls there were now two principes with a five-year tenure. This ingenious device temporarily solved the question of the succession. If Augustus died Agrippa would step into

his place by the sheer compulsion of fact. He alone had
all the strings of government in his hand. Moreover,
Julia had borne him two sons, Gaius in 20 B.C. and Lucius
in 17 B.C., and Augustus, after the Roman fashion, adopted
the children. By universal consent the heir-apparent was
now Agrippa, and his successor in turn would naturally
be Gaius, who would be trained for the task. A form of
hereditary succession was therefore established, but with a
republican flavour and a solid constitutional basis.

Augustus, according to Dio,[1] was also granted for five
years the censorian power. Censors had been appointed
in 22 B.C. but had proved impotent, and it may be that the
Princeps, following his approved practice, acquired the
powers without the office.[2] Something of the kind was essential if he were to achieve the reforms in manners and
morals which he saw to be no less vital than a reform in
government. But it is more probable [3] that the famous
Julian laws on conduct, which will be considered later,
were introduced and put into effect by virtue of the tribunician power. As a preliminary Augustus did what he
had done ten years before and revised the senatorian roll.
This was always an invidious task, for no senator would
admit his unworthiness and voluntarily resign. At first
he tried to work through a committee of senators, but in
the end he was compelled to make the nominations himself and face the odium. He was unable to get the number
below six hundred, which was double the size of what he
regarded as a workmanlike body. The brevity of his reference to the business in the *Res Gestae* is a proof of how distasteful he found it. Moreover, it approached very near
to an act of autocracy, for he was acting only under the
dubious censorian right implicit in his consular power,
which in turn was implicit in his imperium.

[1] LIV., 10.   [2] As in 29 B.C. See p. 137, *supra.*
[3] See the passage in *Mon. Anc.*, I, 37–39.

These were the more prominent features of two years of extreme busyness. He took every branch of public service for his province, and devoted long hours to municipal administration, to army reorganization, to public works, to the intricacies of finance, while all the time problems for his decision flowed in from every part of the globe. One of his chief reforms was to distribute certain duties of the old magistracies among new select commissions, approved by the Senate but controlled by himself. He had his secretariat also to develop,[1] and the new civil service, and he was engaged in carrying out a statistical survey of the empire with a view to a fairer adjustment of taxation. No point was too small for his personal attention. The evidence of epigraphy shows that by a stream of edicts and rescripts and mandates he regulated the minutest details of provincial administration. By and by he created an efficient secretariat, and on questions of policy he had the help of his privy council, but it is clear that the initiative in most cases came from Augustus himself, and that the bulk of the work was his. Agrippa was a great soldier and a builder of genius, but he took little part in the larger matters of statesmanship, while Maecenas was first and foremost a specialist in the imponderabilia of public opinion; his talent was advisory, not executive.

In 17 B.C. Augustus rested for a little from his labours. Most of the preliminary work had been done, and the time had arrived to celebrate the dawn of the new world. There was a living spirit of hope abroad, a sense that the old unhappy days had gone and that Rome was entering upon a second youth. Some great national ceremony was needed to give concreteness to this vision and to impress the imagination of the people. 'It must reunite in picturesque harmony the belief in the regeneration of the

---

[1] Suetonius (*Vit. Hor.*) says that he tried to get Horace as private secretary, but that the poet refused.

world, the social ideas of the oligarchy which governed the
empire, the Etruscan doctrine of the ten centuries, the
Italic legend of the four ages of the world, the oracles of
the Sibyl which announced the approaching reign of
Apollo, the recollections of Virgil's eclogue which had
predicted the Golden Age, the Pythagorean doctrine of
the return of souls to earth, which taught that after four
hundred and forty years body and soul lived again in their
former state, and society therefore returned to its former
condition.' [1] There must be a consecration of the future by
linking it with the past. Virgil had done this in the *Aeneid*;
indeed he had prophetically foreshadowed such a celebration,

> Augustus Caesar, divi genus, aurea condet
> saecula qui rursus Latio regnata per arva
> Saturno quondam.[2]

The ceremonial must be traditional, and an appropriate
precedent was found in the Ludi Saeculares. These had
been instituted in the year of the foundation of the Republic and repeated every century, but the fifth celebration, which should have taken place in 49 B.C., was prevented by the outbreak of civil war. Here was an ancient
ritual which might be adapted to a new purpose, and be
made the occasion for a solemn union of old and new,
religion and policy, church and state.

In February the Senate sanctioned the festival, and
entrusted the duty to the Quindecimviri, the College of
Fifteen, who in turn chose Augustus and Agrippa as their
representatives. The legal adviser of the Princeps,
Ateius Capito, adopted the Etruscan idea of the century
as one hundred and ten years, and found a Sibylline oracle
to support his view.[3] The same oracle provided minute

---

[1] Ferrero, v, 81.

[2] 'Caesar Augustus, son of a god, who shall establish the age of gold in Latium over
fields that once were Saturn's realm.' *Aen.*, vi, 792–94.

[3] For the calculations see Zosimus, ii, 6; Censorinus, *de die natali*, xvii, 10; Nilsson in
Pauly-Wissowa, 1696 *sqq.*

details of the ritual, which Augustus modified and enlarged. Dis and Proserpina had been the principal deities
of the old rite, but now the inspiration should be rather
Apollo [1] and Diana, gods of the sunlight and the upper
world.

No more solemn pageant was ever staged in Rome.
Heralds were sent through all Italy to summon the country people to the capital. Between the 26th and 28th of
May sulphur and bitumen were distributed, for the old
rite had begun with a purification, and first-fruits of wheat,
barley and beans for the sacrificial cakes. Then, on the
last night of May, the ceremonies began. There was a full
moon, and about two o'clock in the morning a great concourse assembled in the Field of Mars — once a swamp,
but now, by the grace of Augustus, the home of splendid
monuments, chief among them the Mausoleum of his own
house. There the Princeps sacrificed nine lambs and nine
kids to the Fates, and repeated a curious archaic prayer
to those goddesses who ruled the destinies of men and nations. Then followed a blaze of torches and fires which
turned the silver moonlight to crimson, and one hundred
and ten matrons offered a ritual banquet to Juno and
Diana.

Next day, the 1st of June, the ceremonies moved to the
Capitol, where the marble of the new temples gleamed
white in the sun. Augustus and Agrippa each sacrificed
a bullock to Jupiter, while on the Field of Mars all day
games and plays continued, and a second banquet was
given by the Roman mothers. That night in the same
place there was again a midnight sacrifice; bloodless this
time, for it was of cakes, and the goddesses honoured were
the Ilythiae who give fertility to women. On the 2nd of
June, at the Capitol, Augustus and Agrippa sacrificed

[1] See on this point C. Pascal, 'Il culto di Apollo in Roma nel secolo di Augusto' in
Bull. del. C. A. (1894), XXII, 52–88.

AUGUSTUS IN HIS EARLY FIFTIES, IN PRIEST'S ROBES
(Museo Civico, Ancona)

each a cow to Juno, in the presence of one hundred and ten matrons chosen from the noblest families of Rome. That night in the Field of Mars there was a ceremony which came down from the earliest days, when Augustus sacrificed a pregnant sow to Mother Earth, and implored her blessing on her children.

June 3 was the great day, for it was the day of Apollo and Diana, the divinities of the new light to whom the Roman mind was turning, as the mind of the Middle Ages turned from the austerities of the Father and the Son to the kindly humanity of the Mother of God. In Apollo's temple on the Palatine Augustus and Agrippa offered bloodless sacrifices, and then, after the crabbed Latin of the ancient prayers, came the Carmen Saeculare, sung by twenty-seven boys and twenty-seven girls. Had Virgil lived no doubt he would have been its author; as it was, Horace wrote it, not overwillingly. It is scarcely his best work; there are finer pieces on the same theme among his odes; but it must rank high among official poems, for it exactly fitted the occasion. Into it he wove every purpose of the ritual — the nocturnal recognition of what was hoar-ancient, the dependence upon the bounty of Mother Earth, the prayers by day to the old Capitoline gods and to the special divinities of the new empire. As the pure voices of the children sang in alternation, first of the reverence due to the Fates, the Earth and the Gods, and then of the achievements and aspirations of their race — Media and Scythia and India offering friendship, Rome herself 'bellante prior, jacentem lenis in hostem' — the listening crowds must have deemed themselves witnesses both to the rebirth of old piety and the advent of a happier world.[1]

[1] The evidence for the Ludi Saeculares is largely epigraphical and will be found in C. I. L. and Dessau. An inscription discovered in the bed of the Tiber in 1871 gives us the official programme, ending with the words, 'Carmen composuit Q. Horatius Flaccus.' C. I. L., VI, 32323. See also J. Gagé, Recherches sur les Jeux séculaires (Paris, 1934).

III

The Ludi Saeculares marked the beginning of two decades of domestic peace. The regular magistrates, assisted by the new special commissions, were perfectly capable of directing affairs in Rome and Italy, and Augustus and Agrippa were free to attend to the trimming of the frontiers and the internal development of the provinces.

The Princeps chose Gaul for his special duty. Its eastern borders were still unquiet, for there were constant little wars with the Alpine clans, and on the Rhine the German tribes, Sugambri, Usipetes and Tencteri, were threatening invasion. The governor, Marcus Lollius, had been defeated by those old antagonists of Julius, and an eagle of the V legion captured, but the invaders had no desire as yet to challenge the might of Rome, and retired across the Rhine. Augustus took with him his step-son, Tiberius, now twenty-five years old, who was that year praetor; Drusus, the younger step-son, now a youth of twenty-two, assumed his brother's praetorian duties, and Statilius Taurus was appointed prefect of the city. The purpose of Augustus in his journey was not, as some believed, the invasion of Britain, or the settlement of the frontiers, where he looked for no immediate danger, but the completion of the romanizing of Gaul. It was his favourite province, the arena of his family triumphs, and the old gateway at Nîmes, inscribed with his name, still stands to remind us of his close interest in the land. The Narbonese, which was quiet and prosperous, had been transferred from the Princeps to the Senate; all he did there was to establish new colonies, of which Nîmes, Avignon and Aix were the most famous. But the three Celtic Gauls, Aquitania, Lugdunensis and Belgica, needed some attention.

His first task was to correct abuses. The imperial procurator in charge of the revenue at Lugdunum (Lyons) was one Licinus, a Gaul whom Julius had taken prisoner and released, and he had degraded his office by shameless extortion. He was dismissed and retired to Rome, but there is no record of his punishment; the price of his immunity may have been contributions to public works out of his ill-gotten gains. Augustus then proceeded to a drastic revision of the financial system, for which his census of 27 B.C. had prepared the ground. Taxation on the Roman plan was a difficult thing to introduce in a society which had a tribal and not an urban basis.[1] There was a land tax and a tax on personalty,[2] and to these he added a small levy on imports and exports. Lyons was made the mint and the centre of the financial administration, and the way was prepared for that complete romanization which was soon to make it politically the second city of the empire.

Gaul was rapidly advancing in wealth, and was already in certain commodities becoming a serious rival to Italy. It had great natural resources, and in its roads, and especially in its rivers, a highly developed system of transport. In the days of Julius it had been a land of hill towns; under Augustus it became a country of river cities, for trade and not defence was now the preoccupation of its inhabitants. The famous old fortresses of Bibracte and Gergovia ceased to exist, and their inhabitants were transferred to new cities in the plains, Augustodunum (Autun) and Augustonemetum (Clermont). But in dealing with native customs he showed himself a far-seeing statesman. He did not interfere with tribal rights in his new division of the provinces, and he permitted old worships and old methods of local government to continue unchanged. How vigorous and idiomatic was the native life is shown by the fact that it is the Gallic tribal and not the Roman

[1] For popular discontent in Gaul, cf. Tac., *Ann.*, III, 40; *Hist.*, IV, 74.
[2] This, and not a poll-tax, seems to be the true meaning of 'tributum capitis.'

urban names which have persisted through history —
Reims, Paris, Amiens and Langres, not Durocortorum,
Lutetia, Samarobriva and Andomatunum.[1] For Gaul
and Gallic ways Augustus seems to have had a special
tenderness. His efforts at romanization were confined
to fostering the growth of cities, improving communications, spreading the knowledge of the Latin tongue, and
establishing a close personal contact by making himself
a readily accessible court of appeal for provincial grievances.[2] The treatment of Gaul remains one of his foremost achievements and the one most fraught with happy
consequences for the future. Its success is proved by the
fact that the land continued so to prosper under the system created by the first Princeps that it was little moved
by the follies of his successors.

But internal well-being could not get rid of the border
problem. As soon as Rome crossed the Cevennes she entered a new world, which had a rude unity as far as the
Cheviots. The conquest of northern Gaul meant sooner
or later the conquest of Britain. So, too, in the east the
Germans might rise again, or a new Mithridates come out
of the dawn, and the straggling, rightangled frontier
formed by the Rhine and the Alps would be ill to defend.
In the latter region disorder broke out in 16 B.C., and for
almost a decade Rome was involved in frontier wars.
Agrippa had gone to the East, where he was to perform
his last great piece of imperial service. Accompanied by
his wife and his two sons, and much troubled by gout,[3]
he went first to Athens, which he treated more kindly than
Augustus, then to the Thracian Chersonese, of which he
was now the owner,[4] and thence to Syria. One of his chief
duties was the establishment of new colonies for veterans.

---

[1] See on this point Rice Holmes, II, 59–60; Arnold, *Studies of Roman Imperialism*, 88.
[2] Jullien, *Hist. de la Gaule*, IV, has a full study of this subject.
[3] Pliny, *N. H.*, VII, 45.　　　　　　[4] Dio, LIV, 29.

There he met Herod of Judaea, and at his request visited Jerusalem and offered sacrifices to the god of the Jews.[1] After a stately progress through the cities of Asia he moved north early in 14 B.C. and settled a dispute about the throne of the Cimmerian Bosporus, which had been seized by a usurper. This kingdom was of great strategic importance, since it was the only barrier against a Parthian domination of the Euxine. He reported, as before, direct to the Princeps, and declined the triumph offered by the Senate. After a winter in Lesbos he returned to Italy early in 13 B.C. The campaigns on the northern front were therefore in the charge of the two young step-sons of Augustus, Tiberius and Drusus.

There was a flickering of unrest all along the border from the Maritime Alps to Dalmatia, partly the turbulence of racial oddments which had found their last sanctuary in the mountains, partly the stirring of powerful tribes who occupied what is now the Grisons, the Tyrol and southern Bavaria. It was a situation which needed young and energetic generals, and Tiberius and Drusus brilliantly rose to it. In the spring of 15 B.C. they contrived an elaborate strategic movement; Drusus advanced from the south by the Adige while Tiberius came in on the enemy's flank from the west. The former defeated the insurgent Rhaeti and Vindelici in a battle near Trent, and followed them across the Brenner, while Tiberius won a victory on the shore of Lake Constance. The brothers then joined hands and conquered Bavaria as far as the Danube. The result was a substantial extension of the empire by the annexation of Noricum and the creation of the province of Rhaetia, to be served by the new Via Augusta along the valley of the Adige. The exploits of the

---

[1] Agrippa went out of his way to conciliate the Jews, and was very popular among them. One of their synagogues in Rome bore his name. Cf. Josephus, *Ant.*, XVI, 2; *C. I. G.*, 9907.

young generals roused the enthusiasm of Rome, and in the odes of his fourth book Horace, at the request of Augustus, celebrated the revival of the ancient Roman 'virtus.' In 13 B.C. Tiberius entered upon his first consulate, and Drusus became legate of Gaul.

Augustus returned to Rome that year with a quiet mind, but the campaigns were not over. There was fresh trouble in Pannonia, which subsided at the threat of Agrippa's advent, but which broke out again in 12 B.C., and Tiberius had to spend the better part of three years on that frontier. But the German border was the main terrain. The Sugambri crossed the Rhine into Brabant, while Drusus was busy consecrating to Augustus the great altar at Lyons which was to be the chief shrine of imperial Gaul. He drove the invaders back across the river, and, with the assent of the Princeps, entered upon a campaign which was definitely intended to advance the Roman frontier to the Elbe, and to put an end once and for all to the German menace. Somewhere near Cologne he bridged the river, defeated the Usipetes and moved against the Sugambri. He had a flotilla on the Rhine, and he cut a canal to the Zuider Zee that his ships might support him by operations along the northern coast. That year he reached the Weser; in 11 B.C. he occupied what is to-day Westphalia, and built a number of forts. In 10 B.C. he dealt with the Chatti, and in 9 B.C., the year of his first consulate, he pushed through the land of the Cherusci and Marcomanni to the Elbe, where he erected a trophy to mark the limit of Roman control.[1] His task was one not only of conquest, but of consolidation, for he left a chain of fortresses behind him, while a line of new garrisons defended the Rhine as far as Strassburg. It was a bold forward movement, of which the wisdom will be con-

---

[1] It is impossible from the ancient authorities to be certain as to the exact order of the events of 11–9 B.C.

sidered in a later chapter; but his achievement was in the nature of an elaborate raid, for there still remained the slow task of subjugation if Germany were to be a second Gaul.

It was the last episode in a brief and brilliant life. On his way home, somewhere between the Saale and the Rhine, his horse fell and he broke his thigh. Tiberius, sent by Augustus to his side, in a day and a night drove nearly two hundred miles, and found him dying. He accompanied the body on foot all the way to Rome, where, after a splendid funeral, the ashes of the dead soldier were laid in the imperial Mausoleum. The loss of Drusus was a greater tragedy for Rome than the death of Marcellus. The beauty of his person was matched by the grace and dignity of his spirit. He was adored by his troops and by all who came in contact with him, for, unlike his brother, he did not suffer from the ingrained Claudian pride.[1] His betrothal to Antonia, the younger daughter of Octavia and Mark Antony, had been hailed by the Roman people as the perfect union of manly and womanly virtue. He possessed, it is plain, military talents as great as those of Tiberius, and a far more humane and engaging character. When death overtook him Rome was coming to regard him with hope and pride as the ultimate heir of the Principate.

The return of the Princeps in 13 B.C. was greeted with widespread popular demonstrations of relief and gratitude. As was his custom, he entered the city quietly by night, and next day ascended the Capitol and placed the laurels from his fasces on the knees of the statue of Jupiter. The Senate decreed that an altar dedicated to the Peace of Augustus should be set up in the Field of Mars and made the scene of annual sacrifices. Rome clung to him as her

[1] 'insita Claudiorum superbia.'

chief security for ordered peace, and whenever difficulties threatened clamoured for his intervention. During his absence in Gaul Horace had pled for his return: 'With vows and prayers your country calls for you ... for with you here the ox plods the fields in safety, Ceres and bounteous Happiness enrich our farms; our sailors sail waters unvexed by pirates; public Honour stands inviolate; chaste homes are stained by no adulteries, and punishment follows swift on crime ... Who fears Parthian, Scythian, German or Spaniard if Augustus be safe? Each man sees day close in peace on his native hills, and trains his vines to the widowed trees, and returns home light of heart to drink his wine and bless thee as god indeed.' [1] In the old Latin, not in the oriental, fashion, the plain man began to take oath by the genius of Augustus, thinking of him not as a remote deity but as an intimate and friendly patron. His 'auctoritas' had now acquired something of the veneration due to one who was god-like, if not yet god. His power had brought him reverence, but his 'providentia,' his affectionate care for his people, was winning him love.

Augustus's extensive travels were at an end, for he had given personal attention to both East and West, and now could make his home in Italy. That year his imperium was renewed for another five years, and Agrippa given the same extension of his joint imperium and his tribunician power. It was renewed again in 8 B.C., this time for ten years. He carried out another revision of the senatorian roll, raising the property qualification, and in 8 B.C. he held a census. The death of Lepidus in 13 B.C. enabled him at last to become Pontifex Maximus. For six years, while the trumpets sounded on the frontier, he was for the most part in Rome, busied with the details of administration, with ceremonies, and with minor reforms. In 9

[1] *Od.*, IV, 5.

B.C. the Ara Pacis was formally dedicated. Of this, one of the noblest of Roman monuments, the sculptured friezes have largely survived, and form a superb pageant of Augustan policy, the pictorial counterpart of the *Res Gestae*. Most beautiful are the children, done with simplicity and tenderness and all the solemn stiffness of infancy.[1] Notable, too, is the place given to Augustus himself, for he takes rank in the groups as an ordinary participant. 'It is not so much with the majesty of Empire that the Ara Pacis strikes one, as with that human and personal conception of the Principate which Augustus wished to stress. There is nothing monarchic about these friezes in the oriental sense, which placed a monarch above his subjects, though the dynastic ideal is manifest in the presence of the many descendants.'[2] Another famous memorial belongs to this period, for in 7 B.C. a monument inscribed with the names of forty-six conquered Alpine tribes was set up by the Senate on the rock of La Turbie above Monaco between the mountains and the sea.[3]

In these years Augustus suffered other bereavements than the death of Drusus. In the spring of 12 B.C. Agrippa died at his Campanian villa, after the threat of his coming had stilled the Pannonian revolt. He had been ailing for several years. Augustus himself delivered the funeral oration, speaking behind a curtain, since a Pontifex Maximus might not look on the dead, and the ashes were laid in the Julian Mausoleum. The honour was well deserved, for Agrippa had been a principal architect of empire and the most loyal, as well as the ablest, of Augustus's col-

---

[1] 'In the Ara Pacis the child makes a triumphant entry into art, and attains a position there from which he has never been dislodged. He is no longer the diminutive man or woman of Greek art, nor are his charms and grace those of the conventional hellenistic *putti*, but real childhood in its infinite variety is pictured here.' E. Strong, *Art in Anc. Rome*, I, 155.

[2] *C. A. H.*, x, 548; cf. Vol. of Plates, iv, 112 *sqq.*, and Colini in *Enc. Italiana*, *s.v.* 'Ara Pacis.'

[3] *C. I. L.*, v, 7817; Pliny, *N. H.*, III, 136.

leagues. No misunderstanding ever clouded their friendship. The Princeps owed him everything, for without his help in the campaigns against Sextus Pompeius and Mark Antony he could not have conquered, and after Actium Agrippa was his chief instrument, both in the ordering of Rome and in the settlement of the provinces. The affection between the two men was shown by Agrippa's leaving to Augustus the bulk of his vast fortune, and by Augustus's long mourning for his dead friend. That career, begun at eighteen and now closed at fifty-one, is one of the wonders of history. Agrippa had military gifts of a high order, and among Roman captains must rank only after Julius and Scipio. He was also a most capable administrator, an adept at carrying out any plan given to him, though in civil affairs he may have been an executant rather than an originator, and his mind a cistern and not a fountain.[1] He came out of obscurity; for a little his house blazed like a comet until it ended in the blood and terror of Nero; but he himself stands alone, a type of all the virtues that Rome delighted to honour. He had the ancient 'gravitas' and 'pietas,' but he was also a man of wide culture with a fine taste in art and architecture; he wrote an autobiography, which is unhappily lost, and he was an eager geographer and prepared a map of the world.[2] His special achievements were to keep the Principate in touch with the middle classes from which he sprang, and by the example of his devotion to the head of the state, in whose name he insisted that all his victories were won, to rivet the loyalty of the army to the civil administration. In habits, in spite of his great wealth and power, he preserved, as one might judge from his honest, blunt features, a fine simplicity.[3]

[1] There is no evidence that apart from army and navy reorganization, and probably the Roman city police, Agrippa contributed much to the main structure.

[2] Pliny, *N. H.*, III, 17. It was finished by Augustus.

[3] 'vir rusticitati proprior quam deliciis.' *Ibid.*, xxxv, 26.

Agrippa is indeed one of the most remarkable figures in history for two reasons. Though a parvenu in an aristocratic society, all men spoke, and continued to speak, well of him. The gossiping Roman annalists, who found specks on every other sun, never suggested scandal or criticism about his public or private life. He was to them, as to Dio,[1] the noblest Roman of his day. Again, he is the chief instance in history of a man of first-class talents who was content to subordinate them to the interests of a friend. He had many times the military gifts of Augustus, and he was loved by the army, but no dream of disloyalty ever crossed his mind. In this there must have been more than personal affection. It is the highest tribute to the moral and intellectual stature of Augustus that he maintained his ascendancy over this mighty servant.[2]

In the autumn of 8 B.C. Maecenas died. He had been a sick man for some years, suffering especially from insomnia, and all his life he had been in delicate health. Maecenas is an eternal enigma. The rugged face was no index to a character which was a compound of the effeminate hedonist and the provident and subtle statesman. He had no vulgar ambitions, for, though one of the three most powerful men in the state, he never held office, or moved out of the equestrian class. At many crises in his career he gave Augustus shrewd counsel, and he did not hesitate to rebuke him sharply when he was in error. More than any other, perhaps, he saw the delicate compromises on which the principate must be built. But it is clear that there was something in him of the antic and the grotesque. He had all the foibles of the aesthete and the foppishness of the *petit maître*.[3] He would fain have been a great writer, but his prose was as harsh as his features — Seneca called it

[1] LIV, 29 — ἄριστος τῶν καθ᾽ ἑαυτὸν ἀνθρώπων διαφανῶς γενόμενος...

[2] 'The dependence of a great man upon a greater is a subjection that lower men cannot easily comprehend.' Lord Halifax, *Thoughts and Reflections*.

[3] Cf. Vell., II, 88; Juv., I, 66, XII, 39; Seneca, *Ep.*, 114.

'drunken' — and Augustus laughed at the 'scent-dripping curls of his verse'; [1] all that remains of the latter is an indifferent fragment in priapeans, glorifying life even if lived in pain.[2] It would seem that Augustus had not the same steady affection for him that he had for Agrippa; there was some estrangement in his later years, due, said Roman gossip, to an affair between the Princeps and Terentia, his beautiful wife who was many years younger than her husband; but there appears to have been a final reconciliation and Maecenas made Augustus his heir. He did invaluable service to the principates service which only he could have performed, for he brought the men of letters, who had formerly been republican, to its side, and thereby made the fame of Augustus immortal. Messalla Corvinus had a small circle attached to him, which included Tibullus, but Maecenas in his house on the Esquiline had the chief *salon* in Rome, with Virgil, Horace and Propertius as its brightest stars. It was his task to feel the pulse of public opinion and to advise the blunter intelligence of the Princeps, and not less to create opinion both for his day and for all time. Literature can give a notable handicap in the race for posthumous fame. In Britain it has taken a century for the reputation of Castlereagh to be cleared from the slanders of the poets.

A few weeks later Horace, as he had predicted long ago,[3] followed his patron to the grave. He was in his fifty-seventh year, and had just finished his *Ars Poetica*. He was a plump little man with hair prematurely grizzled, and he had always been something of a valetudinarian. Towards Maecenas he felt a warm gratitude, and for that strange *poseur* he may also have had a temperate liking, but between him and Augustus there was a strong affection. Horace was a court poet, but no courtier; he was not afraid to laugh gently at Augustus's paternalism and his

---

[1] Suet., *Div. Aug.*, 86.   [2] Seneca, *Ep.*, 101.   [3] *Od.*, II, 17.

belief in making people virtuous by statute, and he cherished and gave constant expression to a kind of literary republicanism. There was never a more independent poet-laureate. The two men, indeed, had much in common, for both looked at life with a cool realism which was not allowed to become cynical; both loved the old ways of the land; both detested snobbery, luxury and ill-bred display. There was a hard core in the mind of each and a pleasing astringent dryness. To the poet, whom he would have made his private secretary, Augustus wrote in the undress style which a man keeps for his intimates. 'Consider yourself a privileged guest in my house... you will be always sure of a welcome.... What a warm feeling I have for you, you can learn from Septimius among others, for the other day I was talking about you in his presence. You need not suppose because you are so grand as to reject my overtures that I mean to get on the same high horse and pay you back.' [1] Yet Horace's urbane and critical soul was fired by Augustus's aims, and he turned the dull things of policy into a poetic vision. In his odes, with their thunder of place-names, he makes vivid the territorial immensity of the empire. He paints with exquisite art the charm of the deep country and the lure of the simple life. He pays to the makers of empire a tribute which has ever since echoed in men's ears. This poet, whose works, like Virgil's, soon displaced in Roman schools the aridities of Livius Andronicus, made it his task to interpret the Augustan ideal to that educated middle class which was the true strength of Rome. Above all he stood by the Princeps in his cult of Apollo, the chosen god of the new humanism. His highest praise for Augustus is that he is Apollo's servant. It is Apollo, patron of enlightenment and peace, who is chiefly celebrated in the Carmen Saeculare, and at the dedication of Augustus's greatest building, the temple

[1] Suet., *Vit. Hor.*

of Phoebus on the Palatine, Horace does not, like Propertius, gloat over the architectural magnificence, but asks
from the god those gifts which Augustus was striving to
bring to Rome:

> What blessing shall the bard entreat
>   Of new-shrined Phoebus as we pour
> The wine-cup? Not the mounds of wheat
>   On some Sardinian threshing floor;
> Not Indian gold or ivory — no,
>   Nor flocks that o'er Calabria stray,
> Nor fields that Liris, still and slow,
>   Is eating, unperceived, away.
> .   .   .   .
>
> Oh grant me, Phoebus, calm content,
>   Strength unimpaired, a mind entire,
> Old age without dishonour spent
>   Nor unbefriended by the lyre! [1]

IV

The death of Agrippa left Julia a widow. Once more
the succession was unsettled, and Augustus set himself to
buttress it. He had Agrippa's sons in mind as his ultimate heirs, but meantime he must find someone in Agrippa's place and provide for Julia. So he compelled Tiberius
to divorce his wife Vipsania, Agrippa's daughter by a
former marriage, and espouse Agrippa's widow. Tiberius
was deeply attached to Vipsania, by whom he had a son,
and he had little respect for Julia, whose manners had a
levity which frightened him, and whose tastes were far
other than his own. With bitter regret he complied with
the Princeps's command, and ever after, when by chance
he met Vipsania, it was noted that his eyes followed her
longingly, and that he could not refrain from tears. Julia
went with him to his Dalmatian campaign and bore him

---

[1] *Od.*, I, 31 (Conington's translation).

a child which died. When, after the death of Drusus, he went north to deal with the Sugambri and the German frontier, she remained in Rome and lived a life of her own.

In 7 B.C. Tiberius was in Rome, where he celebrated a triumph for his northern wars and entered upon his second consulship. He then returned to Germany for two years to complete the settlement of the frontier. So far his career had been one of steady advancement, and he had been on the best of terms with his step-father. Augustus's view of the succession was that Tiberius should succeed to the position of Agrippa and be Princeps in the event of his premature death, while Gaius and Lucius should take the place of Marcellus, and ultimately perpetuate in the highest office the Julian descent. In 6 B.C. Tiberius was given tribunician power for five years. But it was not easy for a proud and ambitious man to accommodate himself to a situation where the heavy work would fall to him and the reward to others. Gaius and Lucius, the one now fourteen and the other eleven years of age, had had a dangerous upbringing. As the heirs-presumptive to the principate all men had flattered them, and it may be presumed that their mother was not the wisest guardian of youth, while their father Agrippa had been constantly abroad on his campaigns. Augustus had done his part by laying down a severe curriculum of studies and providing the best tutors, but he was too busy to give much personal attention to the matter. The consequence was that the boys were spoilt, and were growing up arrogant and headstrong. Already Tiberius found them a trial, and their pride was not abated by the honours which the Senate insisted on showering upon them. Gaius was elected consul, though Augustus would not permit him to accept the post, and both were allowed to become consuls-designate, the holding of office being postponed for five years. In 5 B.C., when Augustus entered on his twelfth consulship, Gaius as-

sumed the garb of manhood, being introduced into public
life by the Princeps himself; the Senate gave him the immediate right of attending its meetings; and the Roman
knights hailed him as 'princeps juventutis.' The direct
meaning of the title was that he was now chief of the
future officers of this army, but the implication was that
its holder was designated as the Princeps's successor.[1]
Three years later, in the thirteenth and last consulship of
Augustus, the same honours and privileges were decreed
to Lucius.

Tiberius found the position impossible. There was
fresh trouble in the East, for Armenia was in process of
revolt, and Augustus offered him the task of bringing it
to order. He declined and, in spite of the entreaties of his
mother, retired to Rhodes, where for the next seven years
he gave himself up to astronomical studies. It was a
strange incident in a life of vigorous action, and Rome
speculated assiduously on the cause. Tiberius's own defence many years later was that, if he remained in Rome,
not only would his military renown overshadow anything
that the young princes might do, but that it would be
hard for him to keep the peace with two vainglorious
boys; and he quoted as a precedent Agrippa's retirement
in 23 B.C. to avoid the appearance of rivalry with Marcellus.[2] Such was perhaps the main motive for his exile,
but another may be found in the growing unhappiness of
his marriage. Julia had entered upon those indiscreet
pleasures which, three years later, were to bring disaster.

The character of Tiberius is hard to assess, for there is
a deep gulf between the marshal of Augustus and the
tired and cynical man who was Augustus's successor. He
was now not far from his fortieth year and in the prime

---

[1] The Pisan cenotaph (Dessau, 140) speaks of Gaius at his death as 'jam designatus
justissimus ac simillumus parentis sui virtutibus princeps.' The title had republican
associations, and is used by Cicero, *ad Fam.*, III, 11.

[2] Vell., II, 99; Suet., *Tib.*, 10.

of his bodily and mental powers. As a soldier he was just short of the first rank, respected but not loved by his troops, a master of detail and a stern devotee of duty. He was a true aristocrat, for he despised popularity and scorned to conciliate an opponent. The evidence shows that in his youth and early middle life he cultivated a republican austerity, and lived, on the whole, hard and temperately, though now and then he had a drinking bout. He was something of a scholar, too, for he knew Greek well, and wrote verses in that tongue, while he was always a keen antiquarian. But he had none of those graces which are implied in the word 'blanditia.' His manners were awkward and unconciliatory, and this was due not to shyness but to a deep spiritual pride. He had in the fullest degree the Claudian arrogance, which was apt in old age to degenerate into a kind of madness. [1]

In the absence of Tiberius, Augustus found his labours multiplied. With Agrippa and Maecenas dead, he had no colleague of his own calibre, and, with the exception of L. Domitius Ahenobarbus, the grandson of Julius's old enemy, and perhaps Quirinius, he had no marshal of conspicuous talent. It is an obscure period in the story of the principate, and it must have been a wretched time for the Princeps. He was ailing and weary, and he was growing old. But he did not relax his labours, and early in 2 B.C. he was cheered by a proof of the gratitude of his people. The Senate voted him the title of 'pater patriae,' which of all the many honours he received he valued most. [2] The resolution was moved by the old republican Messalla Corvinus, who had fought on the right wing at Philippi. 'Good fortune and divine favour,'

---

[1] Suet, *Tib.*, 68; Pliny, *N. H.*, xxviii, 2; Tac., *Ann.*, 1, 4. Tacitus, Suetonius and Dio have drawn a dark picture of the vices of Tiberius, but the first-century writers, like Philo and Velleius, give a different account, and Seneca, Pliny, Josephus, Plutarch, and even Juvenal, are silent on the subject.

[2] *Mon. Anc.*, vi, 24–27.

he said, 'attend thee and thy house, Caesar Augustus;
for thus we feel that we are praying for enduring prosperity for our country and happiness for our city. The
Senate and the People of Rome hail thee Father of thy
Country.' Augustus, with tears in his eyes, replied: 'Conscript fathers, I have attained my highest hopes. What
more have I to ask of the immortal gods than that I may
retain this, your unanimous approval, to the last day of
my life?' [1] The title, with its old republican tradition,
made of the empire a family over which he had the
'patria potestas.' It now became the fashion at banquets
for the guests to drink his health with this formula, rising
and declaiming, 'Father of thy country, Caesar, the best
of men.' [2]

V

Looking round the world at this time one is struck by
the absence of commanding figures. Augustus had a
lonely pre-eminence. There was no man in any part of the
empire likely to challenge his authority, or in the lands
beyond the frontier, though such an one was coming to
maturity in the German forests. Nor, with a single exception, was there any protected prince who rose above
mediocrity. The exception was Herod of Judaea, and his
territory and his people were of all the client-kingdoms the
most interesting to the Roman mind. Palestine, like
Armenia, had high strategical importance in the defence
of the eastern frontier against Parthia. The Jews, now
scattered throughout the globe, were a perpetual conundrum to Rome, and Herod himself, in his extraordinary
career, captured the Roman imagination. He had that
touch of genius which makes a man incalculable.

[1] Suet., *Div. Aug.*, 58.

[2] Ovid, *Fast.*, II, 637–38. The title had been long in unofficial use (Dio, LV, 10; Dessau, 96, 101); both Cicero and Julius had received it, the former informally; Horace
anticipated it — 'Hic ames dici Pater atque Princeps.' *Od.*, I, 2.

There had been a Jewish colony in Rome since the days
of the Gracchi, and now there were perhaps as many of
the race there in proportion to the population as there are
in America today. Rome had been generous to them, and
had granted them exemption from any service inconsistent
with their creed. Julius had given them privileges, and
Augustus and Agrippa had been notably respectful to
their faith. They had considerable underground influence, for their banking business played a large part in
imperial finance. Of their religion the Romans had a very
confused idea. Obviously their rites were very different
from the common heady mysteries of the East. A few of
the educated classes recognized the grandeur of their
monotheism, and some were even converts, but to the
ordinary man their creed was unintelligible. There were
many stories about the great temple in Jerusalem, where
some said the object of worship was a silver ass, and
others a mysterious spirit that dwelt in an old box. In
Rome they lived for the most part in the suburb beyond
the Tiber, and, while tolerated and even respected, they
were not loved.[1]

The ruler of the homeland of this odd people was
Herod, a convert, who had been born in Idumea. The
epithet of 'Great' is not misapplied in his case, for he was
a man of infinite audacity and resource. He had consistently taken the wrong side in the civil wars, and had
always emerged the friend of the victor. He had been for
Cassius against Antony, and for Antony against Octavian,
and in each case had won power by his treasons. Having
obtained by crime the wretched little domain of Judaea,
he made of it a considerable kingdom. He professed Judaism but he was no true Jew, and he repeatedly out-
raged the sanctities of that faith. His aim was to combine

[1] Tacitus's kindest epithets are 'genus invisum diis' — 'instituta sinistra' — 'deter-
rima gens' — 'despectatissima pars servientium.'

Judaism with Hellenism, and to have behind him the strong arm of Rome. Augustus appreciated and supported his purpose, for he wanted someone to control the turbulent populace of Jerusalem and to be a barrier against Parthia.

Herod attempted to ride two horses and failed with both. He did succeed in making Judaea the most important of the client-kingdoms, but he won the undying hatred of all orthodox Jews, especially the aristocracy, and he failed to hellenize his land beyond the surface. On the one side he sacrificed to Jupiter Capitolinus; turned Samaria into Sebaste, and created the great port of Caesarea, both in honour of Augustus; made of the High Priesthood a family benefice; filled his court with Greek-trained Jews, like Nicolaus of Damascus; established theatres and games on the Roman model even in Jerusalem; made his subjects swear by the name of the Princeps, and sacrificed daily in his honour. About 18 B.C. he paid a state visit to Rome. At the same time he professed himself a devout Jew, pled the cause of the Jews in Asia Minor before the Princeps, and began on a magnificent scale the rebuilding of the Temple at Jerusalem. About 8 B.C. he fell out of favour with Augustus, who said bitterly that he would rather be Herod's pig than his son.[1] After that, till he died in 4 B.C., a sense of failure sharpened his passion for cruelty. He broke every law of Jewry, put his sons to death, massacred the Pharisees, and descended to the grave in an orgy of blood. It is probable that he had become mad. The way was prepared for the end of the client-kingdom, the transformation of Judaea into an ordinary Roman province, and that exacerbation of Jewish feeling which ended in the destruction of Jerusalem.

---

[1] The pig was, of course, anathema to the Jew. The point of the saying is the use of the Greek words ὖς and υἱός.

In 7 B.C. Quirinius, the governor of Syria, who had just completed a successful campaign against the brigands of the Taurus, decreed a census of this distracted little land, that census which, for taxation purposes, was held every fifteen years. All Jews had to attend at the centre of their tribe. A certain Joseph — a carpenter from Nazareth in the pleasant country of Galilee — was compelled to journey south in the winter weather to Bethlehem in the Judaean uplands, the city of David, for he was of the tribe of David. With him went Mary, his betrothed. There on December 25, in a hovel where the stars shone through the thatch, a son was born. The name given to the child was Jesus.[1]

[1] Luke, II, 2. Tertullian makes Saturninus the governor of Syria (*adv. Marc.*, IV, 19), but see Sir W. Ramsay in *Expositor*, Nov. 1912, and *J. R. S.*, VII, 273; cf. also Lewin, *Fasti Sacri*, XXIII *sqq.* and Hastings' Dictionary of the Bible *s.v.* 'Chronology.' The likeliest date for the Nativity seems to be 7 B.C.

PATER PATRIAE

BOOK FOUR

I. THE COMPLETE PRINCIPATE

It has long been a grave question whether any government, not too strong for the liberties of its people, can be strong enough to maintain its existence in great emergencies.

ABRAHAM LINCOLN, Nov. 10, 1864.

THE principate was now in substance complete, and it is our business to examine in more detail the structure as it left Augustus's hands. We must therefore anticipate a little and include the modifications which he introduced up to the end of his life. Since it was an organic thing, framed to permit of growth, it is necessary to be clear as to its various elements. There were parts which remained intact so long as the empire endured. There were parts which he deliberately left fluid to change as conditions might change. There were principles which he believed would last and which were to alter for the better; and there were elements which he held not less essential, and which were to be altered for the worse.

I

The huge mechanism was, as we have seen, based upon two principles which lay deep in Rome's history. The first was that the People were sovereign, the sole fount of power; the second, that this power was delegated, in the shape of an imperium, to a magistrate, and that in an emergency such a delegation might be all-embracing and universal. If the emergency seemed to the People to be a permanent thing, then the authority delegated would be perpetual. But at the most it could not persist beyond the life of such a magistrate. On his death it must return to the People and be freshly conferred; it could not be transmitted directly from person to person; it must preserve the character of a special commission. The principate, as Augustus conceived it, was, to begin with, mainly an interweaving of existing institutions, with all their traditional authority and historic appeal. He must have foreseen that some of these institutions would prove feeble stuff, and that others would take a different colour in the new fabric; but at the start the materials must be familiar. Novelty would lie in the pattern.

But even more vital than the elements of the constitution was the central control. The speech which Dio [1] puts into the mouth of Maecenas at the beginning of the principate goes to the heart of the matter. 'Our city, like a great merchantman manned with a crew of every race and lacking a pilot, has now for many generations been rolling and plunging as it has drifted this way and that in a heavy sea, a ship without ballast.' Certain structural changes in the vessel were required, and a more expert crew, but the crying need was a pilot. When Galba, in A.D. 69, adopted a successor he stated what had come to be accepted doctrine. 'If the immense body of the empire could stand and keep its balance without anyone to control it, then I would gladly restore the Republic. As it is, things have long come to such a pass that my old age can give the Roman people no better gift than a good successor, nor your youth anything better than a good emperor.' [2]

A Princeps deriving his mandate from Senate and People; and a mandate which could be revoked and which therefore entailed the duty of governing in accordance

[1] LII, 16.　　　[2] Tac., *Hist.*, I, 16.

with popular opinion — such was Augustus's conception of a system which would be the Republic made practically efficient and adapted to the needs of empire. He saw clearly the dangers. If a temporary and provisional office were made permanent, as it must be, there was always a risk of it drifting into something like a monarchy, and of the first citizen becoming a master and not a leader. When Pliny and Dio Chrysostom lectured Trajan on politics, they stressed the difference between 'dominatio' and 'principatus.' [1] For the defect of the principate — its defect and also its strength — was that it could not be fully expressed in any code of law or body of institutions; it was rather in the nature of a general conception, the content of which must be left to each Princeps to determine for himself. Augustus interpreted it in one way; a successor might interpret it in another, and seek to be a god-king like Caligula, or a tyrant like Domitian. Fate was to drift it gradually towards monarchy, so that with Commodus the word 'dominus' could be used for the Princeps, and with Diocletian it became an official title. Yet so strong was the personal prestige of Augustus that he was able to establish a tradition which, while it might lapse in a Nero, a Domitian or a Commodus, could be restored by the great Flavians and Antonines.

The principate being so fluid a thing, the question of the succession was of supreme importance. He could, of course, lay down no permanent law, but he could make provision for his own successor, and thereby create a precedent. Mere popular election was impossible, and Rome would not accept the hereditary monarchy of which Julius had dreamed. The plan which Augustus devised was to select a colleague who received the proconsular imperium and the tribunician power, and who, since he understood the whole mechanism of government, would in-

[1] Pliny, *Pan.*, II, 24; Dio Chrys., *Or.*, I, 22, III, 48.

evitably succeed him, unless the civic fabric dissolved altogether. He chose Agrippa for this purpose, and, after his death, Tiberius. But he not unnaturally hankered after a successor who would perpetuate his blood and the Julian family tradition.[1] There was some justification for his view. Under the Republic son had often succeeded father in office; the family always meant much to Rome; the prestige of the Julian house was great and his own 'auctoritas' colossal, and these would provide powerful sanctions for any new Princeps. Moreover, the army, which in the last resort was omnipotent, had a partiality for his race. So first Marcellus and then Gaius and Lucius were selected as his ultimate heirs, and it was only when there were no males left of his blood that he fell back upon his adopted son, Tiberius.

The drawbacks to this quasi-hereditary system are obvious, and that he should have accepted it was one of his rare blunders. It provided no protection against a Caligula, a Nero, a Domitian or a Commodus. If the nominal successor were not the strongest man in the state there would be a perpetual temptation for such an one, if he existed, to aspire himself to the throne; for a Princeps could not always count upon the selflessness which Augustus found in Agrippa, and Vespasian in Mucianus. It worked well enough at his death, since Tiberius was the ablest man in the empire, but later it provided a lunatic in Caligula, a loutish pedant in Claudius, and a monster in Nero. Galba broke away from it by his nomination of Piso Licinianus, but the family compact returned with the Flavians. After Domitian came a better system which flung the principate open to the best men and produced great emperors like Trajan, Hadrian, Antoninus Pius and Marcus Aurelius. The last introduced the custom of ap-

---

[1] Augustus's views on the hereditary principle may be gathered from his letters in Suet., *Tib.*, 21, and Aul. Gell., xv, 7.

pointing in his lifetime not a lieutenant, but a colleague, so that at his death the succession was already determined. After him there was a return to the dynastic fashion, varied by occasional lucky pretenders, until it culminated in the fourth-century system of two Augusti.

II

Rome was the heart and pulse of the empire, the citadel of which Italy was the glacis, and on its well-being hung the future of the civilized world. Its citizens were a ruling class, the People from whom the Princeps derived his mandate, and who must provide the staff for imperial administration. Our first question is, Who were the Roman citizens? To begin with, the free inhabitants of Italy; but citizenship in the nature of things must expand, and through his imperium the princeps had the right of conferring it, both in its complete form and in the modified version known as the Latin status. Julius had been very free with the franchise. His colonizing activities made that inevitable, but he also dreamed of an empire which would be one great Rome, and of which all free men would be citizens. The extent of his grants may be judged from the fact that in 70 B.C. there were only 450,000 on the civic roll,[1] while forty-two years later, at the first census of Augustus, there were 4,063,000. The meagreness of the grants of Augustus is witnessed by the number at his last census, held forty-one years later, which was 4,937,000,[2] an increase little more than the natural increment.

Conservative sentiment, no doubt, had a part in this policy, for he was in strong reaction against Julius's ideal of a uniform empire. But there were also weighty reasons of statecraft to influence him. The integration of Italy was not complete; when he began his rule the peninsula

[1] Livy, *Epit.*, 98.   [2] *Mon. Anc.*, II, I–II.

had only been incorporated with Rome for twenty years, and it was very necessary to foster Italian patriotism and self-respect. In Cicero's day the Italian provincial was at a discount compared with the metropolitan; it was essential to remove this stigma, and that could only be done by making the new metropolitan status of all Italy likewise a privileged thing. Again, there was a financial reason — citizenship meant freedom from certain taxes; there was a military reason — the prospect of the franchise was an inducement to the overseas provincials to serve in the army. Most important of all, his scheme of romanization was largely based upon urbanizing the provinces, and Augustus was resolved to do nothing to lower the pride of the provincial cities. He did not wish to cheapen the citizenship of Lyons by making too many of its people citizens of Rome. His conception of the Roman citizenship was as a thing wholly different from the exclusive citizenship of fifth-century Greece, a thing which was compatible with loyal membership of a lesser municipal unit, a thing complementary, inclusive and imperial,[1] and to such an idea the world would take a little time to become accustomed.

The conservatism of Augustus was therefore an expedient to serve an immediate purpose. Of its reality there is no doubt. He refused to grant the citizenship to a Greek protégé of Tiberius unless the man appeared before him in person and convinced him of his worthiness. He declined Livia's request on behalf of a Gaul, offering instead to let him go tax-free, since the loss to the exchequer was preferable to the prostitution of the Roman dignity.[2] In the testament left at his death he enjoined his successor not to create too many new citizens, since Rome must be exalted among the subject peoples.[3] But

[1] This seems to be implied by the tone of the third of the Cyrene Edicts.
[2] Suet., *Div. Aug.*, 40.   [3] Dio, LVI, 33.

he was aware that the time would come when this exclusiveness would have served its purpose, and the advice which Dio puts into the mouth of Maecenas — to make all free men within the empire citizens of Rome — would become practical politics. With Claudius more liberal ideas prevailed; under him the number of citizens grew to almost six millions.[1] The conception of a dual citizenship, local and imperial, had, by the time of the Antonines, become an accepted thing. The orator, Aelius Aristides, could declare that 'the empire is a city made up of cities,' and that, 'what each city is to its own land that Rome is to the whole world'; and Marcus Aurelius turned the same formula into a mystical vision of human society — 'Man is the citizen of a Supreme City in which the other cities are like houses.' [2] Half a century later the edict of Caracalla conferred citizenship upon all free men within the empire. It was in the dark days of the fifth century that a Gaul, Sidonius Apollinaris, summed up in a famous phrase this great enfranchisement. 'Rome,' he said, 'is the city where no man is an alien save the barbarian and the slave.'

In examining the social structure of Rome it is well to remind ourselves that the division was by classes and not by castes. A man, if he were fortunate, could pass freely to a higher rank. The aristocracy was one of office not of blood; he who served the state in a high post ennobled his descendants. By this channel the middle classes, the equestrian order, passed readily into the senatorian, while they in turn were constantly recruited from the third estate of the plebs.

At the bottom lay that canker of the old world, slavery. The wars of Rome during her great period of expansion had filled the city and the country districts with slaves, most of them from races of a high civilization. In a rich

---

[1] Tac., *Ann.*, XI, 25.   [2] *Med.*, III, 12.

family there were men and women skilled in every task from the most menial to the most expert. There was no need for a Roman to go outside his household for any craftsman. Slaves were secretaries, copyists and accountants; carpenters, metalworkers, jewellers, weavers and plumbers; cooks, bakers and coiffeurs; managers of country estates as well as rural labourers; painters, artists and builders; physicians, surgeons and oculists. Their economic value put a certain bridle upon a master's caprice, but their position was always precarious. They could be flogged or branded at their master's will, in a criminal trial their evidence was given under torture, and strict limits were set to their acquisition of property. It was the fashion to expose a sick slave in the temple of Aesculapius on an island in the Tiber, and leave his recovery to chance. Towards the close of the Republic a more humane attitude was appearing, due largely to the Stoic doctrine of the brotherhood of man, and this developed fast in the early empire.[1] Augustus took the lead in the matter. He set his face against senseless brutality to slaves,[2] and their wholesale punishment in the case of the death of an unpopular master.[3]

The question of their manumission forced itself early on his attention. The close of the wars of conquest had greatly lessened the flow of slaves from abroad, but their numbers were kept up by those bred in Rome, and many still arrived in the ordinary way of trade. This latter supply was of a different type from the earlier; those had been either of kindred races to the Roman, or of a not inferior culture; these were often of barbarian stock and of uncouth traditions. It was impossible, even if he had so desired, to restrict the increase of slaves, but he set him-

[1] Cf. Seneca, *Ep.*, XLVII, 1, 13, 18; Pliny, *Ep.*, II, 17, VII, 16; Mart., III, 1.
[2] See the story of Pollio's dinner party in Dio, LIV, 23.
[3] Seneca, *Nat. Quaest.*, I, 16.

self to regulate their admission into the free life of the city, for otherwise Rome would soon become a polyglot rabble. Manumission was getting too popular and too simple, and there was no security for the good character of those set free.[1] Formal manumission, conferring full citizenship, required a process before a magistrate and the payment of dues; but there was an easy and inexpensive kind of informal manumission by mere declaration, which gave the substance of liberty. By a series of laws Augustus checked this abuse. A law of 17 B.C.[2] gave a legal position to slaves informally manumitted and made their children free-born, but drastically restrained their power to acquire and bequeath property. In 2 B.C. he put a limit to the number of slaves whom a master might free by his will,[3] and four years later he severely restricted a master's right to liberate during his life. Slaves who had anything against their character were subjected, after manumission, to heavy disabilities,[4] and gained nothing but their personal freedom. The result of these measures was to keep the freedman class within reasonable bounds. For the rest it was a class to which Augustus showed himself well disposed. He permitted freedmen to hold high rank in the fleets and to serve in the city police and fire brigades; he conferred equestrian rank on distinguished freedmen, like his physician Antonius Musa; he made a freedman, Licinus, his procurator in Gaul with disastrous results, and from freedmen he drew his private secretaries.

What of the dwindling free-born population of Rome? The day had long gone of the stalwart burghers who had won the battle with the patricians and had been the mainstay of Roman arms. They had fought and died in the

---

[1] Cf. the account of Dionysius of Halicarnassus, IV, 23 *sqq.*

[2] *lex Junia.* I accept Prof. H. Last's view as to the date, *C. A. H.*, x., *note* 9. It was repealed by Justinian, for it had served its purpose.

[3] *lex Fufia Caninia.*   [4] *lex Aelia Sentia.*

wars of conquest; many were settled in colonies throughout the empire; some, no doubt, driven by slave competition, had disappeared into the wilds like the 'poor whites'
in the American South; [1] too many had sunk into the
pauperized urban mob. Their quality as well as their
numbers had declined, for there is a Gresham's Law
for human society as for currency, and servile labour ousts
free labour. The higher industries of the empire were
staffed by freedmen and the lower by slaves.[2] What,
indeed, was there for the Roman workman to do when
every avenue was blocked to him, even the humblest, by
men who had behind them the patronage of the rich?
He could seek a patron, but most patrons were already
pledged to their freedmen, and the merry days had gone
when he was of some public importance and could enlist
under the banner of a Clodius or a Milo. Now he mattered
little to the state, except as a potential source of unrest.

Augustus was alive to the problem and not unsympathetic. He was not prepared to dismiss those humble
fellow-citizens contemptuously as the 'cesspool of Romulus' or the 'rabble of Remus.' His legislation on manumission was designed to create a greater demand for free
labour. Rome always accepted the duty of the state to
relieve destitution, and he increased the maximum of
those entitled to free corn.[3] Apart from the regular doles
he gave special gifts of food and money, and for this purpose seems to have spent in the first twenty-seven years
of his rule something like £400,000.[4] Two other steps he
took with a view to giving the Roman plebs duties as well
as rights. One was his division of the city into districts

[1] Tenney Frank, *Econ. Hist. of Rome*, 332.

[2] See Kühn, *de opificum Romanorum conditione* (1910).

[3] Julius had limited it to 150,000, with a means test (Suet., *Div. Jul.*, 41); Augustus
raised it to 200,000 (*Mon. Anc.*, III, 19–21).

[4] The value of such money gifts (*congiaria*) is obvious, for they might enable a decent
citizen to rise permanently above subsistence level.

(*regiones*) and municipal boroughs (*vici*), and the provision in the latter of some kind of elective local government. It was not a very successful attempt, but it reveals his desire to give the populace a direct interest in public affairs. A second step was to try to find a substitute for the old rowdy political clubs by the development of the trade guilds (*collegia*). These had been largely suppressed by the Senate in 63 B.C., and all but a few had been dissolved by Julius after his need of them had gone; but they had come to life again and required watching. As the holder of the tribunician power, Augustus regarded himself as the protector of the poor. He sought to encourage the guilds, to amend them, and also to control them, for no activity must be outside the pale of the integrated state at which he aimed.[1] He therefore decreed that every guild must be licensed, and be to some extent under government supervision. They were strictly benefit societies and not trade unions, for slave labour made the latter impossible. A strike in Rome would have been the idlest folly.

With the decline of the Assemblies the political importance and interest of the Roman poor had vanished. Augustus, true to his wish to give all classes an organic function in the state, would fain have revived these within limits. As it was, the Assemblies were like the Accession Council [2] in Britain, which derives from the old Witan — an antiquarian relic without serious functions. The Assembly of the Curies had become a farce, and no one wanted to revive the Assembly of the Centuries; but at the outset it looked as if something might be done with the Assembly of the Tribes. Julius apparently had thought to restore it, if we may judge from his provision of a new meeting-place in the Saepta Julia, and a grant of citizenship

---

[1] In the third century, under Severus Alexander, all industries were incorporated in licensed guilds.

[2] Anson, *Law and Custom of the Constitution*, II, I, 269.

to a provincial by Octavian in his second triumvirate is so phrased as to suggest that the franchise would be exercised in the Assembly at Rome. The difficulty was time and distance. As things stood, only members of the urban tribes were able to vote, and the voice of the People was only the voice of its least worthy part. Augustus himself wished, for very obvious reasons, to revive the Assembly, and restore to it, within limits, its ancient elective and legislative rights.[1] He devised a scheme by which the votes of members of municipal senates in the Italian country towns could be forwarded in ballot boxes to Rome and counted along with the urban votes.[2] But the thing was still-born, partly no doubt because of the technical difficulties, and partly because Rome at the moment was undergoing a conservative reaction and had no inclination for novelties. The practical obstacle might have been got over by some method of representation, but it is curious how alien the whole representative conception was to the ancient world.[3] Burke's famous doctrine would have seemed to it wholly unintelligible. It understood delegation, but the conception of one man appointed to think and decide for a multitude, because he was typical of their modes of thought and so had their confidence, was remote from its political philosophy. The task awaits some scholar of investigating the way in which the representative idea entered the world. It owed something to the Christian church, and more to the tribal habits of the northern races. Lacking it, constitutional government in the modern sense was impossible.

The Assembly slowly lapsed into desuetude. Nominally it approved elections, but it was only a formal assent,

[1] Vell., II, 99.

[2] Suet., *Div. Aug.*, 46. See Gardthausen, II, 315, for an interesting suggested emendation of the text of Suetonius.

[3] The nearest approach to it is found in local government in the provinces under the empire.

and Tiberius, in the first year of his rule, transferred even
this slender prerogative to the Senate.[1] Augustus began
by using it as a legislative body, but as he grew older he
dropped the habit; in the first twenty years of his principate it passed twenty-one laws, but in the second twenty
years only four. The Saepta Julia, inaugurated with so
much pomp, drifted into a kind of zoological gardens,
where gladiatorial shows were held, and on one occasion
a rhinoceros was housed. A kind of Assembly did indeed
continue for nearly three centuries, when the People were
solemnly summoned under the old republican forms to
ratify some power of the Princeps, and the red flag flew
from the Janiculum, but it was a shadow of a shadow.
This particular bit of republican technique Augustus had
perforce to abandon. The People could still make their
will felt, but it was by mass agitation and not by legal
process.[2] The popular element in the principate lay in the
tribunician power of the Princeps. The true successor of
the Assembly was the new army, and such the Assembly
had been in the beginning.

Above the plebs came the middle class, which was
roughly identical with the equestrian order. It was a
mixed body, for in its social character it included many
who did not possess the gold ring of the knight; poets,
philosophers, and men of letters were admitted to it as
gentlemen by courtesy. On one side it was like the unen-
nobled gentry of England, for some of the equestrian
families could boast of long descent. On another it represented the self-made men who had made fortunes by commerce or banking and were on the fringe of the aristocracy.

The rehabilitation of this order was one of Augustus's
principal and most lasting achievements. He looked upon

---

[1] Tac., *Ann.*, 1, 15. Velleius (11, 124) says that this was done on the instructions of
Augustus.

[2] Cf. the rioting on behalf of Julia and the family of Germanicus, and against Tiberius,
Sejanus and Nero.

it not, like Gaius Gracchus, as a political makeweight, or,
like Julius, as a plutocracy which could be milked, but as a
social grade of high value from which he could draw the
staffs of the army and the chief civil servants. To enter
the class a man had to be free-born and of good character, to possess a fortune of from three to four thousand
pounds, and to receive a specific grant from the Princeps.
He need not be domiciled in Rome or in Italy, and the emphasis laid on the order was one of the forces making for
imperial unity. For Augustus this great middle class was
a special care. He laid stress upon its military character,
and himself took the salute on horseback at the parade of
the knights each July. A legate of a legion must be a senator, but the tribunes were knights, and a centurion attained the rank on his discharge. A young man of the order might rise to command the Household Brigade, govern
an imperial province, like Noricum, Rhaetia or Mauretania, or in Rome control the corn supply and command
the city police. Above all, he might aspire to be viceroy of
Egypt. If the knights lost their old privilege of farming
the taxes they were given all the principal financial posts
in the empire. Wherever the personal interest of the Princeps was concerned, the official was a knight. The order
therefore became not only the exploiters of the rapidly
growing commerce of Rome, but the principal source from
which the imperial bureaucracy was drawn. It was a wise
provision, for the middle classes were the strongest stock
in the Roman world. Unlike the aristocracy they had no
violent class pride which stereotyped their character.
They were continually being recruited from below, and in
turn provided recruits for the Senate. They offered to
able youth a brilliant career, and they had the vitality
of men with a horizon and the realism of men who were
the architects of their own fortunes. More than any other
class they still possessed the tough virtues which had made

the Roman state. The history of the principate is the history of the steady advance of the knights until they ousted freedmen from the emperor's cabinet and had all the strings of administration in their hands. The empire at its most prosperous stage was ruled by the upper middle class.

At the top of the social fabric was the senatorian aristocracy. This was no longer the Optimates whose power Julius had challenged. The famous old houses were fast dying of exhaustion. The oligarchy, which, in the name of liberty and the Republic, had fought to retain its exclusive powers, had crumbled by the inexorable laws of nature. It was the policy of Augustus to cherish what was left of that historic blood, and by grants of money to enable the poorer members to sustain their rank.[1] But meantime the enrichment of the Senate by promotion from the lower orders enabled him to build up a new nobility, and by his censorian power he could insist upon a standard of quality. Early in his rule he had been empowered to create new patrician families. This policy was continued by his successors until the patriciate drew recruits widely from the Italian and provincial bourgeoisie and from the army commanders. Vespasian first brought in provincials, and among those whom he admitted were men like Trajan and Agricola. Of this nobility the Princeps was an ordinary member, for Augustus set his face against the creation of a royal caste. His distinction lay in office, not in rank. The senators were his peers, his colleagues;[2] never, like the equestrian procurators, his servants.

III

On this social basis was raised the fabric of the principate. The Senate is the first part of the structure to be

---

[1] Juvenal (1, 106) mentions a Corvinus who was a labourer on a sheep-farm, and in A.D. 58 a Valerius Messalla was granted £5000 to lift him out of 'blameless poverty.'

[2] ὁμότιμοι is Dio's word.

considered. Here the task of Augustus was less creation than conservation. He extended its bounds by his 'adlectio,' the admitting of competent men who had not yet attained nobility through office, but that was no more than what the popular party in the Republic had always demanded. Its old position as supreme authority in the state had indeed gone, but that had been surrendered of its own volition, since the task of government had grown beyond its powers. To Augustus it was vital to preserve the Senate's dignity, since it was the chief bridge with the past, the only body which represented the continuing identity of the Roman state, and whose members had some experience of public service. In the division of functions, as we have seen, he left it a great part to play. It administered a large number of the provinces; its members held the highest official posts; it had charge of the public finances; it had replaced the Assembly as a legislative authority; it had extensive judicial powers. Its real sovereignty was gone, since it had no longer the command of the armies, but it was given many rights and duties unknown to its republican counterpart. Augustus sought to make of it a true colleague and in every way to enhance its prestige and dignity. As we have seen, he had large powers of determining its constitution and controlling its debates, but he wished to keep those powers in the background, and to let the Senate freely deliberate and decide. He sincerely wanted assistance in his immense task, and above all he laboured through the Senate to keep in close touch with educated opinion. While his health allowed him, he attended its meetings in person, he gave his own view last in a debate, lest he should influence a decision unfairly, and he did not mind heckling or even rudeness.[1]

The partnership was not destined to succeed. The relations between Senate and Princeps were to vary during the

[1] Dio, LIV, 12; LV, 34. Suet., *Div. Aug.*, 53.

empire; they were bad under Caligula, Nero and Domitian, reasonably good under discreet men like Vespasian,
Hadrian and the Antonines, but never truly cordial. A
Princeps could find individual senators loyal colleagues,
but not the Senate. For this there were two reasons.
The body had lost corporate vitality, like the nobility itself; its members were no longer the stern kings who had
stricken into silence the invading Gauls. They were inclined to be captious and childish, and to shirk their duties. In order to secure a full house Augustus had been
forced, as early as 29 B.C., to forbid senators to leave
Italy without his permission. In 17 B.C., and again in 11
B.C., he had to increase the fines for non-attendance. He
stopped the publication of its minutes, which Julius had
inaugurated, no doubt in order that the world should not
see the nakedness of the land. The second reason was that,
even had the Senate been dutiful and competent, its legal
supremacy was bound to be impaired by the practical efficiency of the Princeps. It had, in theory at least, a voice
in foreign policy, and Augustus on various occasions referred such questions to it, but, since he controlled the
armies, the decision must rest with him, and the Senate
was compelled to turn the matters back on his hands.[1]
It had new and enlarged judicial functions, but the Princeps had the right to remove any case from its jurisdiction
to his own. It was the normal legislative body, but, when
in an hour of panic it gave him the power to issue edicts,
it paved the way for a new type of law-making, which was
far simpler and speedier than the old clumsy methods.
No Princeps claimed legislative powers before Hadrian,
but from Augustus onward they made both administrative and private law.[2] An executive authority must have

[1] Dio, LIII, 33, LV, 33; Josephus, *Ant.*, XVII, 229.

[2] Cf. Greenidge, *op. cit.*, 381. 'The Romans had lived for centuries mainly under the
rule of interpreted or judge-made law, and now the Roman world, enlarged and unified,
looked for guidance not to the "comitia," which were in decay, or to the Senate, whose

some rapid means of making rules for emergencies. Augustus, too, owing to the difficulty of getting a full Senate, was forced to make use of a privy council,[1] and, with succeeding emperors, this tended to be less a committee of senators than a cabinet of personal friends. The decisions of this camarilla were given the validity of senatorian decrees.[2] Had the Senate been of higher quality it would still have found it hard to preserve its status in the face of the multitude of executive tasks which the Princeps alone could perform. As it was, it became more and more a dignified anachronism, peevish if unskilfully handled, tractable under a discreet Princeps, but with no inherent power of initiation or resistance. It is not without significance that Augustus, in the first of the Cyrene Edicts, speaks of 'the Senate and I' and in the last of 'I and the Senate.'[3]

The republican magistrates — consuls, tribunes, praetors, aediles and quaestors — continued in their traditional functions. The principal changes made by Augustus in the hierarchy of office was that any man with ambitions for the public service must begin in the army, and that before holding the quaestorship he must have filled one of the twenty minor urban posts. The elections nominally lay with the Assembly, but, by his right of nomination and commendation, he could secure the success of any candidate. In general he held strictly to the rule that the highest dignities could only be obtained through

contact with the provinces was ever becoming less, but to the one interpreter who was known to every judge and every litigant, and whose utterances could be heard at the furthest ends of the earth. It was the force of circumstances, not any constitutional theory, which made the Princeps the highest of all legislative, because the greatest of all interpreting authorities.'

[1] See p. 148, *supra*.

[2] Josephus (*Ant.*, XVI, 6) cites an edict of Augustus beginning, 'It seems good to me and my councillors'; cf. also Dio, LVI, 28.

[3] ἡ σύγκλητος καὶ ἐγώ — ἐγώ τε καὶ ἡ σύγκλητος.

the traditional sequence. It was not always easy to find candidates for some of the offices because of the poverty or the slackness of the senatorian class, and Augustus was more than once forced to exercise compulsion.[1] A busy-body like Claudius further depressed the status of the republican magistracy, for, says Tacitus, 'he attracted all the functions of the laws and magistrates to himself.'[2] The existence of the imperium of the Princeps in Rome itself tended to make the magistrates increasingly dependent upon him, and the new civil service took away many of their tasks. The praetorship, for example, lost some of its duties to special commissions, which worked under the eye of the Princeps, and which handled the chief urban services, like the corn supply, the water supply, and the care of the streets. Augustus had discovered that useful person, the professional committee-man.

The one office which he tried to keep sacrosanct and make the goal of ambition was the consulship; but in order to have enough consulars for high posts he was forced to increase their number by the system of 'consules suffecti,' who held office only for a few months, so that in any one year there might be four or five consuls. After A.D. 2 this became the regular custom. The office was given dignity from its frequent tenure by the Princeps: Augustus held it thirteen times, Tiberius five, Caligula four, Claudius and Nero five each, while Vespasian and his sons had twenty-one consulships between them. Caligula and Nero might set themselves to degrade the office,[3] but the wiser emperors treated it with respect. But no antiquarian zeal could keep the consulship alive, and it survived in the fourth century only as a municipal dignity. Republican magistracies were killed in the long

---

[1] Dio, LIV, 26; LV, 24.   [2] *Ann.*, XI, 5.

[3] Caligula invited two consuls to dinner and suddenly broke into guffaws. When asked why, he replied that he had only to give the signal to have them both strangled. Suet., *Gaius*, 32.

run by the wider scope and the greater efficiency of the imperial service.

The administration of Rome had become a major problem, for which Augustus made special provision. His work in this sphere was indeed one of his chief successes. 'In the Rome of Augustus, not less than in the London of today, there was need of non-political bodies capable of dealing with the practical problems of local government. . . . He did not, indeed, create a city-council independent of the Senate, but by the end of his reign all the departments of local administration were in experienced hands, and Rome was a healthier and more peaceful city than she probably had been at any period of her history.' [1] He gave her superb public buildings — temples, baths, libraries and places of assembly; he gave her an efficient police and a vigilant fire brigade; he pulled down slums and supervised new building areas; he protected her from the Tiber's floods; he saw to it that she should never want for bread. Above all, he gave her civic pride. He taught her his own creed of a world where the Latin culture should be universal, with Rome herself as the source and guardian of this proud tradition, a city 'with no peer and no second.' [2]

Julius, with his Oppius and Balbus, laid the foundation of an imperial secretariat, but it was left to Augustus to extend it into a civil service. This service was gradually to develop into a complex bureaucracy, which was the cement which held the empire together. Augustus laid down the main lines, for he created important posts which could be held by knights and freedmen, and made his own household the centre from which all the wires radiated. Such a change was not unattended by friction, for the imperial secretaries and stewards were regarded

[1] *C. A. H.*, x, 199.   [2] 'cui par est nihil et nihil secundum.' Mart., xii, 8.

with disfavour by the older aristocracy, and, like all bureaucrats, they tended to magnify their office. It was not till Claudius that the service was fully organized with a secretary-general (*ab epistulis*), a financial secretary (*a rationibus*), a petition secretary (*a libellis*), and a judicial secretary (*a cognitionibus*), highly skilled freedmen who between them constituted one of the most businesslike bureaus in history. In Hadrian's time knights replaced freedmen in charge of the main departments, but the general organization endured as long as the empire.[1] These men were salaried officials, unlike the republican magistrates, and they were graded in a hierarchy as strict as the old 'cursus honorum.' They were not, in the modern sense, ministers of state, though they were the executive heads of great departments; they were the personal servants of the Princeps, responsible only to him — a conception which owed something to the Hellenistic monarchies, but more to the old Roman fashion by which the household of a grandee was itself a microcosm of government. The Merovingian kingdoms are another instance of the extension of the methods of a royal household into the administrative fabric of a nation.

Government, for the first time in Roman history, became expert and professional. This was one of the most lasting of Augustus's reforms, and without it Rome and the empire would have lapsed into chaos. The bureaucracy was to change its colouring; with Hadrian it became more closely linked with the army, and acquired a military precision; in the time of Diocletian it had grown so rigid and so intricate that it was an incubus on the empire. The freedmen whom Augustus used may, as administrators, have been less honest, but they were probably more competent and liberal than the retired colonels of a later period. The Augustan system suffered from the defect

---

[1] Suetonius was for a time Hadrian's secretary-general.

of all bureaucracies in that in time the machine became so grandiose that officials looked only to its smooth working, and not to the purpose it was meant to serve, the needs of the people. Nevertheless, for several centuries it provided as inexpensive, clean and efficient a government as any empire has ever enjoyed. Gibbon did not exaggerate when he wrote: 'If a man were called to fix the period in the history of the world during which the condition of the human race was most happy and prosperous, he would without hesitation name that which elapsed from the death of Domitian to the accession of Commodus. The vast extent of the Roman empire was governed by arbitrary power, under the guidance of virtue and wisdom.' [1]

IV

So much for the fabric; it remains to consider the services built up within it. First comes the essential business of finance. The Republic had raised its revenues from two main sources; in Italy, from customs dues, rents of public land, and a five per cent tax on manumitted slaves; in the provinces, from various direct taxes on real and personal estate, as well as from rents, customs and mining royalties. Direct taxation was repugnant to the Italian temper, but there had been a little god who gave his countenance to indirect taxes.[2] The republican revenues were not large — Cicero says that of the provinces only Asia paid for its upkeep — and they were most wastefully collected, while the fact that they were in charge of magistrates with short periods of office made a continuous financial policy impossible. On the other hand the expenses were small in time of peace; there were no social services, no national debt, and most officials served without salary.

[1] *Decline and Fall* (ed. Bury), 1, 78.
[2] 'genius portòrii publici.'

Augustus's reconstruction changed all this. Experiments in paternalism, a salaried civil service, much public building, and a long-service and better-paid army greatly increased the cost of government. He was forced, therefore, to drastic financial reforms. The system of tax-farming in the provinces was greatly modified, and all the direct taxes there were collected by his own procurators. An elaborate register of the inhabitants prevented tax-evasion. In Italy he took a bold step. Frontier wars and the better provision for soldiers' pay and pensions had swollen his military budget, and he had met this increase at first out of his own pocket, but by A.D. 6 the thing had grown too large for private munificence. He created a special military chest into which he himself paid a sum equivalent to one and a half million sterling, and he laid on Italy two new imposts, death duties and a tax on sales. The upper classes were scandalized, for such direct taxes seemed to them an insult to the Italian people, but they capitulated when Augustus, pointing out that the money must be raised, offered instead to revive the old 'tributum' or property tax which had not been levied since 167 B.C. Apart from the army chest, the 'aerarium militare,' there was the ordinary 'aerarium Saturni' or exchequer, nominally under the Senate but really administered by prefects appointed by the Princeps. Into this all revenues, Italian and provincial, were paid, except those earmarked for the military chest. There was also the privy purse ('patrimonium Caesarum'), the property which he had inherited or received by way of legacies, and out of which he made benefactions to the state. He had a special financial office in his house called the 'fiscus,' where his slaves and freedmen kept exact accounts of the whole finances of the empire. This was a bureau and not, as has been argued, a private treasury which was separate from the exchequer and into which were paid the revenues of Egypt. These, like all other receipts, went to the 'aerarium.' It was not until later that the 'fiscus' acquired the character of an additional treasury.[1]

The principate was self-supporting, but it clearly was no more. Taxation was not high, and under Augustus expenses were rigorously scrutinized. Thereafter solvency depended upon the Princeps. Tiberius was frugal, Nero extravagant, the Flavians were parsimonious, while from Trajan onward there was a steady adverse balance, so that Marcus Aurelius was compelled to sell the imperial jewels to raise money for his wars. In the third century came a financial crisis which led to a debased currency, and after that the controls slipped, and the central machine moved steadily towards bankruptcy. In this, as in other things, the success of the Augustan policy depended upon the continuance of the Augustan tradition. In finance he was faithful to his plan of slowly and obliquely winning control by superior efficiency, and not less of getting full value for every denarius expended.

Augustus left to his successors, as a principal maxim of state, an injunction not to extend the area of the empire. This had been his policy from his first accession to power, and he spent his life in the quest of a defensible frontier. For two sides he had no fear, since he had the desert in the South and the Atlantic in the West; but in the East he had a precarious border-line with Parthia, and in the North there were the uncertainties of the Danube and the Rhine. As a consequence this lover of peace had to give much of

[1] On the difficult question of the 'fiscus' under Augustus see Vell., II, 39; Suet., Div. Aug., 101; Momms., Staatsr., II, 998; Hirschfeld, Die Kaiserlichen Verwaltungs-beamten, 1–52; Mattingly, The Imperial Civil Service, 14 sqq.; E. Meyer, Kleine Schriften, I, 461; Hammond, The Augustan Principate, 317–18. It is not possible to arrive at any exact estimate of the imperial revenues; cf. Arnold, Rom. Prov. Administration, 211. Augustus left to his heirs a private fortune of about a million and a half pounds, only one-sixth of what he had received in legacies, and to the army and people just under a million. He was probably no richer a man than Crassus under the Republic, and he died poorer than he began. See Tenney Frank, J. R. S. (1933), XXII, 143–48.

his time to outland wars, and he made greater additions than Julius to imperial territory. When he died, Egypt, Galatia, Moesia, Pannonia, Rhaetia, Noricum and upper and lower Germany were under the sway of Rome.

On the seas there was no danger. The Romans were not a race of sailors, and the most required of him was to keep the Mediterranean clear of pirates, and occasionally to use a fleet, as Drusus did, to assist a land campaign. He retained part of the navy which fought at Actium, and established naval bases in west and east Italy, at Misenum on the bay of Naples, and at Ravenna near the mouth of the Po.[1] Most of the naval ratings were slaves, though in the time of Claudius we find free provincials serving; the officers were either freedmen of the Princeps or ex-legionaries of equestrian rank. Battleships had gone out of fashion, and the light galley replaced the trireme.

The army was regarded as primarily a frontier defence force, with police duties in the less settled border provinces. Augustus was little of a soldier, and the legionaries were never 'commilitones' to him as they had been to Julius; but he had the statesman's instinct for a strategic danger-point, and he had the gift of choosing able commanders in the field. As we have seen, he linked army commands to civil administration, and, regarding soldiers as citizens and not as mercenaries, he vastly improved their lot. His army was never very large. After Actium it was reduced to not more than twenty-seven legions; under him its normal strength was about 300,000, and probably at no time during the first three centuries of the empire did the total military establishment reach a figure of 450,000. It was recruited for foreign service only, and after the close of the triumvirate there were no legions quartered in Italy until Septimius Severus. Following the

---

[1] Ravenna at that time was situated on a network of lagoons connected with the sea; it is now four miles inland. There was a third minor naval base at Fréjus to protect the western trade-routes.

example of Julius, Augustus endeavoured to encourage
professional skill and *esprit de corps* and to make the life
of the soldier attractive. It was a long-service army, at
first for sixteen years and then for twenty; it was raised by
voluntary enlistment, except in time of crisis; it was
drawn not from Italy only, but from all parts of the empire,[1] and the auxiliary forces came wholly from the
provinces. The chief inducements to serve were the pen-
sion and the right of citizenship which awaited a soldier
on his discharge. The pay, too, was adequate, and under
Augustus there was no difficulty in finding recruits.[2]

In addition to the regiments of the line there were nine
regiments of household troops, the 'praetorians' who
formed the imperial bodyguard and preserved law and
order in Italy. They were strictly a bodyguard, and were
not liable to active service unless the Princeps, or some
member of his family, took the field. They were commanded by two prefects of equestrian rank. This force
was the invention of Augustus, though republican precedents could have been found for it, and, while something
of the kind was necessary, it was an experiment full of
danger for the future. At the start it had no concern with
the capital, and order was preserved there by the city
police. Augustus was always careful to station only one-
third in Rome, and it was not until Tiberius that all nine
cohorts were camped outside the north-east gate — a step,
due to the ambition of Sejanus, which was fated to have
momentous consequences.

Augustus desired no hard and fast distinction between

---

[1] As early as Tiberius the non-Italian element was the strongest part of the army.
Tac., *Ann.*, III, 40.

[2] The disposition of the legions at Augustus's death seems to have been somewhat as
follows: one in Africa, two in Egypt, four in Syria, seven in the Danube area, eight on the
Rhine, and three in Spain. A legion, with its auxiliary troops, was roughly the equiva-
lent of the modern division. On the whole question of the legions under Augustus, see
R. Syme in *J. R. S.* (1932), XXII; Ritterling, in *Pauly-Wissowa, s.v.* 'legio,' and Parker,
The Roman Legions (1928).

civil and military life, and therefore insisted upon em-
bryo statesmen serving for some time with the eagles.
This valiant non-professionalism had been well enough
in the early days of the Republic, when 'the hand had to
keep the head' and every man was trained to arms. But
now it was an anachronism. The ex-praetor or ex-quaestor
who, as legate, commanded a legion, was no more than an
amateur. Soon military enthusiasm died in the Roman
upper classes, while the retention of the army on the
frontiers killed the interest in defence among the population at large. The world inside the protected borders
became not only unmilitary, but unmartial, and could not
defend itself against an invader who had forced the outer
lines. Here lay one of the weaknesses of Augustus's army
policy. Another was that, though conditions of service
were reasonable, discipline was not strictly enforced, and
in the officer class there was some corruption.[1] It was an
instance of that weakening of fibre at the centre which was
ultimately to destroy the empire.

The strength of the army lay in its non-commissioned
officers, the centurions drawn from the Italian yeomanry.
For the Roman army was still strong, and was to remain
for centuries one of the marvels of the world. A vast territory was never more economically garrisoned: twelve
hundred men at Lyons kept order throughout the whole of
Gaul. Wherever the legions went they spread Roman
ideas and the Latin tongue; they were a force of unity in
another sense, for the troops were often of the same race
as the men they supervised or fought against, and so the
gulf was bridged between Roman and barbarian. Famous
cities sprang from the field-force canteens which grew up
beside their permanent camps. On little but wheaten
porridge they faced the suns of the East, the snows and

[1] Cf. for the beginning of Tiberius's rule, Tac., *Ann.*, I, 16–30; Dio, LVII, 4; Vell., II,
125.

forests of central Europe, and the desolate barrens of
the North, and made of the desert a habitable place.
For generations their morning reveillé was to sound at
the outposts of empire and their harness to clank on the
world's horizons, and they held the gates of civilization
long enough to preserve for the future the most vital part
of the bequest of Rome.

Of that bequest law formed a principal part. The Romans as a race had legal genius, and their juristic conceptions, elaborated early in the Republic and codified by the
great jurisprudents of the later empire, were the foundation of the law of the mediaeval and modern worlds. This
is not the place to attempt a summary of the judicial system of the Republic. It was an intricate structure built
up slowly, cell by cell, and if it was clumsy it was compre-
hensive. Both in civil and criminal cases the ordinary
tribunal was the jury-courts presided over by the praetors. The praetor, at a preliminary hearing, had to grant
a type of action, and new types were invented to meet new
circumstances, just as English lawyers in the past had to
devise new kinds of writs. Especially, new formulas had
to be found for cases where one of the parties was an
alien — the beginning of private international law. Criminal procedure up to the time of Sulla is obscure, but we
know that he created a variety of criminal courts, each to
deal with a special class of crime, and that his system continued under the empire.

The chief of Augustus's changes lay in the judicial
powers now accorded to the Senate and to the Princeps
himself. The Senate was the consuls' court which had always claimed jurisdiction in certain cases, but now it was
made a regular high court, both of first instance and of appeal. Its importance lay chiefly in criminal cases, especially
offences against the state, all that came under the wide

heading of 'majestas' or treason. In theory there was no appeal from the Senate's verdict, but in practice the Princeps had effective rights of intercession and veto. The Princeps himself could bring cases before the Senate and preside in person, and he could appear and give evidence in the ordinary jury courts, but his real power was in his direct jurisdiction. This covered every penal offence, and could be exercised by his delegates. In theory it was based upon his imperium, and it arose in practice, perhaps, from the necessity of dealing with appeals from the provinces. Two things are to be noted about the whole judicial system. There was no legal process by which a citizen could enforce his rights against the state. There was an elaborate machinery of appeals ending with that to the Princeps himself, but there was no tribunal to judge between the state and the private person, nothing to correspond with the English 'action against the Crown.' The principate was always judge in its own cause. Again, the jurisdiction of the Princeps was of a different type from any other, being executive rather than judicial, an application of executive power to matters properly justiciable. This gave it great freedom of action, and made it certain, in time, to override every other form of tribunal. The 'appeal to Caesar' was to become the cardinal fact in the law of the empire. That Rome accepted it so readily was due perhaps to her traditional preference for judge-made law.[1]

The new judicial powers of the Princeps were an inevitable growth, as vital to effective government as his army command. In this matter Augustus moved slowly and tactfully. He was no lawyer, and he had not the fussy interest of Claudius in the work of the courts. He had not the wide vision of Julius, who began that codification of Roman law which was continued by Hadrian and com-

---

[1] Cf. Greenidge, *op. cit.*, 381, quoted on p. 217, *supra*.

pleted by Justinian. His reforming zeal was shown
rather in the lesser methods of procedure. Apart from the
creation of his own new tribunal, he enlarged the ordinary
jury-lists, so as to provide a wider area of choice, and he
made them more democratic by admitting men of small
fortune.[1] He made bribery difficult, by preventing any
relations between litigant and jurors. To clear the cause-
lists he increased the number of days on which the courts
sat, and he put a limit on the length of trials.[2] He exercised his special jurisdiction sparingly, taking no more
than he could help, and showing himself very ready to
delegate to the Senate and the jury courts. He gave evidence at a trial modestly, like an ordinary citizen.[3] He
provided legal assistance for all who applied to him, after
the traditional custom of the Roman nobles, and he dignified the legal profession by creating a panel of skilled
lawyers to advise him. More, that very principle of Julius
of a uniform empire, which he had rejected on the political
side, he accepted on the legal. He permitted Greeks to sit
in judgment as well as Romans,[4] thereby paving the way
for an ultimate imperial citizenship. The independence
of the judiciary, which is an axiom of modern constitutional government, was impossible in the throes of a world-
wide reconstruction, but it may be said that Augustus, as
a judge, used his supreme executive power in moderation
and with due regard to the precepts and conventions of
the law.

The economic policy of republican Rome was one of in-
dividualism and *laissez-faire*. In those pleasant days, before the advent of the economist, this was an instinct
rather than a reasoned creed. Julius had held a different

---

[1] Pliny, *N. H.*, xxxiii, 1; Suet., *Div. Aug.*, 32.

[2] Gaius, *Inst.*, ii, 279; iv, 104.   [3] Suet., *Div. Aug.*, 56; Dio, liv, 3.

[4] This is clear from the Cyrene Edicts which reversed the practice of the old *lex Rupi-
lia* (Cic., *in Verr.*, ii, 13).

view. From what we know of his plans it would appear that he meant to give state-aid to commerce and make it a unifying force throughout the empire. Augustus accepted this paternalism, for he saw what a power for integration lay in a world-wide mercantile network with Rome as its centre. On one point only he differed from his predecessor, for he was determined that Italy should be on a different plane from the rest of the empire. Economic conditions were to bring this about without any effort on his part, for under his rule Italy sprang into undisputed commercial pre-eminence,[1] and there was no need to erect tariff walls. During republican times there had been an attempt to protect Italian agriculture by forbidding the production of wine and oil in the provinces,[2] but the experiment was not repeated. The Roman empire began and continued as a free trade area.[3]

The causes of this economic prosperity were many. Foremost came the Augustan peace, under which, by sea and land, trade could move in security. Another was the rise of the middle classes, the bankers, merchants and industrialists, who had now a major influence in the state. There was the opening up by conquest and annexation of new markets; the spread of Latin as a world tongue; a universal gold and silver currency; the making of new harbours and the improvement of old ones; the steady urbanization of the provinces and the growth of new tastes; a marvellous road system running from Rome to the ends of the earth. The consequence of this activity was that in the Western and Northern provinces Italy had a huge market for her manufactures, and for exports like oil and wine. In the East she was principally a buyer,

[1] Rostovtzeff, *Soc. and Econ. Hist. of Rom. Emp.*, 74.

[2] *e.g.*, in southern Gaul. Cic., *de Rep.*, III, 9.

[3] It was unnecessary to protect Italian agriculture against the importation of grain from Egypt and elsewhere, for by the time such grain arrived in Rome the cost of freight had raised its price above that of the homegrown product.

since countries such as Egypt exported to her not only corn, but a multitude of oriental luxuries, like spices, silks, gems, rare foods and condiments, and manufactured articles of a type beyond her rivalry. The provinces paid their tribute in gold, which explains the eagerness of the poorer West and North to find mines of the precious metals. This gold returned to the East in payment for oriental merchandise, since the East took little in the way of Italy's products. As Gaul became herself a manufacturing country and developed an export trade of her own, the way was prepared for an adverse balance of trade against Italy, and for the economic perplexities of the later empire.

This mercantile intercourse was one of the chief centripetal factors in the empire, a power which automatically held the parts together till the political cement had time to set. The impetus came from Augustus, and his principal contributions were his experiments in the quest of new markets and his elaborate roadmaking. Like Julius, he was a keen geographer and a lover of maps, and he infected his people with the same passion. The early empire was a heyday of exploration. By land, communications were always open and notably rapid. There were two great lateral routes, one down the Danube to the Black Sea, and one from the Black Sea across Anatolia to Syria and Egypt; and in every province there was a network of roads following the configuration of the country. Augustus took special charge of the Italian highways, and his legates abroad followed his example, as we know from tablets found everywhere from the Carpathians to the Taurus, and from the Pyrenees to Lebanon. The care of the roads was entrusted to a special commission, with a curator for each of the main roads, and in 20 B.C. a golden milestone was set up in the Forum to mark the spot where all the ways of the world converged. An imperial postal service was also introduced, under which government messages went regularly by relays, though private citizens had still to find their own means of transport. This service was at first a burden upon the communities through which the road ran, a burden which continued until the cost for Italy was transferred to the state under Nerva, and under Septimius Severus for the whole empire.

Augustus desired for Rome, as the heart of the empire, not only political reform, but a moral and religious regeneration. In a later chapter we shall consider the subtler aspects of this work; here we are concerned only with its embodiment in institutions and laws. The Republic had always possessed a state church, with a recognized list of deities, and a ceremonial which was supervised by public officials. It made no inquisition into a citizen's private beliefs, but as a state it professed a certain creed, of which it required public recognition. It was very ready to accept new worships as supplements, for Rome was immensely tolerant and had no wish to offend any god; but it decided what temples should be permitted inside the city walls, and, after the Punic War, had suppressed the mysteries of Dionysus as a public danger.

Augustus set himself to revive the state religion, the cult of the Olympians, as part of his policy of linking up past and present, and as an instrument in securing the restoration of the old morality. It was in its essence a conventional thing, a guarantee of public decorum, a religion of external observance, and not of fervour or personal holiness — best described, perhaps, by the Greek word *eusebeia*.[1] As Pontifex Maximus, and so official head of the state church, he put life into the valley of dry bones. The spirit which prompted the celebration of the Ludi Saeculares appears in much of his work. He compelled the

[1] See Nock, *Conversion*, 10.

Senate to open its meetings with an act of worship — the offering of incense. He gave the Vestal Virgins the official residence of the Pontifex Maximus and increased their prestige and privileges. He prepared a revised edition of the Roman scriptures, the Sibylline Books, and a copy lay for four centuries in Apollo's new temple on the Palatine until it was burned by Stilicho.

In this work Horace was his assiduous helper. We can trace the influence of the poet, too, in the one addition which Augustus made to Roman worship, the cult of the Princeps. This — in Italy, a modest respect paid to his 'genius,' but elsewhere in the empire a special state religion and in some parts almost a mystery cult — was more than a political expedient, and will be discussed later in connection with the profounder aspects of his spiritual regeneration.[1] The campaign for moral reform had also Horace behind it as a vigorous propagandist. It is not likely that Augustus believed that the heart could be purified by outward observance and vice eradicated by statute, but he took the view of the practical statesman that externals count for much, since they sway opinion, and opinion sways fashion, and fashion is reflected in conduct.

In a study of the mind of Augustus the important point is the fact that he undertook this campaign, not the complicated details of his restrictive legislation, from the Julian laws of 17 B.C. to the Lex Papia Poppaea of A.D. 9.[2] He saw that Roman morals were slipping into a perilous state. Peace and security had brought an increase in luxury and raised the standard of living; but, since incomes had not risen proportionately, marriage was at a discount, the birth-rate had fallen, and the idle legacy-hunter courted the celibate and the childless. We have seen how he attempted by statute to regulate the

[1] See p. 285, *infra*.
[2] The subject is fully discussed in *C. A. H.*, x, ch. 14, and Ferrero, v, ch. 3.

manumission of slaves and limit the freedman class. Following the example of Julius, he passed sumptuary laws restricting the amount spent on banquets and wedding feasts, in the hope of making ostentation vulgar. The Julian laws were directed to the rehabilitation of marriage. They forbade the marriage of senatorians with certain types of women; made divorce less easy; gave the wife more power over her own estate; provided heavy penalties for seduction and adultery; laid severe disabilities on bachelors; and granted substantial privileges to the parents of large families.

Such legislation was bitterly unpopular, especially among the middle classes, but Augustus stuck to his policy, and it was continued, with modifications, for three hundred years. It was, indeed, wholly consistent with Roman tradition and with the best Roman habit of mind.[1] But means of evasion were soon found, and beyond question his laws were in advance of general public opinion, an opinion which grew laxer as the years passed. Law should be regarded as an elastic tissue which clothes a growing body. That tissue, that garment, must fit exactly; if it is too tight it will split and there will be lawlessness; if it is too loose, it will impede movement. It should not be too far behind, or too far ahead of, the growth of society, but should, as nearly as possible, coincide with that growth. Augustus's experiments were in advance of Rome's wishes, and though they might remain on the statute-book they suffered the fate of the recent prohibition laws in the United States.

> Quid leges sine moribus,
> vanae proficiunt?[2]

Celibacy did not go out of fashion. Horace and Virgil

---

[1] It was apparently criticized by the conservative lawyer, Antistius Labeo, as a departure from tradition; Aul. Gell., XIII, 12, quoted by Ferrero, v, 64 *n.*

[2] Hor., *Od.*, III, 24.

died unmarried, and it was ironically noted that both the
consuls who gave their names to the Lex Papia Poppaea
were bachelors. Tacitus reports that six years after
Augustus's death the laws were a failure in practice,[1]
and Tertullian calls them 'vanissimae leges.'[2]

Yet the purpose did not wholly fail. Morality by acts
of parliament is an unattainable ideal, but such acts may
do something to create a 'climate of opinion.' They acted
as a brake, though a feeble one, upon one sort of ethical
decline. But the true purpose of Augustus was not
achieved by his restrictive and penal legislation, but by
his positive work in inspiring his people with a new faith
and a new outlook on life. In the latter task, as we shall
see, he won a notable success.

V

Italy outside Rome, in the early years of the principate,
was perhaps the most fortunate part of the empire, her
agriculture flourishing, life and property secure, her ancient cities winning wealth by trade, and the new military
colonies rising into cities. Much of her strength lay in
that municipal life which Julius had fostered;[3] the *graffiti*
on the walls of Pompeii show how vigorous was the popular interest in local government. Augustus also developed
a specific Italian tradition by encouraging an old institution, the League of Youth, which trained boys in sport and
arms and held regular contests known as the Trojan
Games. Italy's well-being was to remain the chief care of
succeeding emperors, even of those who were not Italian
by birth. Tiberius gave one million pounds out of his
own pocket to relieve the agrarian crisis of A.D. 33;
Claudius passed a law against absentee landlords and the

[1] *Ann.*, III, 25.   [2] *Apol.*, IV.
[3] By the *lex Julia municipalis. C. I. L.*, I, 120.

speculators who turned tillage into pasture; Vespasian stopped Italian recruiting in the interests of agriculture; Domitian and Trajan spent large sums on rural Italy; and Hadrian brought her municipal life under his special supervision. By the third century the great decline had begun, and it is a proof of the soundness of Augustus's judgment that there was no serious weakening of the empire till it decayed at its Italian heart.

The provision for the government of the overseas provinces was the largest and most intricate of the tasks of Augustus. He fell heir to a wise tradition. Rome in her history had never shown any pedantic love of uniformity, and in this respect he was a true Roman. His aim was unity not of letter and of form, but of spirit. He was faced with a remarkable variety of laws and institutions, worships, languages, social habits, economic aptitudes and cultural traditions, from the nomads of Africa and the Celtic tribes of Spain and Gaul to those eastern lands which were the debris of Alexander's empire. His policy towards these was much the same as that which Britain has followed in her Asiatic and African possessions. He was respectful to local cults, suppressing only a barbarous practice like Druidism, which had an ugly political connotation. He held aloof from them, refusing when in Egypt to visit the Apis calf, and commending his grandson Gaius for keeping away from the temple at Jerusalem; but he left them to their own devices. Perhaps he interfered too little, for it was not until Hadrian's time that human sacrifices to a Phoenician god were abolished in Africa. From the provinces he asked nothing except that they should keep the peace among themselves, pay their tribute, and provide recruits for his army. He took no account of racial divisions, and recognized no colour-bar. He kept local customs intact and accepted local modes of administration; in Africa, for example, he followed the

modern British practice of 'indirect rule,' and left native
tribes in charge of their own chieftains. What he sought
was unity of sentiment, not an unfeatured uniformity, and
he attained it. He found the solution of what is the chief
political problem of the modern world, 'how communities
might live together and yet live their own lives.' [1] His
methods were to give honest government and an assurance
of peace, to inspire in the subject peoples gratitude to and
reverence for Rome, and by his institution of the worship
of his own Genius to provide a personal object for this attachment. The Gaul who gazed upon the great altar to
Rome and Augustus at Lyons, the Asiatic who brought
flowers and incense to his shrine at Ephesus, the Egyptian
who sacrificed to this new deity as to a member of his own
pantheon, saw in him one who fulfilled all the duties of a
tutelary god.

We have seen the general scheme of government — the
division of the provinces between Senate and Princeps.[2]
A province might be transferred to the Princeps from the
Senate, and to the Senate from the Princeps, according
to the risk of war within its bounds, and the latter had always the right of entry for purposes of defence. The new
system provided for continuity of policy, the careful selection of governors, ample means of getting grievances to

---

[1] *C. A. H.*, xi, 853.

[2] At the end of the life of Augustus the allocation was as follows (Arnold, *Rom. Prov. Admin.*, 278–79):

Senatorial —
1. Under consular proconsul: Asia, Africa.
2. Under praetorian proconsul: Sicily, Baetica, Gallia Narbonensis, Macedonia, Achaea, Bithynia, Pontus, Cyprus, Crete with Cyrene.

Imperial:
1. Under consular legati: Hispania Tarraconensis, Pannonia, Dalmatia,
Moesia, Syria.
2. Under praetorian legati: Lusitania, Aquitania, Gallia Lugdunensis, Gallia
Belgica, Galatia.
3. Under procurator: Rhaetia, Alpes Maritimae, Noricum, Sardinia, Judaea,
Cilicia.
4. Under prefect: Egypt.

headquarters, and, through the imperial procurators, a rigorous supervision of finance. The scandals of the republican regime were now impossible. There were procurators even in the senatorian provinces, so that financial policy was uniform throughout the empire. The Princeps was kept informed about every part, and the governors, conscious of working under his eye, and aware of the career open to merit, had every inducement to be efficient and honest. Taxation was, on the whole, very light; a good shepherd, as Tiberius said, should shear and not skin his sheep.[1] Egypt was a special case. One of the secrets of empire, according to Tacitus,[2] was that Egypt should have a peculiar status. It was kept as a closed territory, and senators and knights were not allowed to enter it except by permission of the Princeps. For this there were two reasons. It was the principal granary of Rome, feeding the capital for four months in each year, as later it fed Constantinople.[3] Again, in Egypt Augustus was the successor of the divine Ptolemaic kings, and had for the Egyptians a royal authority, which it was desirable to preserve, if the complex social and economic system were to continue; but, since it was an anomaly in the empire, it was necessary to segregate it. Accordingly he governed the country through his own viceroy,[4] and maintained most of its native institutions.[5]

In provincial administration Augustus followed two purposes — a steady romanization, and a vigilant regard for the traditions of provincial life. The latter was in the end so successful that Rome herself became semiprovincialized, for the senatorian and equestrian orders were full of non-Romans, provincials commanded legions,[6] and pro-

---

[1] Suet., *Tib.*, 32.   [2] *Ann.*, I, 59.   [3] Pliny, *Pan.*, 31.
[4] Though a knight, the viceroy of Egypt had the imperium of a proconsul. Ulpian, I, 17.
[5] See M. A. Levi in *Aegypt* (1924), v, 231–35.
[6] Cf. Tac., *Hist.*, IV, 74.

vincial emperors sat on the throne. But not less thorough
was the romanizing — by trade, by government, by the
presence of the army, by the emigration of Italians, both
as military colonists and as ordinary settlers. Seneca wrote
with truth: 'Wherever Rome conquers she makes her
dwelling.' [1] Part of the success of Augustus was due to his
emphasis upon urban life, as shown in the cherishing of
old cities and the making of new ones. He thought of the
empire as principally a union of city-states. The 'civitas,'
which he recognized as a unit, might in the West be a
tribal community, but in the East it was generally a city.
Those cities had different relations with the central power,
some having special privileges, but all had a modicum of
self-government; indeed, without this degree of local
autonomy the administration of the empire must have
broken down from the sheer weight of the burden on Rome.

There can be little doubt about the vigour of the provincial municipalities; indeed, in prosperous times their
members competed with each other in their desire to assume public burdens and to spend lavishly. The lesser
units were also grouped in larger organisms, which could
give voice to public opinion and influence imperial policy.
In the West the 'concilia' represented groups of cities and
tribes, and formed a kind of local parliament; in the East
the old Hellenic *koina* had the same function. Both began
with a religious purpose, to which they gradually added a
secular interest. In the East Augustus found the system
ready to his hand, but in the West he created it. It was not
democratic in the modern sense, for the local senates and
councils were in the hands of the local plutocracy, but it
at least preserved the idiom of provincial life. 'A Roman
province,' in the words of Goldwin Smith, 'was far above
a satrapy, though far below a nation.'

Outside the comity of the empire, beyond the border

[1] *Cons. ad Helviam*, VII, 7.

provinces and client-kingdoms, lay the unknown lands and the strange peoples. Every now and then some pressure from afar off drove them up against its battlements. The day of the Roman 'limes' or Pale was still distant, when only a mound of earth separated civilization from savagery; for on most frontiers there was still an extensive no-man's-land to serve as a buffer. Rome did not suffer from narrow horizons. In the East she looked down the road to India and Cathay; in the South over pathless deserts to a domain of magic and terror; in the North to a land of mists and snows and infinite forests; and West, beyond the Pillars of Hercules, to the fairyland of the poets where the Hesperides drowsed in a shoreless ocean.

VI

To recapitulate briefly. — The foundations were the overriding power of the Princeps, a power drawn from the People, revocable in theory, but irrevocable in practice — a power, according to the plan of Augustus, to be shared by each holder of the office with a vicegerent who would be *ipso facto* his successor. This power was executive, legislative and judicial, but principally the first. It rested in law upon a popular gift, but in fact upon the command of the army and a personal 'auctoritas' which was fortified by the cult of his Genius. His prerogatives were shared with the Senate and the regular magistrates, who were encouraged in their duties, but the Princeps had, in all important matters, the ultimate say. The provinces were divided for actual administrative purposes, but the Princeps had a general right of supervision over all. His salaried bureaucracy was the executive both in Rome and abroad, and it drew its members largely from the middle classes. The constitution was strictly an unwritten one, and was avowedly subject to revision in the light of new developments.

This vast fabric was the work of one mind. Augustus drew upon tradition and used existing institutions, but that he modified and those he transformed, and he added much that was new. His additions were effected so patiently and obliquely that they met with little criticism, even from the most conservative. He achieved not only a formal, but a spiritual unity. He provided a system of defence which lasted for centuries, till the barbarians from the North and the Persians from the East broke in on its bounds. Moreover, though we may call it a 'perverted republic,' [1] it was in the main a commonwealth, and neither satrapy nor kingdom. He provided in his bureaucracy, and in the universal reverence for Rome, a mortar which held the walls together when the storm broke, and did not yield till the hurricane became an earthquake.

I have purposely tried to present the work of Augustus as a practical solution of a number of urgent problems. It would be easy to clothe it in the language of a later constitutionalism, and to show how unorthodox was the blend of executive responsibility, legislative power and financial control. Easy, but futile; for these conceptions have a long history behind them, which has given them, for us, a special atmosphere, and they were not present in their modern dogmatic form to the Roman mind. The ancient world had its own complexities, but it was not, like ours, heavily overlaid with the debris of speculative systems. The Augustan construction was the linking together in one polity of a set of solutions forced upon a most practical mind by the stern compulsion of facts.

As we study it, the defects are patent, and it is not likely that they escaped its maker's candid eyes. In all nation-building there is an element of gambling and the architect must take his chance. Too much was laid upon the Princeps, and the system assumed for its continuance a race

[1] Greenidge, *op. cit.*, VIII.

of men of the first quality, if not of demigods. The partnership with the Senate was soon to break down, and the immense load of business to fall on the shoulders of the Princeps alone. The last watchword of Septimius Severus was 'Laboremus.' [1] 'An emperor must perish standing,' said the dying Vespasian. The mere volume of work was enough to crush the most diligent of rulers and depress the most vital. Only the bureaucracy saved the situation when a Princeps was a fool or a debauchee. Again, there was no provision for that change, without which according to Burke a constitution has no means of self-preservation, save the will of the Princeps, and the caprice of one man is an imperfect means of evolution. Again, the Princeps had nothing between him and the people, when the Senate ceased to be of weight, nothing to take the shock of popular criticism or be a guide to popular feeling. The only buffer was the bureaucracy, and that was not enough. To this lack of touch with ordinary opinion and ordinary conditions of life was due the ultimate downfall. Even a conscientious emperor was unaware of the decline of quality in his people and the growing economic confusion, and when the throne passed to rude soldiers from the frontier the end was not far off. 'Seldom did one of them comprehend even the elementary social and economic needs of the Empire, and none were remotely aware of the traditions that had made Rome powerful. Their simple task was to hold the Empire together by force so as to keep intact the taxing machinery which enabled them to pay for that force. When this system wasted the resources, weakened the machinery of production and distribution, and, by the institution of serfdom, incapacitated the citizenry of the Empire for army service, the dull emperors hired German mercenaries to protect the frontier, until those mercenaries took over as their own the Empire

[1] *S. H. A.* (Severus), 23.

which they were paid to guard.' [1] Finally, Augustus erred in his estimate of his 'auctoritas.' Great as that was, it could not be indefinitely transmitted.

Yet it was transmitted for very long. The restoration of unity by Aurelian postponed for more than a century the final collapse, and his restoration was on Augustan lines. For three hundred years every wise emperor invoked the name of Augustus and thereby won popular assent for his regime. It is as if the government of modern Britain were still under the shadow of Oliver Cromwell, or the French polity of today inspired by the creed of Richelieu. The more we study the making of the principate, the more we shall be impressed with the grasp and foresight of its founder. It was a far greater and more intricate task than the Napoleonic reconstruction of France, and it may well rank among the foremost political achievements of the human genius.

[1] Tenney Frank, *Soc. and Econ. Hist. of Rome*, 511.

II.   CAESAR'S HOUSEHOLD

What is the price of Experience? do men buy it for a song?
Or wisdom for a dance in the street? No, it is bought with
    the price
Of all that a man hath, his house, his wife, his children.

WILLIAM BLAKE.

I

A GREAT man may be fortunate in his ordering of the
state, but have no such felicity in his own household, for
the reason, perhaps, that the qualities needed in public
affairs are too hard and stiff in texture for the little enclave of the family. In the famous Paris cameo,[1] which
dates from the early reign of Tiberius, the Julio-Claudians
are represented as a happy group, with the deified Augustus brooding above them. That is the figure he would fain
have presented, but, in the very year when the ambition
of his life had been gratified and he was hailed as the
Father of his Country, he stood before the world as an indifferent father of a family. Rome was convulsed by the
disgrace of Julia, his daughter and only child.

The Julias had been the principal ladies of his house.
There was his great-great-aunt, the wife of Marius, whose
funeral eulogy Julius himself had spoken. There was his
grandmother, the sister of Julius. There was the daughter
of Julius, who had died young and had been married to
Pompey, twenty years her senior, the first of several ill-

---

[1] In the Cabinet de Médailles, reproduced in *C. A. H.* (Plates), IV, 157. See Bernoulli, *Röm. Ikonographie*, II, 275 *sqq.*

fated political matches. His own daughter, Julia, had been born on the very day on which he divorced Scribonia, the wife whose temper he had found intolerable.[1] The elder women of the Julian race had been, like Octavia, gentle and faithful, but this Julia seems to have had something of her mother's waywardness. Now, at the age of thirty-seven, she was embarked on the high tides of scandal.

It is surprising that writers of romance, who have so diligently combed the ancient world for subjects, have neglected this daughter of Augustus, for her career had many of the true elements of tragedy. Rome, at the time, was a difficult place for women, especially for such an one as Julia. Their life was at once dangerously trammelled and dangerously free. They played a notable part, as in all aristocracies. In the heroic age of Greece women had been potent figures; with the democracy of the city-state they sank into obscurity; in the essentially aristocratic society of Rome they again became prominent. Under the patriarchal regime of the Republic a wife had been subject to the control of her husband, but even by the law of the Twelve Tables the women of the family had their rights, and intestate inheritances were divided equally between sons and daughters. In time the old solemn type of marriage was largely superseded by what was no more than a personal contract. The husband's control became only a form, and a wife managed her own property. Divorce was simple and expeditious. A great lady could remain a dutiful wife and mother, and at the same time play a large part in social life; such was Cornelia, the mother of the Gracchi, who had a famous *salon*; such was her granddaughter, Sempronia, who was implicated in Catiline's conspiracy. The lust of power turned some of them into unsexed viragos, like Antony's wife Fulvia, or mischievous wantons, like Clodia. But women could ex-

[1] Suet., *Div. Aug.*, 62.

ercise great influence in public affairs without losing their character. 'We rule the world,' said old Cato, 'but our women rule us.' [1]

Marriages among the aristocracy were matters of arrangement, on financial or political grounds, and might or might not be accompanied by affection. We have many instances of the tenderest devotion between husbands and wives, and the beautiful epitaph from a tomb on the Appian Way might have been written of countless Roman matrons.[2] Women like Octavia did their duty uncomplainingly under the cruellest handicaps. But there was no guarantee that a marriage arranged in cold blood would have this happy consequence. Chastity in a wife was important, but there was no bilateral monogamic idealism. A husband might take his pleasure where he pleased without criticism. Sex to the Romans was a plain fact of nature with little glamour about it and less chivalry, and the Roman temper was far removed from the *Frauendienst* of the Middle Ages. Love was a terrible thing, a tragic madness, as in the Greek dramas, and in the passion of Catullus for Lesbia's 'burning eyes'; [3] or it was a placid domestic affection; or it was common sensuality. The ancient world, on the whole, was of Dr. Johnson's opinion that it 'had no great influence upon the sum of life.' The only love tragedy in the *Iliad* is the story of Anteia and Bellerophon, which occupies six lines out of fifteen thou-

---

[1] Cf. the account given by Cicero (*ad Att.* xv, 11) of the family council where Brutus and Cassius were present, and Servilia, the mother of Brutus, took the leading part. Well-born women, too, interested themselves in literature; examples are Cornelia, Sulpicia, who belonged to the coterie of Messalla Corvinus, and the younger Agrippina, who wrote memoirs.

[2] 'Stranger, what I have to say is quickly told; stop and read it to the end. Here is the unbeautiful tomb of a most beautiful lady. Claudia was the name her parents gave her. Her husband she loved with her whole heart. Two sons she bore; of them the one she leaves on earth, the other she buried beneath the sod. Charming in discourse, gentle in mien, she kept the house, she made the wool. I have finished. Go thy way.'

[3] The tale of Dido and Aeneas is often taken as an instance of romantic love, but it seems to me to be on the same plane as the ἄτη of Medea and Phaedra.

sand. In Roman literature there is scarcely a hint of the romance of young love and its innocence. The Cynthias and Delias and Pyrrhas of the poets were slave girls or courtesans.

A woman, born into such a society, could, if she were happily wedded, find satisfaction in husband and children; but if she missed that, the only other avenues were ambition and adultery. She could set her heart on power or on pleasure. Julia seems to have had something of the fineness and *esprit* of her father's race, marred by the caprice of her mother Scribonia. Her portraits show that she had beauty,[1] but her dark hair was early streaked with grey, which gave her much concern. Her childhood in the house on the Palatine cannot have been gay. Livia, her stepmother, was a woman of the old school, with strict ideas about the upbringing of youth, and Augustus, while anxious to play a father's part, was too busy to see much of his daughter. A girl was not likely to find much charm in the grave and preoccupied Agrippa, or in a dry lawyer like Ateius Capito, or in the airs and attitudes of Maecenas. Julia, as a child, seems to have been on easy terms with her father, and to have been allowed to chaff him and to answer him pertly. She was carefully shielded from young men, and was inordinately proud of her rank, having little else to think about.[2]

At fourteen she was married to her cousin Marcellus, which might have been well enough had Marcellus lived; but at sixteen she was left a widow, and was promptly espoused to the elderly Agrippa. She bore him five children, Gaius, Lucius, the younger Julia, Agrippina, and a posthumous son, Agrippa. She seems to have been reasonably happy with him. She accompanied him on his

[1] There is a bust in the Uffizi gallery at Florence, and her head appears with Agrippa's on a gem. See Bernoulli, *op. cit.*
[2] Macrob., *Saturn*, ii, 5.

eastern travels, was nearly drowned in the Scamander, and was hailed as a goddess in various Asian cities — a bad thing for a woman with her overweening pride of birth. But it was the old story of crabbed age and youth. She had much time on her hands when Agrippa was abroad on duty, and she amused herself with books, but principally with dress, and won a name for extravagance. She began, too, to see too much of young men, especially of one of the Gracchi. Augustus scolded her but failed to keep an eye on her, though Livia was a vigilant duenna.

Agrippa died, and Julia was again on the market. Presently at the age of twenty-eight she was married to Tiberius, who was three years older. Her new husband, whose heart was with the wife whom he had been compelled to divorce, was ill-fitted to be the mate of a brilliant and audacious woman. At first she seems to have done her best, for she accompanied him on his Dalmatian campaign, and there bore him a son who died. But after that the breach widened. Julia in Rome lived wholly among the younger set, and stories began to circulate of her doings. She was seen with drunken revellers in the streets, and was a frequent guest at dubious male parties. Tiberius was well aware of the scandals and suffered them in silence, but the position, for a proud man, was intolerable, and was one of the reasons for his retreat to Rhodes.

Then suddenly Augustus learned from Livia what was happening, since all Rome rang with the story. He was wounded to the quick in his pride and selfrespect. At the very time when he was attempting to purify Roman morals his own child was revealed as the leader of that light-witted raffishness which he detested. He must have been aware, too, that he was not free from blame, and in the extremity of his anger we may detect the prick of conscience. He referred the business to the Senate and asked for the legal penalty. Her two chief lovers were a son of Mark Antony and Fulvia, and the young Gracchus; the former committed suicide and the latter was banished. Julia herself was exiled to the island of Pandataria, off the Campanian coast.

Such was the fate of this bright and brittle creature who, under happier circumstances, might have been great, for she had an excellent mind, and, as her popularity with the Roman mob showed, the magic of personality. Neither her father nor her husband ever saw her again. She was denied the simplest luxuries, and, though she was later allowed to live on the mainland, her exile was never rescinded. When she died a few weeks after Augustus, her ashes were forbidden the imperial Mausoleum. Nor did her tragedy end at Pandataria. Her daughter, the younger Julia, who married L. Aemilius Paullus, travelled the same road. In A.D. 9 she was detected in adultery and was banished to the island of Tremesus on the Apulian coast, where, supported by a scanty allowance from Livia, she lived miserably until her death twenty years later. Her fall crushed the wings of a butterfly poet, for Ovid had apparently been privy to the affair and was himself exiled to the bleak shores of the Black Sea. The tragedy of his daughter weakened the prestige of Augustus in Rome, for a strong Julia party came into being, and it left a deep scar on his soul. In the words of Suetonius, 'he bore the death of his kin with far more resignation than their misconduct.' [1]

II

With his daughter in disgrace and Tiberius sulking in Rhodes, Augustus turned with an almost passionate affection to the two grandsons with whom rested the hope

[1] *Div. Aug.*, 65.

of the Julian succession. The boys suffered all the disad-
vantages of heir-presumptives, for they had been forced
into public prominence too soon and had not borne their
honours discreetly, and they were surrounded by flatterers
who increased their arrogance. In 1 B.C. Gaius was sent on
a roving commission to the Eastern provinces, being invested with a special proconsular imperium. He had as his
chief-of-staff M. Lollius, who had not been very successful
with the legions on the Rhine. His grandfather, in bidding
him farewell, wished him 'the integrity of Pompey, the
courage of Alexander, and his own good luck.' Tiberius
arranged to meet him, but the interview was not satisfactory. Lollius had poisoned the mind of Gaius against
his stepfather, and the grandson wrote to Augustus a
damaging report; the consequence was that the request of
Tiberius for permission to return home was refused.[1]
There had been trouble in Parthia, for Phraates, the king
who had restored the standards to Rome, had been murdered and succeeded by his son Phraataces, who also
organized a revolution in Armenia, where Artavasdes was
replaced by Tigranes. The first task of Gaius was therefore to settle this new frontier problem. He met Phraataces on an island in the Euphrates and patched up an un-
satisfactory truce. Lollius, owing to the revelations of the
Parthian king, fell into disgrace and was dismissed. His
successor, Quirinius, one of the best soldiers of the day,
was a friend of Tiberius, and, principally owing to his influence, Gaius agreed to his stepfather's return to Rome,
a consent which Augustus had made a condition of his
own approval. Livia had been pressing the point, and the
wiser heads in Rome, seeing the clouds banking in the
North, had clamoured for the employment of the ablest of
Roman commanders. In A.D. 2 Tiberius was back in the

---

[1] Accounts differ as to the place of meeting and the nature of Tiberius's reception
(Dio, LV, 18–19; Vell., II, 101; Suet., *Tib.*, 12), but the balance of evidence seems to support the view given above.

capital, though he was not yet allowed to take part in public affairs.

The hopes which Augustus had set on his grandsons were destined to a melancholy defeat. In August A.D. 2 Lucius, the younger of the princes, who had been sent on a mission to the West, died at Marseilles on his way to Spain. Gaius moved north to Armenia, where Tigranes had been slain, and, with the assent of Augustus, gave the crown to Artabazanes, the king of Media. His next purpose was an expedition to Arabia, but in quelling a local Armenian revolt he was badly wounded. Sick and dispirited, he gave up his Arabian plan and started on the return voyage to Italy, but in February A.D. 4 he died at Limyra in Lycia. It was the last of the family bereavements of the Princeps, and it seems to have been felt acutely, for he had come to regard his grandsons with a doting affection. 'Light of my eyes,' he had written to Gaius two years before, 'I miss you desperately when you are away from me, especially on such a day as this. Wherever you are, I hope you have kept my sixty-fourth birthday in health and happiness, for, as you see, I have passed the grand climacteric, which for us old men is the sixty-third year. I have prayed to the gods that I may spend the time that remains to me in a prosperous Rome, while you are playing the man and learning to take up my work.' [1]

The deaths of the princes left Tiberius as the only possible successor. Augustus accepted the inevitable, and that year he adopted him as his son, while Tiberius in turn adopted Germanicus. He was also given the tribunician power for ten years. He was therefore both the colleague of the Princeps and the heir-apparent, and, as the bodily strength of Augustus declined, the actual administrator of the empire. The imperial family now consisted of the Claudians — Tiberius; the younger Drusus, the son of

[1] Aul. Gell., xv, 7; Malcovati, 13.

Tiberius by his first wife; the sons of the elder Drusus, Germanicus, now a youth of nineteen, and Claudius (the future emperor), a loutish boy of fourteen: the Julians — the surviving children of Julia and Agrippa, the younger Julia, Agrippina (who was to marry Germanicus) and Agrippa Postumus. There were also collaterals, the children of Octavia. Agrippa Postumus is a puzzling figure. He seems to have been a case of arrested development, perhaps half an idiot. He had great bodily strength, but showed an aptitude for nothing except field sports, and he took insensate dislikes to his relatives, especially his grandmother. On these facts all our authorities agree.[1] But it is possible that Livia had given him cause for his dislike of her, and that with gentler handling something might have been made of him. He was a keen fisherman, and few anglers are altogether vile. His adoption was rescinded and he was banished, under strict surveillance, to an island on the way to Corsica. There is some evidence that Augustus, in the voyage taken just before his death, wished to visit the exile with a view to a reconciliation,[2] for he was the only male left of his own blood.

III

Livia was to survive Augustus for fifteen years and to reach the great age of eighty-six; fifty-two years was the span of their married life. When she died she was the mother of the empire, an institution like the principate, and to speak against her was to slander the majesty of Rome. In the provinces she was 'Mater Patriae' and 'Genetrix Orbis,' and in many parts of the East she was identified with the local goddess. But there had always been a party, the party of the exiled Julias, which hated

[1] Tac., *Ann.*, I, 3; Suet., *Div. Aug.*, 65; Vell., II, 112; Dio, LV, 32.
[2] Pliny, *N. H.*, VII, 150.

her; they regarded her as the cruel stepmother of the fairy-tales, and whispered dark libels in secret. Later, when the Julio-Claudians had degenerated into mountebanks and monsters, a cloud of suspicion arose against the woman who was responsible for the Claudian strain. She was accused of a series of murders in the interests of her own offspring — of Marcellus,[1] of Gaius and Lucius, of Agrippa Postumus, of Augustus himself.[2] The gossip-writers, and even the grave Tacitus out of his hatred for Tiberius, hint at, or explicitly charge, a succession of crimes, which, if true, would make her one of the great criminals of the world. For such scandals there is not a shadow of evidence; they are simply the old legend of the 'gravis noverca' which human nature is always prone to credit, supported by the popular repute of certain later empresses like Messallina and Faustina. Tiberius was quite capable of accomplishing on his own account the death of Agrippa Postumus; it was physically impossible for Livia to have murdered Gaius and Lucius; Marcellus perished in the midst of an epidemic; and as for her husband, we have ample proof of her lasting devotion. The wholesale nature of the libels provides their refutation.[3]

There are no portraits of Livia in the beauty of her youth, when Augustus was her devout lover. The bust in the Uffizi gallery shows her in early middle life, with features nobly moulded and a grave matronly comeliness. The Copenhagen head [4] is of an older woman, for the

[1] It is possible that this rumour may have arisen from the grief of Octavia. The distraught mother, we are told, 'oderat omnes matres et in Liviam maxime furebat.' Seneca, *ad Marciam*, II, 5.

[2] Tac., *Ann.*, I, 5, III, 19, IV, 71, V, 1; Dio, LIII, 33, LV, 10, LVI, 30. Modern historians (Merivale, Drumann, Gardthausen) have shown themselves ready to believe improbable scandals about Livia. The matter is intelligently discussed by C. C. Barini in *Rend. Linc.* (1922), XXI, 25–33.

[3] The scandals about Livia contained in Tacitus and Dio have been critically examined by M. P. Charlesworth in *A. J. Phil.* (1923), XLIV, 145–57.

[4] In the Ny Carlsberg Glyptotek. The head and shoulders of a statue, generally identified as Livia, are in the Villa dei Misteri at Pompeii. From the pigment remaining she seems to have had brown hair and eyes.

cheeks have begun to fall in and the eyes are sunken; the hair, dressed elaborately in bandeaux and curls, frames a countenance of notable dignity and grace. Strength and urbanity are in the clean-cut jaw and exquisite nose, and the delicate lines of the mouth. She was a type of the true Roman aristocracy, with all its virtues and all its limitations, and in this lay part of her appeal to her husband. She embodied in her life the ideal of the Roman matron, shunning publicity, scrupulous in her domestic tasks, spinning her own wool and making with her own hands her husband's clothes, setting an example of simplicity and good-breeding to a world where fastidiousness was going out of date. Her chastity was beyond the breath of scandal.[1] She saved the lives of some nudists who met her in the street by saying that to a woman such as herself naked men were no whit different from statues.[2] Augustus was tolerant of ribaldry at his own expense, but would suffer no insult to Livia.[3] Though she accompanied her husband on many of his travels she would not permit any advertisement of her doings; for her a woman's life should be the 'fallentis semita vitae.' Virgil does not mention her, nor Horace, nor Propertius, and we may be certain that this silence was her own wish.

There was a gentle side to her character. Even Tacitus admits that she did much to curb the severities of Tiberius, and that her apartments in the palace were a sanctuary for those in trouble. Her advice to Augustus was always on the side of lenity. She seems to have had moments when she could unbend and forget the *grande dame* in the woman. She was charitable to the sick, and maintained at her own cost many orphan girls and boys. She provided dowries for poor brides, and assistance for

---

[1] The circumstances of her marriage to Augustus were a little shocking to Roman tradition. It is just possible that Drusus, who was wholly different in character from Tiberius, was Augustus's son.

[2] Dio, LVIII, 2.   [3] Seneca, *de ira*, III, 33.

the parents of large families, and decent tombs for her slaves.[1] She was a fond, almost too fond, mother, and a most dutiful wife, and to the end she retained the affection of her husband, which would have been beyond the power of a mere model of the chilly virtues.[2]

But her chief attribute was a calm, balancing wisdom. She made a haven of domestic peace for the busy master of the world. Once she confessed that her power over Augustus came from 'doing gladly whatever pleased him, not meddling with any of his affairs, and, especially, pretending to be blind to the favourites with whom he fell in love.'[3] This wise complaisance made her husband her slave as soon as the passions of youth were gone. She never offered an opinion until it was asked for, but Augustus came to her frequently for counsel. When he conferred with her he was accustomed to make notes of what he wanted to say — a remarkable tribute to her critical acumen. There is a letter from him to her on the subject of how to treat her difficult grandson, Claudius, the future emperor, which shows how he strove to carry her with him in all family decisions.[4] With this respect for her brains there was mingled, perhaps, a certain awe of her person. The grandson of the country banker could not rid himself of his reverence for pure aristocratic blood, and his practical genius had its moments of unwilling admiration for a long-descended and unpractical pride. Both her husband and her son seem to have been a little afraid of the stately woman who spun on the Palatine. When the Julian laws were before the Senate Augustus was unwise enough to tell the senators that they should admonish and command their wives, and they replied gleefully that they would like to know how he admonished and commanded Livia.[5]

---

[1] *C. I. L.*, vi, 2101.

[2] Suetonius's words are 'dilexit et probavit unice et perseveranter.' *Div. Aug.*, 62.

[3] Dio, lviii, 2.   [4] Suet., *Div. Claud.*, 3; Malcovati, 6–7.   [5] Dio, liv, 16.

IV

We have seen the main features of the construction to which Augustus gave his life, and in the next chapter we shall consider that more subtle and intangible thing, the soul which he sought to build up in his people, since he knew well that without the requisite spirit the letter was dead. That is to say, we are engaged in the study of a creative mind. Of the character apart from the mind there is not a great deal to note. It can be said truly of Augustus that the mind was the man. His moral qualities were in full accord with his intellectual powers; they were such as were needed for the fulfilment of his task; in his work he completely realized himself, and there were no unsatisfied longings left over, no gift or quality which missed its mark. His public life was also his private life, and he had no secret world hid from his fellows. All his days were passed in the glare of publicity, and to his contemporaries, as to later generations, he was fully intelligible; a man like themselves, only built on a grander scale, a figure as obvious as the Zeus of Olympia, revered, saluted, but not discussed, for there were no mysteries about it. The gossip-writers a century later found much to admire in him, but little of personal interest to record. The picture they give is on the whole a pleasant one, but it is colourless; to them he was something statuesque, grandiose, marmoreal, with few of the ragged ends of life.

He was a man with a mission, which he pursued with as austere a devotion as any saint or prophet, but there was very little mysticism in it. He began with two purposes — to avenge his great kinsman, and to make himself the first man in the state, and these he followed with cold resolution in the face of desperate odds. Then came the purpose of using the power he had won to build an orderly world. In later life his task was the perfecting of his new mechanism. He was sustained, to begin with, by the zest of overcoming difficulties, and later by a personal pride in his achievement. Such a career meant constant toil, a campaign in which there could be no discharge. There was little chance of an inner life for one whose waking hours were crowded with urgent practical duties. No man in history was ever forced to labour so continuously and decide daily on graver issues. We can see from his portraits what toll this took of body and spirit. In all of them there is the same fine modelling of forehead, mouth, and chin, the same calm, forward-looking eyes; but the Octavius of the British Museum is a boy of sixteen with the world before him; the Augustus of the Prima Porta is the man who has founded the principate and received back from Parthia the lost eagles; in the Ancona head he is in his early fifties, at the zenith of his powers, the high priest of the Roman faith and the ruler of the world; while in the statue from the Terme museum age has come upon him, the forehead is lined, the shoulders a little bowed, and the eyelids a little weary.[1]

The essentials of his character have already been made clear in his work. He had his passions, but they were never allowed to interfere with his efficiency. As we have seen, there is every reason to discredit the charges made by Mark Antony against his youth, and repeated by the gossips; but in sexual matters he was no precisian, for sexual licence was to the Romans as natural and pardonable as an extra bottle of wine at dinner. Cicero plumed himself on flirting with disreputable actresses; the lawyer Hortensius wrote lascivious poetry,[2] and no one thought the worse of him; it was all what Horace called 'permitted indulgence.'[3] Of adultery, the only serious charge is Dio's about the wife of Maecenas; but the story does not hang

---

[1] *C. A. H.* (Plates), IV, 146-51.
[2] As did Augustus, if we may believe Martial (XI, 20).   [3] *Sat.*, I, 4, 113.

together, and in any case it is improbable, since Augustus at the time was beginning his puritan crusade. In middle life his conduct was irreproachable. The cruelty with which he was charged in his youth was wholly absent from his maturity. He was severe, and with cause, to erring servants, and he was implacable towards his daughter and granddaughter, but in the latter cases he had good grounds of public policy. He had schooled himself by a long discipline to do nothing, and to overlook nothing, which might interfere with the success of his work.

Yet the man, so far as we can see him behind the colossal façade of his achievements, was friendly, easy of access, affable to all, the *honnête homme* whom everybody could understand, Henri Quatre without the gasconnade. The house on the Palatine was a very modest palace, being without mosaics or marbles, and having a colonnade of plain Alban stone. He slept there in the same room summer and winter, but sometimes, when his health was poor, he would retire to the villa of Maecenas on the Esquiline, which was believed to be more salubrious, and which, from a disused graveyard and refuse-heap, had been turned into a garden paradise. He had several country houses, but far fewer than the great nobles. One was nine miles out of Rome on the Flaminian Way, one was on a spur of the Alban mountains, one at Praeneste, and one at Tibur. All these dwellings were austerely furnished, but the parks were elaborately laid out. Business was apt to follow him there, and occupy most of his time, so when he wanted a true holiday he went yachting along the Campanian coast, using a modest villa at Capri as his base.

Part of his strength lay in his retention of the tough bourgeois common sense of his upbringing. This was more than the self-conscious simplicity of the old type of aristocrat, and it gave him his power with the middle class, who were to be the backbone of the empire. He had

the countryman's sturdy good-humour, which could give
and receive plain words. He could never be made ridicu-
lous, for he was always ready to laugh at himself and to
prick the bladder of fulsome praise. He met every man
squarely on his own ground, and if he were proved wrong
he admitted it. Like Cromwell, he welcomed frank and
honest speech. The stories handed down may or may not
be apocryphal, but, taken together, they prove the kind
of repute he left behind him. He could be trusted to deal
fairly with opponents, and there was a brusque kindliness
even in his reproofs. Tiberius, the true aristocrat, was offended by the free speech which he permitted, but Augustus comforted him: 'My dear fellow, don't be childish and
worry because people say hard things of me. It is enough
if we can prevent them *doing* us any harm.' [1] He had pride
of the deepest, but he was without vanity and the malad-
justments of vanity. But he would tolerate nothing which
lowered the dignity of his office. Offensive lampoons, and
above all offensive panegyrics which might bring the principate into contempt, were sternly suppressed. There was
a line beyond which no man might venture without drawing the lightnings of his formidable eyes.

His tastes were those of the better type of Roman
country gentleman. Working from morn to night, he had
no time for frills, but ample leisure would not have disposed him to luxury. His clothes were home-made and of
an old-fashioned pattern. He preferred the plainest food
and the commoner sorts of wine, and his diet was always
frugal. He liked to have his family about him at meals,
especially the younger members, and he was fond of good
talk. Now and then he gave a gala banquet, with professional entertainers and handsome gifts for the guests.
Games of chance he found a recreation, but he does not appear to have played for high stakes. The routine of his

[1] Suet., *Div. Aug.*, 51; Malcovati, 9.

AUGUSTUS IN HIS OLD AGE
(Museo delle Terme, Rome)

days was to rise an hour or two after daybreak — he had often bad nights and liked his morning sleep; to work until noon; then a light meal and a short nap without undressing; a little air and exercise before he dined at any time between four and seven; then work again until bedtime. He rarely dined out. His daily exercise was a short walk or run, or a game with children, and when he allowed himself a holiday he went yachting or fishing.

He had no serious hobbies. As a young man he had dabbled in letters and written a tragedy; in later life he composed an occasional epigram, prepared his memoirs, and made a collection of his letters and speeches. Horace might hail the Muses as the consolers of great Caesar's leisure, but he was never more than their casual worshipper. He knew that he was an imperfect scholar and an indifferent writer, and he refused to inflict his compositions on the world. But he read widely, especially in Greek literature, and he was a fastidious critic both of the written and the spoken word, hating anything which savoured of the fantastic or the turgid.[1] He was also keenly interested in geography and exploration, and was what Tertullian said of Hadrian, 'a seeker after everything strange.'[2]

There could be nothing narrow about a life so rich in varied duties, but, though the palace was filled all day with a multitude coming and going, its master lived a solitary life. As there were none to share his responsibilities, so there were none to share his confidence. He cannot be said to have had any real intimate, not even Livia. Agrippa was his trusted lieutenant and the architect of much of his fortunes, but Agrippa was primarily a soldier. As for Maecenas, the grasshopper must often have become a burden. Virgil he loved and revered, but he had no opportunity to see much of him, and Livy's smooth, rhetorical mind must have palled on one who liked sharp edges

---

[1] Suet., *Div. Aug.*, 84–89.   [2] 'curiositatum omnium explorator.'

and clear colours. Horace, perhaps, was nearest to him in temperament, but Horace was not disposed to be a courtier. He had no favourites among his officials and no underling had any influence over him.

In the life he led, with leisure only to cultivate his family, the one chance of an intimate was among his immediate kin. Tiberius would have met his needs, and the fragments which we possess of his letters to his stepson have sometimes a note of wistful affection. 'Good-bye, most delightful of men! Success to you as you war for me and for the Muses.' ... 'When anything turns up that troubles me or calls for special thought, I long desperately for my dear Tiberius.' ... 'When I hear that you are worn out by constant hardships may heaven confound me if my own body does not ache in sympathy. I beseech you to spare yourself, lest the news of your illness kill your mother and me and put the empire in peril. It matters nothing whether or not I am well if you are ill.' [1] But there can have been little response from Tiberius; the Claudian and the Julian were very different strains, and the shadows of Vipsania and Gaius and Lucius stood between them. Augustus had stores of affection which were never expended except upon Livia and small children. He had a great capacity for friendship, for, says Suetonius, 'though he did not readily make friends, he clung to them with the utmost constancy.' [2] Yet, except for a very few, these were tepid friendships. Augustus never found his true intimate; indeed, his position and his duties forbade it and forced him into a magnificent loneliness. The state was to him more of a spouse than Livia, more of a comrade than Agrippa.

[1] Suet., *Tib.*, 21; Malcovati, 10–12.   [2] Suet., *Div. Aug.*, 66.

III. ANIMA ROMAE

Non tu corpus eras sine pectore.
                                    HORACE.

'NOTRE ignorance de l'histoire,' Flaubert has written, 'nous fait calomnier notre temps.' Of no period is this more true than of the early principate. 'It is a grave error to think of the ordinary man in the Roman Empire as a depraved and cruel fiend, dividing his hours between the brothel and intoxication, torturing a slave from time to time when he felt bored, and indifferent to the sufferings and poverty of others.' [1] The common conception is based on the later gossip-writers and satirists, whose lurid pictures have too often been taken for fact. They were either men of humble origin who found pleasure in exaggerating the vices of a class to which they did not belong, or artists who darkened the colours to get a dramatic contrast, or lovers of the past who mourned an imagined degeneracy. Satirists and sentimentalists are always doubtful guides. The picture of Britain after the Great War, drawn by writers with damaged nerves, presented a deranged, anaemic and neurotic youth, when all the time our young men were facing a difficult world with exemplary fortitude. In the Rome of Augustus there was luxury, no doubt, but it was only for the few, and it never reached the extremes of many later ages; there were instances of vulgar ostentation, but they were not admired;

[1] A. D. Nock, *Conversion*, 218.

there were many who led vicious lives, but their vices
were not applauded. Popular opinion was strong on the
side of what was decent and simple. There were degen-
erates among the aristocracy, but most of its members
lived dully and reputably. Among the middle classes in
town and country the average household was as wholesome as in any age. A happy family life, such as we find
in the story of the younger Pliny, was nearer being the
rule than the exception. Roman life was a frugal thing,
sparing in food, temperate in drink, modest in clothing,
cleanly in habit, and spent largely in exercise and in the
open air.

We know something of the Roman nobility and bourgeoisie, but we know very little of the common people.
Lord Acton has told us that the historian must learn to
take his meals in the kitchen, but it is hard to penetrate
to the humbler Roman kitchen. Yet of the kitchen Hera-
clitus said, 'Here also there are gods,' and it is necessary
to be just to a society which history has somewhat misrep-
resented. The calumnies come from the Romans themselves. Their men of letters were apt to despise a class
from which most of them had emerged. Tacitus, for example, was not free from snobbishness, though he was no
aristocrat by birth. He thought it a blemish in the younger
Drusus that he had an equestrian strain in him; one of his
chief grievances against Sejanus is that he was an obscure provincial; he does not mind the sufferings of gladiators since they are of low birth.[1] Even high-minded men
like Lucretius and Cicero [2] show scarcely a trace of sympathy with the poor as human beings, and to most Romans they were like the grains of gunpowder, to which
Coleridge uncharitably compared the French nation —
dangerous in the mass, but 'each by itself smutty and con-
temptible.'

[1] 'vili sanguine,' *Ann.*, I, 76.   [2] *e.g.*, Cic. *de Off.*, II, 42, 150.

Their lives were hard and comfortless, though Augustus gave them humaner bankruptcy laws and some protection from a violent end, and the state kept them from starvation. Their livelihood as porters, messengers, craftsmen, and small tradesmen was subject to the competition of slaves and well-patronized freedmen. They had little in the way of homes, lodging in garrets at the top of tenement blocks in insanitary areas, and forced to spend much of their time in the streets. No statesman was interested in what they might think or feel, since politically they were negligible. Their rations were corn from the public purse, and occasionally oil, supplemented by a little cheese, cheap vegetables and a thin *vin ordinaire*. Meat they never saw. They had the use of the public baths, and free entry to the public games to fill their too ample leisure. Having no household gods in life, they had not the decency of a tomb in death, for, unless they belonged to a funeral club, their bodies went to the common burying place. The idea of a pampered proletariat must be revised. The corn dole was a necessary form of outdoor relief, which could be amended but not terminated, though it had the disastrous effect of attracting rural paupers to the city,[1] and it was never more than a bare subsistence. The games and shows were not a piece of public benevolence, but an attempt, almost obligatory, to give an underemployed populace something to think about.

Of this great class, as I have said, we know little directly from the aristocratic literature of Rome, so we must judge it from epigraphy, from indirect evidence, and from proven facts. One of these facts is that Augustus respected it, and endeavoured, by restricting the supply of slaves, limiting manumission, and reconstructing the guilds, to protect its rights, and by gifts of money to the reputable to build up a solvent working class. He recognized the

[1] Sallust, *Cat.*, 37; App., II, 120.

danger to the state of a plebs whose only interests lay in
'panem et Circenses,' and he believed that the ancient
quality was not dead in it. The kitchen might be squalid,
but it still held the gods. The poor of Rome were more
than the rabble which we might deduce from Latin literature. They were coarse-grained like most Romans, naturally insensitive to suffering, and further hardened by the
brutal sports of the amphitheatre.[1] But they were capable
of pity. The cruelty to the elephants at Pompey's games
sickened them, and they were shocked by the chains of
Arsinoe, Cleopatra's sister, in Julius's triumph in 46 B.C.[2]
There must have been elements of good taste in a class
which provided the audiences for, and established the
fame of, playwrights like Plautus and Terence and actors
like Roscius, which could appreciate the greatness of the
Aeneid, and which could write epitaphs which have often
a salt wit and a moving tenderness. Above all, courage
and devotion had not died in it, for from it came the first
Christian converts.

The intellectual circle, to which Augustus looked to
provide the spiritual foundation of his polity, drew from
both the upper and the middle classes. Decades of unset-
tlement had given it a conservative bias, a longing for the
old good times, and, as a corollary, a keen antiquarian
zest. As the vision of the empire opened, a livelier interest
awoke in foreign lands and foreign ways. The class was
receptive to new modes of thought, new cults, and the
glamour of new horizons; but the literary influence of
Alexandria declined as Rome began to cherish her own

---

[1] The Romans were curiously apathetic about blood, as is shown not only by their
sports, but by religious usages like the 'taurobolium' and the 'criobolium.' This trait
was shared by the early Christian church. The metaphors of Cowper's hymn, 'There
is a fountain filled with blood,' which sound crude to us, would have seemed natural
and proper to a Roman.

[2] Cic., *ad Fam.*, VII, 1; Dio, XLIII, 19. See also Tac., *Ann.*, XIV, 42 *sqq.*

native forms of art, and experiment with new ones, not
as an imitator, but as a creator. The best men were highly
cultivated and widely read, but it does not appear that
there was any large educated class in the strict sense.
There was no national system of education.[1] The sons of
the well-to-do went to private schools generally managed
by learned freedmen, where they read the old Latin texts
till these were superseded by Virgil; but the real education
was in the home, where they were trained in manly sports
and good manners.[2] Later they studied rhetoric and law
under some famous practitioner. Julius seems to have
toyed with the notion of establishing an educational system when he invited foreign teachers to Rome and promised them citizenship. Augustus contented himself with
founding two great public libraries, providing a private
school for members of the imperial family, and exempting
teachers from the law expelling foreigners from the city
during a time of famine.[3] As for university education, that
was first introduced by Vespasian, and under Hadrian
was established on a permanent basis with state endow-
ments.

The Roman was no theologian, nor, in a constructive
sense, a philosopher. Nor was he a scientist. He was a
great inventor and builder, but in the speculative and
theoretic side of science he had little interest. Men like
the elder Cato, Varro, and the elder Pliny liked to record
the curiosities of nature, but they had not the systema-
tizing impulse, the restless passion for order, of the Greeks.
Pure science seemed to the Roman a waste of time, though
he welcomed applied science. So he was a good field natu-
ralist but no biologist; a good engineer but a poor mathe-

---

[1] The only general educational system was found in the provinces, owing to the desire
of provincials to acquire the Latin language.

[2] See Warde Fowler, *Soc. Life at Rome*, ch. VI.

[3] Suet., *Div. Aug.*, 42. See on this subject C. Barbacallo, *Lo stato e l'istruzione publica
nell' impero Romano* (1911).

matician; a successful calendar-maker but an indifferent
astronomer. He was a mighty traveller, but his serious
geographical work was done for him by foreigners. He
was a soldier and a conqueror, but he made no contribution of value to military science. In everything he undertook he demanded a utilitarian purpose and a practical result. We find among the Greeks germinal concepts which
are a vital part of modern thought. Pythagoras first
taught that physical science was based on measurement
and that therefore number was the key to the structure of
the universe; Hippocrates laid down the cardinal principles of medicine; Archimedes founded hydrostatics;
Anaxagoras and Aristarchus of Samos anticipated the
modern doctrine of the nature of the sun and the rotation
of the globe; Hipparchus, in 125 B.C., calculated the lunar
month, and was no more than a second wrong from the
modern point of view; Eratosthenes measured the earth's
circumference; in Aristotle, and in Empedocles before
him, there is implicit the theory of evolution, and in De-
mocritus the atomic theory. The Greeks had the disin-
terested curiosity of the scientist; 'a new diagram,' said
the Pythagoreans, 'means a step in advance, but we do
not draw it to make a threepenny-bit'; [1] while the Roman
asked for an immediate cash return. Only Lucretius, a
lonely figure among his people, is a link between the free
speculation of Greece and our own day.

It was human conduct and human government that interested the Roman, and therefore the one science in
which he excelled was jurisprudence. The practice of law
involves a study of the art of persuasion, the impact of the
spoken word on the minds of others. Hence rhetoric was
for Rome both an art and a science, the principal art and
science. It had obvious utilitarian value, and its materials
were not only exact logical concepts, but the sonorous

[1] σχᾶμα καὶ βᾶμα ἀλλ' οὐ σχᾶμα καὶ τριώβολον.

words and the noble rhythms which were the glory of their
tongue. The staple work of the schools was declamation.
A new book was recited to an audience — that was, indeed, the only way of publishing it.[1] We cannot get the
full enjoyment of Latin poetry unless we realize that it
was composed for the ear rather than for the eye, and was
read aloud slowly and carefully, each syllable being given
full value — a method necessary with a close-textured
language, which admits both quantity and stress. Rhetoric was in the very fibre of the Roman's mind. He had
to speak his thoughts aloud. St. Augustine was amazed
when he saw St. Ambrose reading to himself silently without moving his lips.[2]

With such a background philosophy meant to the Romans not the metaphysics of being and knowledge, but a
reasoned rule of life, and a gnomic wisdom which appealed
both to the intelligence and to the emotions. A confused
world sought a principle of order, and distracted minds
cast about for helpful maxims of conduct. The eye of the
rhetorician turned inward, since he could no longer hope
for a public career like Cicero's. The Romans had little
originality of thought, but they could appreciate the work
of the Greek ethical teachers and reproduce it with a Latin
accent. So it befell that those who were not content with
the simple civic religion of observance, supplemented it
by studies which offered a key to the meaning of things
and which answered conundrums beyond the scope of the
conventional creeds — which above all promised liberation
from those caprices of fortune of which they had had recent and bitter experience. Philosophy for them was an
agōge, a scheme of living. Its great inducement was that

[1] For an account of the practice, see Persius, I, 15 *sqq.*
[2] *Confess.*, VI, 3. I owe this reference to Mr. C. S. Lewis, *The Allegory of Love* (1936),
64–65.

it gave a sense of freedom, of existence simplified and self-sufficient and beyond the reach of fate. Since the drama of life had to be played, it was well to have a set of rules. Philosophy was a hospital for sick and puzzled souls; [1] it provided a foothold for man above the torrent of circumstance, an armour for the spirit which the shafts of fate could not pierce, and which even death could not shatter.[2] It was a supplement to religion, or even a substitute, for it enabled its votary 'to beseech no man for his helping and to vex no god with prayer.' But in general it was tolerant of the popular divinities, who were treated as aspects of the divine unity.[3]

The fashionable philosophic creeds were all imported. Stoicism was the most potent, for it best suited the Roman character. It may be defined as puritanism stripped of its element of rapture. It offered freedom through the acceptance of the great order of nature — which was no other than the universal Reason — and the direction of life accordingly. It might equally well produce saints like Marcus Aurelius and Epictetus, or pious time-servers like Seneca. The Epicurean differed from the Stoic only in his metaphysics, for while the latter believed in a World-Soul immanent in man, the former held that there was no traffic between the human and the divine. In practice the Stoic *autarkeia*, or self-sufficiency, differed little from the *ataraxia*, or tranquillity, of the Epicurean. The Cynic preached abstinence from all common ambitions, rank, possessions, power, the things which clog man's feet — an attempt, in Dean Inge's words, 'to balance our accounts not by increasing our numerator but by diminishing our denominator.' All these creeds sought to make man in-

---

[1] A phrase of Epictetus, III, 23, 30; cf. Persius, III, 66 *sqq.*

[2] Cf. Hor., *Ep.*, I, 16, 73; Plato, *Apology*, 29.

[3] 'Deus pertinens per naturam cujusque rei, per terras Ceres, per maria Neptunus, alii per alia poterunt intelligi.' Cic., *de nat. Deorum*, II, XXVIII, 71. Observe the construction 'Deus . . . poterunt.'

vulnerable, to deliver him from the bondage of fear, whether of life or of death or of the hereafter. They increased his consciousness of his dignity as a human being, and not only pointed the way to, but gave him a motive for, the good life. They taught him to live, in the phrase of Marcus Aurelius, as on a mountain top. Moreover, they brought into ethics a soldierly spirit. Virtue was now conceived as very different from the bland, effortless morality of the Aristotelian Good Man. Life was a campaign from which there was no release, a perpetual war of soul against flesh, of the members against the spirit; [1] it was a pilgrim's progress, like Bunyan's, from the City of Destruction to the City of God. [2]

Philosophy was therefore a bracing regime for the comparatively small class which was worthy of it. But it was no evangel for the average man. Its theism was too abstract and detached, and behind it, even in the best, was an abiding pessimism, so that Marcus Aurelius could write of human life, 'What is the end of it all? Smoke and ashes and a legend — or scarcely a legend.' [3] The decadence of the Republic and the years of war had produced a kind of listlessness, not unlike the mediaeval *accidie*, which was perhaps aggravated by the increase of malaria through a long-continued neglect of public hygiene. There seemed to be a decline of intellectual and spiritual energy, as if old age had come upon Rome. The readiness with which the principate was accepted made its first stage easy, but the second stage was the more difficult because of this very docility, for the impulse to revolt is a proof of life in the body politic. There was little hope for Rome if its spirit became that of the common epitaph for slaves: 'I was not. I was. I shall not be. I do not care.' To revive the soul of the Roman people, and to put one

---

[1] Seneca's words are almost those of the New Testament; cf. *Ep.*, LI, 6, LXXVIII, 16.
[2] *Ibid.*, CVII, 2.   [3] *Med.*, V, 33.

into the empire at large, were the most delicate tasks which Augustus had to face.

II

What were his own beliefs? It is hard to say. He held, beyond doubt, to some form of God, some divine power which governed the world. Like Julius, he had his private superstitions,[1] which were not permitted, however, to govern his conduct, and he had faith in his star, which was no more than a romantic expression of self-confidence. He was a fatalist, like most great men of action. He had imbibed from Posidonius in early life a mild Stoicism, and had written an 'Exhortation to Philosophy,' based apparently on Cicero's *Hortensius.* Cicero's work is lost, but we know the profound influence which it had on St. Augustine,[2] and if we possessed it we might learn more of Augustus's creed. We may believe that it had no speculative subtlety and was held with little devotional fervour. He faced life calmly, like one at home in the universe, not concerned about absolute truth, and willing to accept the conventional religion as something to go on with; above all things a pragmatist and a realist. He might have taken Bishop Butler's words for his own: 'Things and actions are what they are, and the consequences of them will be what they will be; why then should we wish to be deceived?' But in one thing he firmly believed, the need for religion and the right kind of religion in the state.[3] He looked round the Roman world and discerned beneath its scepticism and indifference a great longing. He saw all the materials for a religious revival.[4]

His problem was threefold so far as concerned the soul

[1] Suet., *Div. Aug.,* 90–92.   [2] *Confess.,* III, 4. See p. 58, *supra.*

[3] Cf. Ovid, 'expedit esse deos et ut expedit esse putemus,' *Ars amat.,* I, 635.

[4] This point is well brought out in Rostovtzeff's *Augustus* ('Univ. of Wisconsin Studies,' No. 15), 134 *sqq.*

of the people. In the first place he must give each class
and section its proper niche in the state. He had created
a huge and intricate polity, and it must have the articulate
life of an organism and not the mere functional differentia-
tion of a machine. Quality must not be lost in quantity,
or kind in scale. It would be fatally easy for the empire to
become a soulless mechanism, in which case its doom
would be as certain as that of the old slave monarchies of
the East. The sharp idiom of the Republic must somehow
be preserved, or rather, since it had been blurred in the
past century, it must be restored. Edge and accent and
colour must be regained. The individual must not be
stifled by the state, or the locality by the empire. His aim
was to rekindle a sane vitality in the whole body politic.
In the second place the ancient religion of Rome must
again be given due honour, since it was the basis of civic
decorum, and the chief link with the past. The empire
must be felt not as an artificial novelty, but as the natural
extension of the republican tradition, with all the sanctions of the old faith. Finally, since Roman religion was
in its essence a local thing, some new faith must be found
which would be common to the whole empire. That empire, as it stood, was full of disharmonies, a mosaic of
creeds and beliefs, many of them fantastic and alien to the
Roman austerities. There was already a basis for imperial
patriotism in the widespread gratitude to the man who
had given it peace and was now giving it prosperity; but
there was a danger that this patriotism might grow faint
from its very extension in space, so it must be vivified by
some kind of mystical attachment to Rome, which could
only be attained through a personal devotion. In his
spiritual reconstruction Augustus, like the scriptural
householder, had to bring forth from his store things old
and things new.

A bureaucracy is usually the death of idiom, and a

bureaucracy in large part the empire must be. Augustus realized this peril, and his eager desire to preserve individuality is seen in every aspect of his work. We see it in his determination to give each class its function, even at the cost of much trouble to himself; his powers shared with the Senate and the republican magistracies; his opening of careers to talent and his encouragement of youth; his use of the equestrian order; his reconstruction of the popular guilds, and his attempt to give the urban plebs some form of local government. We see it in his zealous care for local rites and customs in Italy. We see it in his preservation throughout the provinces of traditional worships, in his refusal to interfere with any form of government which did not endanger the empire, in his encouragement of municipal life and provincial councils. But the main proof is his attitude towards the Roman citizenship. Julius would have made that universal and set Italy on the same plane as the provinces, for he conceived of the empire as a unitary state, and dreamed of one imperial culture which would include the best that Rome and Greece and the East could furnish. To Augustus such an ideal had no charms, for he believed that it would end in a uniform drabness. He desired the Italian culture to be inviolate and predominant, not that it might override but that it might inspire the others. The citizenship of Rome should be a privilege which could be attained by service and merit, an aristocracy on the broadest basis, a new feature in the life of the world.

III

So much was clear; the two other tasks were more intricate, since they dealt with less ponderable things. The West had vanquished the East, the Roman gods had defeated the dark gods of Egypt, the native deities were still potent things in the nation's life. Such was the feeling of most men, however sceptically inclined. The Roman religion was concerned less with belief than with ritual. Three major Italian divinities, Jupiter, Juno and Minerva, had emerged from the mass of local cults; then, as the stately household of the Olympians moved west from the Greek world, the Roman trinity was identified with the Greek trinity of Zeus, Hera and Athene, and the hospitable Roman mind soon added to its pantheon the other Hellenic gods and goddesses. But in Rome religion had always a special relation to the state. Worship was a public duty, a civic function, carried out by an official lay priesthood. To obey the state was to obey the gods, and to worship the gods was a public obligation. It was a case less of an established church than of the identification in the last resort of the civic and the ecclesiastical. With the major deities there was little private worship: officials performed the rites for the whole people, relieving the individual of his duty, so that under a good government he could sleep peacefully, knowing that Heaven had been propitiated. No Roman concerned himself with the origin of his pantheon. The Olympians were there, odd in their behaviour, if the poets spoke truth, and with their numbers increased by generous adoptions; they must be mollified if the people were to prosper, but they had less personal meaning for the ordinary Roman than the most distant star in the sky. Augustus put a new life and dignity into this impersonal worship. He restored old temples and he built new ones; he held the great priestly offices, and saw that their duties were scrupulously performed; he advanced the honour of certain deities, like Apollo and Venus Genetrix; he revived ancient rites and festivals and games. With the help of the poets he made the Olympians bulk large in the popular imagination, potencies which, for all their remoteness and splendour, were part of the Roman state and the guarantors of its peace. Their cult was a kind of national anthem.

Private worship and a more intimate devotion were reserved for the lesser deities, the friendly little godlings who presided over the routine of daily life. Here among the plain people of Rome and Italy we find religion in a truer form, a sense of the mystery of life and the immensities which overshadow man, a desire to walk humbly and to propitiate the unseen, not only by ceremonial, but by a grave and reverent spirit. This is the *religion of Numa,* which was found in many urban households, and above all among the country dwellers. There was a numen in every wood and water, every meadow and fold of hill. Each incident of life had its protecting deity and its simple festival. The Saturnalia came at the time of sowing, and the Consualia at the time of harvest. Janus presided over the cottage door, and Vesta over the hearth, the Penates over the store-room, and the kindly Lar over the whole economy. Some of the deities had a wider range, and Hercules and Silvanus won a prestige beyond Italy. It might seem superstition to the philosopher, but it was more potent than his rationalism, for it was intertwined with the facts of life. It was the most enduring thing in Rome, and when the proud hierarchy of Olympus faded away those household and rustic cults retained their worshippers. The last enemy which Christianity had to face was not the Graeco-Roman gods and goddesses, but the brownies of the 'pagani,' the country folk. It was with these and not with the Olympians that St. Augustine strove, and even in defeat they left their mark upon Christian practice.

Augustus laboured to preserve and dignify these homely cults. For example, he gave the Roman poor a worship of their own in the *Lares compitales,* the spirits who presided over crossroads, and he joined his own Genius to the ritual. The step was part of his scheme of urban local government, but his policy is shown by the religious significance with which he endowed it. He awoke in Rome a lively interest in this legacy from the past, and turned even the lightest of poets into pious antiquarians. Propertius, the Rossetti of Latin literature, in the third book of his elegies abandoned his Cynthia for the chronicling of 'holy rites and holy days,' and Ovid in his *Fasti* used his deft imagination to tell of old religious usages instead of the art of love.

It was in the writers, especially the great poets, that in this task Augustus found his chief helpers. While he was still a child a poet had died who had left no mark on his generation. Lucretius had drawn his singing robes about him, and kept himself haughtily aloof from the troubled lives of men. His remedy for human ills was an arid philosophical creed, which he held with the passion of a religious devotee. His faith was 'quietism in this life and annihilation afterwards'; the world was old and its wheels were fast running down; there was no help to be looked for from the gods, who lived far away in the

> lucid interspace of world and world,
> Where never creeps a cloud or moves a wind,
> Nor ever falls the least white star of snow,
> Nor ever lowest roll of thunder moans,
> Nor sound of human sorrow mounts to mar
> Their sacred everlasting calm.[1]

The proud self-sufficiency of Lucretius was no cure for a distressed world, and the writers whom Augustus gathered around him had a very different evangel. Livy, for instance, thrilled to the ancient glories of Rome, and drew his inspiration from her record. His life was practically co-extensive with that of the Princeps, and his work was a

---

[1] Tennyson's paraphrase of *de rerum natura*, III, 18–22.

valuable auxiliary to the Augustan plan. Interfusing
rhetoric with history, he made the average Roman realize
the grandeur of the past and the magnitude of his heritage.

But with the new poets there was a livelier hope and a
broader sweep of imagination, for they were concerned
not only with things past but with things to come.
Horace provided the man of the world with what has been
called a secular psalter, a code of reasoned discipline and
rational enjoyment, based upon instincts deep in the
Roman nature, and expounded in golden verse. He gave
poetry to those not ordinarily sensitive to poetry, and a
philosophy of conduct to those who fought shy of philosophies. His verse enshrines the inspired common sense of
the Augustan age. He met one part of Rome's need — for
balance and poise, self-criticism and laughter. Moreover,
his love of his country and its ways provided a fresh hope
of their continuance; Rome's past was a warrant for
Rome's eternity —

> dum Capitolium
> scandet cum tacita virgine pontifex.

In Virgil we find that divine afflatus which transcends the
most balanced wisdom and the deftest technical skill.
He spoke not only to the plain citizen but to every range
of temperament and mind. It is difficult for those, to
whom, like myself, Virgil is a constant joy, to judge how
precisely he impressed his contemporaries. We feel his
underlying sadness and unsatisfied longings, but Rome
may have felt more strongly than we do his hopefulness
and pride. They may have greeted him in words like
Victor Hugo's —

> 'Quel dieu, quel moissonneur de l'éternel été!'

He gave them not the intimate and the homely, but the
high translunary things, but his sublimity was a Roman
sublimity, and the path he pointed out wound its way up-

ward from a familiar world. He offered his people a new
reading of the past, a new vision of the state, and a new
way of life. Virgil was Dante's guide to the Inferno and
the Purgatorio, but not to Paradise; but to the dreamers
of his age it was to Paradise that he led with the firmest
step, that returning Golden Age when Rome should accomplish her destiny and 'nations should come to her light
and kings to the brightness of her rising,' and she should
be a city like Plato's dream-kingdom, whose 'walls could
be suffered to sleep in the earth' since there would be no
more strife among men.

We know that Virgil was popular among the masses,
but his beatific vision was not for everyone. The state
religion and the religion of Numa, lit by the genius of the
poets, made their appeal to those who still held by the
Roman tradition. But there were many to whom that
tradition meant nothing, since they were strangers from
overseas, and there were many even of Roman stock who
asked for something more intimate and emotional. Ever
since the close of the Punic War foreigners had been
thronging to Rome, bringing with them their foreign cults,
and she had permitted these worships unless they were
clearly against public morals. Such cults offered something
new in the way of secret rites and private sodalities, ceremonies of purification, and a hope of immortality, and
therefore appealed to the cravings of the subconscious
soul in man. Even orthodox Romans were ready to suffer
these novelties, for Rome was wonderfully tolerant;[1] she
was always willing to admit with Symmachus that there
was no one road to the great secret; and, while faithful
to her orthodoxy, to accept new cults as a kind of re-insur-

---

[1] Cf. the account in Livy (xxxix, 8 *sqq.*) of the moderation displayed in the suppres-
sion of the Bacchic rites in 186 B.C., when provision was made for conscientious worshippers.

ance; indeed, by a mysterious process of syncretion and
conflation she might even link them to her own creed.
Such things to her were supplements, not substitutes.
Further, the decline in prestige of the famous oracles had
created a demand for what might be called the magical
side of religion. So Greeks and Easterns brought to the
capital their own special worships, which were not only
tolerated but largely patronized by the Romans themselves.[1] At the beginning of the principate the streets were
often noisy with exotic rituals, and at any corner one might
be jostled by foreign priests, 'sly slow things with circum-
spective eyes.'

The underworld of Rome, and much of the upper world,
had become a museum of strange faiths. Some, like the
cult of the Great Mother, had been there for generations;
Cybele, indeed, being traditionally linked with the origin
of Rome, was highly respectable, and Augustus gave her
a temple on the Palatine;[2] her worship had not yet developed the awful ceremony of the 'taurobolium,' or blood-
bath, by which a man might be 'renatus in aeternum.'
Dionysus was a more doubtful character; he had been
once expelled and was always on sufferance. The Orphic
and Pythagorean cults were half philosophies and appealed
only to the few. Both offered a clearly defined way of
salvation, but the former seems to have fallen into the
hands of quacks, and the latter was too difficult for the
plain man to comprehend. More important was the ritual
of Isis, which came from the East through the avenues of
trade, and which made converts in all classes. It had every
appeal of a mystical religion, for it was capable of a profound as well as of a superficial interpretation, and it
adapted its rites to changing circumstances. Popular dis-

---

[1] Old-fashioned people were a little troubled at the invasion. Propertius (IV, I, 17)
describes the earlier Rome as a place where 'nulla cura fuit externos quaerere divos.'

[2] There is a striking picture of her cult in Lucretius, II, 608 *sqq.*

trust of Egypt put it in the shade at the beginning of the principate, but its vogue soon revived. Its splendid ritual appealed to the eye, but at heart it was more ascetic than orgiastic. Moreover Isis could be identified with a host of other goddesses, with Ceres and Venus and Diana, with Minerva and Proserpine, even with Juno, so her devotees became honorary members of all religions.[1] The cult of Mithras had been brought from the East by Sulla's soldiers — a pure and beautiful faith, born in the Persian uplands, which was soon to become a potent religious force in the pagan world. It was especially a soldier's creed, viewing life as an unending battle between light and darkness, and recognizing no class distinctions among its votaries. There were the Jews, too, who held severely to their observances and managed to win privileges for them, and whose rigid monotheism was not unattractive to certain circles in Rome. They had no outdoor processions, though they had odd rituals on their Sabbath;[2] but most of the other cults had their public festivals, when the staid Roman citizen was repelled by the wild dances and the frenzied paeans, and shocked to see in the press of dark foreign faces some of his own friends and kin.

What was the appeal of this welter of mystery cults? To the poor and the unlearned there was the excitement of corybantic processions, various types of 'salvation army' with torches and cymbals bringing colour to drab lives. There were also countless tales of miracles performed by this or that foreign deity, and gossiped about in taverns — sailors drawing fresh water in mid-ocean, the blind made to see and the lame to walk. We know from the satiric comments of Lucian and from the ingenuousness of Pliny the deep credulity of the average Roman. Among the educated there was the desire for a new thing

---

[1] See the story of Lucius as told by Apuleius in Book XI of his *Metamorphoses.*
[2] Cf. Persius, v, 179 *sqq.*

which might give them what they missed in the state cults, a personal religion, a closer link with the unseen.

> Quis caelum poterit nisi caeli munere nosse
> et reperire deum nisi qui pars ipse deorum est? [1]

The mysteries could tell them something of what lay behind the veil of sense, those hidden things about which the Olympians were silent. They might give some hint of the land beyond the grave, and insure the safety of the soul hereafter. The old snug world of their forefathers had gone, when a man could live simply in a little enclave protected by his familiar gods. Wars and revolutions had thrown down geographical barriers, and with this expansion of horizons a great uncertainty had come into human life. A man was now terribly at the mercy of fate, and clutched at any possible safeguard. The soul, that spark of the divine in mortal clay, had come to mean more to its possessor as his earthly fortune became precarious; disasters were construed as a proof of guilt, and this guilt might be removed by rites of purification. Release from the burden of sin, security against death and judgment, knowledge of hidden things which were vital to their peace — such were the motives which led men to these new ways of salvation. Most of the worshippers were no doubt foreigners who clung to their ancestral cults, but there was a spirit abroad to which thinking Romans could not be insensitive. It was a phenomenon which seems to appear in cycles, a failure of nerve and a consequent revolt against mere intellect. What men craved for was not a doctrine but a revelation.

Many of the cults had elements of beauty and wisdom comparable to the regimen of those who sought a bodily cure in a temple of Aesculapius.[2] The story of Lucius in

---

[1] Manilius, II, 115.
[2] This regimen is described by Walter Pater in *Marius the Epicurean*, ch. 3.

Apuleius [1] is a story of a true initiation, followed by a constant advance in the spiritual life. By the help of Isis he was brought 'to the harbour of calm and the altar of mercy,' and the goddess gave him not only ease of mind, but considerable success in his profession as a lawyer. But there was no chance of any of these cults developing into a universal gospel. For one thing their appeal, when they transcended common magic, was limited to men of a certain education; for another, initiation was a costly business. The mysteries were not democratic. The bath of bull's blood in the worship of the Great Mother was expensive, as were the Orphic and the Dionysiac rites, and even membership of a Neo-Pythagorean brotherhood. But their real weakness lay in the fact that they were supplements, something tacked on to life, and involved no new vision of the universe, no radical transformation of the soul. Their strength lay in their social character, for they were brotherhoods, secret brotherhoods, and they ministered to those who, with the breakdown of familiar things, were feeling a little lost in the world.

This loneliness and disquiet were a *praeparatio evangelica* opening a path for a new revelation. It is easy to see how potent would be the appeal, a century later, of the Christian faith. Christianity brought a saviour and a promise of immortality. It carried on the Platonic teaching that this earthly life was sacramental, a shadow of eternity. It had its rites, but also its philosophy. It gave freedom from sin, knowledge of the truth, an armour against fate, a discipline of life. Moreover, it used the language of every race and class and clime. 'Except with regard to its fundamental tenets, it adapted itself to the needs and customs of the various nations. In the famine-stricken regions of Anatolia its preachers promised a heaven with

[1] *Metamorphoses*, Book XI. It is retold by Prof. Nock in his *Conversion*, ch. XI, a work which deals brilliantly with the whole question.

ever-bearing fruit trees; for the overworked serfs in Egypt it provided refuges in monasteries; to the Berber mountaineers of Africa it gave a holy cause for crusading, especially against rich and oppressive land-owners; to educated Romans, like Minucius Felix and Lactantius, it permitted the reading of Cicero and Virgil, nor did it attempt to deprive the real Greeks of Homer and Plato.' [1] Above all, it welcomed to its fold the poorest and humblest. When Celsus disputed with Origen, one of his charges against Christianity was the baseness of its converts. 'Let us hear whom these people invite: *Whosoever*, they say, *is a sinner, whosoever is unwise, whosoever is foolish* — in a word, *whosoever is a wretch — he will be received into the Kingdom of God.*'[2] What had the state religion to say to those who were not citizens, or the religion of Numa to those who had no household gods, or Mithras to the sick in body and mind, or the costly mysteries of Isis and Cybele to the penniless, or any of those creeds to the weary and heavy-laden?

IV

Augustus had no concern with exotic things except to keep them in order. His business was not a *praeparatio evangelica* but an *instauratio ecclesiae*. But he saw the necessity of supplementing the Roman faiths, and perhaps replacing the exotic faiths, by a new cult which should have a universal appeal, and should have for its basis his own Genius and the majesty of Rome. He realized that the Greek city-states had failed because they had no centre of conscious unity, no continuing link between past and future, and that if the empire was to endure some mystic and indivisible chain must be forged. Rome furnished

---

[1] Tenney Frank, *Aspects of Soc. Behaviour in Anc. Rome*, 63.
[2] Quoted by Nock, *op. cit.*, 206.

such a bond, but she was too abstract a goddess to appeal
to distant and ill-informed lands, so to her must be added
a personal object of devotion. This could only be the
Princeps, and the new imperial church must be conse-
crated in the name of 'Roma et Augustus.' Such a policy
was no piece of self-glorification. Augustus was as free
as any man who ever lived from whimsies about his own
divinity. He could laugh at such pomposities as readily
as Vespasian, who, on his death-bed, exclaimed, 'Alas! I
fear I am becoming a god!' [1] His purpose was to find a
universal object of devotion, which could be given a priesthood to serve as a kind of provincial 'honours list' and could
provide a minor form of representative government. In
this, as in all things, he was what Napoleon claimed to be,
'tout à fait un être politique.'

The antecedents of emperor-worship lay far back in
history. In the East kings had always been divine, and
the Greeks, with their extreme anthropomorphism, had
blurred the distinction between mortal and immortal. A
hero like Herakles, and a man like Alexander, could have
a divine as well as a human father, and a saviour of
society was as a matter of course accorded the honours
of a deity. [2] In republican Rome there was no such tradition, but there, too, the distinction was blurred, as we
understand it. 'Deus,' covering a multitude of small
divinities, had a meaning very different from our mono-
theistic 'God.' The ancient state was also a church, and
a saviour of the state naturally attracted a religious veneration. [3] As the empire extended Roman generals had
divine honours from many foreign states. In the second
century B.C. Flamininus received them from the people
of Chalcis as the liberator of Greece, Rhodes and Smyrna

[1] 'Vae, inquit, puto deus fio,' Suet., *Div. Vesp.*, 23.

[2] Examples — before Alexander — are Lysander after Aegospotami in 405 B.C., and
Dion in Syracuse in 356 B.C.

[3] Semi-divine honours were proposed for Scipio Africanus. Livy, xxxviii, 56.

set up altars to Rome, and Cicero in his Cilician procon-
sulate was threatened with the same dignity. Before the
close of the Republic Rome was moving nearer to the hero-
cult and the anthropomorphism of Greece. With Julius
a bold step was taken, either by his own wish or by the
intrigues of Mark Antony. His statue was carried in the
procession of the gods and placed in a temple, he was
hailed as Deus Invictus, a new guild of priests was established in his honour, and at his death — first of Romans
— he was formally deified.

Augustus had therefore a distinguished precedent behind him, and he was quick to make use of it. From the
start of his career he claimed the title of 'Divi Julii
Filius.' There he was on safe ground, for the deification
of Julius was in line with the old Roman worship of the
'Di manes' and the custom of consecrating altars to the
dead, and the founders of nations were always believed
to have ascended to heaven.[1] But *divus* was different
from *deus*. It was one thing for a great man to become a
god after death, and quite another for him to be like the
Ptolemies, a god in his lifetime. Augustus kept aloof from
any such folly. He repudiated a personal divinity, and
in this matter Tiberius scrupulously followed him. The
most he claimed was a share in the divinity of the state.
He declined an altar in the Senate-house, and he had
certain silver images of himself broken up. He forbade any
formal worship in Rome or Italy. The poets might identify
him with Apollo or Mercury, Propertius might hail him
as 'deus,' and Horace see him drink nectar among the
immortals, but that was only poetic licence. The most
that he permitted was the cult of his 'Genius,'[2] 'Lar' or
'Numen,' the guardian angel which dwelt in every man
and which the simplest householder shared with the Prin-

[1] Latinus became Jupiter Latiaris, and Romulus was worshipped as Quirinus.

[2] 'Genius' had a double significance — a god as a creative spirit, and the daemon of
the individual (cf. Augustine, *Civ. Dei*, vii, 13), and the latter meaning was slightly influenced by the former.

ceps. What Rome could venerate was his mission, the work which the gods had permitted him to do for the state. It was fitting that this work should be commemorated at the little street-corner shrines.

Overseas it was different. Even in Italy in his lifetime, especially among the Greek peoples of the south, a real emperor-worship had begun.[1] In the provinces, so long as his name was joined to that of Rome, there was no restriction on the cult. It had begun in 29 B.C. when temples were dedicated by the Romans in Asia to Rome and Julius, and by the Greeks to Rome and Augustus. Presently in certain places, like Cyprus and Pontus, Rome was omitted. In Egypt the Princeps succeeded naturally to the divinity of the Ptolemies. The custom spread throughout Greece and Asia, Syria and Palestine and Africa, and Augustus became the successor of the local god-kings. He was hailed as 'saviour' and 'bringer of good tidings,' and even as 'God the Son of God.' In the West, too, the fashion grew, though there a certain amount of government initiative was required. There were temples and altars built throughout Spain and Gaul and the German border, and even in Moesia and Pannonia, and the great altar dedicated by Drusus at Lyons was a seal upon Gallic loyalty. Colleges of lay priests, the Augustales, came into being to supervise the cult, and so a certain modicum of representation and local responsibility was introduced into the imperial fabric.[2]

This cult, devised with a cool judgment of facts, was one of the most successful parts of the Augustan structure. He kept it strictly within bounds in Italy, confining it to forms which had ancient sanction and general approval,

---

[1] At Cumae, Puteoli, Pompeii, Beneventum and elsewhere. See Rushforth, *Lat. Hist. Inscriptions*, 51–61.

[2] This subject has been exhaustively studied by Warde Fowler, *Religious Experience of the Roman People* (1911) and *Roman Ideas of Deity* (1914), and in the monographs of L. R. Taylor, *The Divinity of the Roman Emperor* (Amer. Philolog. Ass., 1931) and *The Worship of Augustus* (Amer. Philolog. Ass., 1920). See also P. Wendland, *Die hellenistisch-römisch Kultur* (1907).

but abroad he let it take the colouring of each race. The
imperial church, which had a uniform inspiration, had an
infinity of local idioms. It was a close link with Rome,
for, as I have said, it was like an honours list on which
the provincials based their social rank, and the priestly
colleges were to last for centuries. 'Titles such as Asiarch,
Syriarch, Phoeniciarch, derived from the high-priesthood
of Caesar's cult, were respected by Constantine's legislation and survived like ghosts of the pagan past to haunt
for a time the life of the new oecumenical church.' [1] It
met the demands of a world which was looking for a Mes-
siah by pointing out that one had come, who had proved
his title by bringing gifts of peace and fortune to men.
To the august legend of Rome it added the interest of a
personality, and thereby provided for the world a common
religious impulse. A universal religion was made a basis
for a universal allegiance. Each citizen of the empire felt
that the fate which directed his life was now a beneficent
thing which he could gratefully admire. Let it be said,
too, that the standard of godship was raised when a
genuine human benefactor joined that dubious pantheon.

The civic religion thus instituted was not state-idolatry
as we understand the phrase today. Augustus would not
have subscribed to the Hegelian view that 'the state was
its own end and object' and that its interest overrode
those of the individual. On the contrary, he held that its
justification was the individual's comfort and happiness,
for he set little value on philosophic abstractions. He
desired not a single iron, overriding loyalty, but a multitude of intimate devotions. His aim was to create a
communal patriotism which would appeal to the imagination of all classes in the empire, and not less to their
common sense. How did the citizens of Roman blood
regard it? As a summing up of the old loyalties and traditions of Rome, coloured by a personal devotion to the man

[1] Greenidge, *op. cit.*, 444.

who had rescued them from chaos. And the provincials of other races? As a confirmation also of their own ancestral faiths, which remained sacrosanct under a new protector. They admitted a fresh divinity into their pantheon without rejecting any of the old. 'Roma et Augustus' was not a juggernaut to obliterate the ancient landmarks, but a bulwark set up to defend them.

V

In Rome Augustus re-created a soul which was fast dying, and left an ideal to which the best men were to cling for many generations. But that soul could not keep the high levels to which he and his poets had led it. *Accidie* returned and material prosperity weakened its power. There was soon a satiety with high endeavour, and the taut bow relaxed. Even in the lifetime of the Princeps Ovid succeeded Virgil, and Ovid was not a cause but a symptom of a moral decline; the poet only described what he saw. But one part of the work of Augustus did not fail. He had made Rome a symbol of human aspiration, and her eternity an article of faith for every civilized man. The time was to come when her voice, once so imperious, became

> 'confusae sonus urbis et inlaetabile murmur.'

But in the dark days, when the barbarian beat at her gates, the Augustan tradition endured, and remote provincials mourned her sorrows as the end of their world. With Rome fell a church as well as a state, a church still under the vast shadow of its founder.

> Come, behold thy Rome, who now doth mourn
> Lonely and widow'd; day and night she cries
> 'My Caesar, wherefore leav'st thou me forlorn?' [1]

[1]
> 'Vieni a veder la tua Roma che piagne
>   vedova e sola, e dì e notte chiama:
>   "Cesare mio, perchè non m'accompagne?"'
>   DANTE, *Purgatorio*. Canto VI.

IV. THE AUGUSTAN PEACE

Venient annis saecula seris,
quibus Oceanus vincula rerum
laxet, et ingens pateat tellus,
Tethysque novos detegat orbes,
nec sit terris ultima Thule.

SENECA, *Medea*.

AUGUSTUS gave the empire a soul, and he laboured also to correct the disharmonies of its body. In the half-century before Actium travel throughout the ancient world was a gamble with fate. The man who took the road on his lawful occasions had to reckon with certain discomfort and almost certain danger. In Italy the highways were infested by brigands and runaway slaves, and the traveller might disappear for good and all in one of the slave-dungeons. In the provinces the wars had put many of the roads out of repair, and except in the vicinity of the cities there was no police system. Dues on merchandise were capriciously and corruptly levied, and merchants had often to buy security by paying blackmail. On the seas the trader was at the mercy of privateers — the Cilician pirates in the Levant, and enthusiastic amateurs like Sextus Pompeius in the western Mediterranean.

The Princeps wrought a miraculous change. In Italy he put down banditry with a strong hand, and he drove the pirates from every sea. His legions policed the provinces up to the extreme barbarian confines. He made the

Italian roads a marvel of efficiency, and established or completed a similar network overseas. Mile-stones and pillars at the crossroads gave the traveller his bearings. Maps were found in every educated household, and by their means a Roman girl could follow the movements of her lover serving on some distant front. A great chart of the world, prepared by Agrippa for Augustus, was displayed in the Porticus Vipsania in the Field of Mars for all to study. Geographers and explorers were patronized and assisted by the government. The old cosmographical notions had changed; the idea of an encircling Ocean stream had been abandoned, and the general conception was now of Africa and Asia joined together somewhere in the south. Imperial posts facilitated official communications between every part of the empire; the inns improved with the roads, and there were posting stations every five or ten miles. The slave-dungeons were frequently inspected to prevent cases of wrongous imprisonment. The harbours were everywhere improved, and the corn supply of Rome was stabilized by the institution of regular lines of sailing.[1] Ports like Ostia and Puteoli had a huge mechanism of ship-owners, ship-chandlers and marine-brokers.

Travel by land on the well-paved highways was principally by coach, carriage and litter; on the inferior roads, which were liable to landslips and floods, men journeyed on horseback or on foot. The ships were often of considerable size, up to a thousand tons register,[2] and many of the largest had as their ports of origin distant places in Spain and Arabia. On land a journey was probably speedier and more certain in the civilized countries than at any

---

[1] Claudius introduced something very like state marine insurance in order to encourage winter voyages. Suet., *Div. Claud.*, 18, 19.

[2] *e.g.*, the vessel in which Caligula brought an obelisk from Egypt. Pliny, *N. H.*, xvi, 20. The ship which took St. Paul to Rome had 276 passengers, and Josephus sailed in one which carried 600.

later time before the age of steam.[1] The news of Nero's death came to Galba in thirty-six hours over three hundred and fifty miles of Spanish roads, and these were not always of the best. The ordinary traveller could average five miles an hour, and twenty miles a day was in the power of the foot-passenger. At sea a ship with a favourable wind could reckon on at least five knots an hour, and there are records of some remarkable voyages; the distance from Alexandria to Puteoli could be covered in nine days, and that from Gades (Cadiz) to Ostia in seven. But this was for summer weather; in winter the Mediterranean was practically closed to sea-borne traffic, and all that could be done was to creep from port to port round the coast. The Etesian winds, too, blew in mid-July from the north-west, and while they made the journey fast from Rome to the East they practically cut off for six weeks all navigation westward. Yet it may fairly be said that communications by sea were as fast as anything known in Europe before the nineteenth century, and that in many parts of the Mediterranean basin — in Syria and Palestine, in Asia Minor, in Thrace and Macedonia — there was a standard of comfort and security under Augustus which is not reached today. The tribute of Epictetus was well deserved: 'Caesar has won for us a profound peace. There are neither wars nor battles, robbers nor pirates, and we may travel at all hours and sail from east to west.' [2]

In 20 B.C. at the north end of the Forum the Golden Milestone was set up, which bore on its gilded bronze the names of the chief cities of the empire and their distance from the capital. From it, like the spokes of a wheel, radiated the highways which led to the Italian coast or frontier, the first stages in foreign journeys. From the

---

[1] Aelius Aristides in the middle of the second century A.D. took 100 days to reach Rome from Anatolia, but he chose the difficult route round the north coast of the Aegean.

[2] III, 13, 9.

Porta Capena ran the Great South Road, the Via Appia, already three centuries old. To begin with it was a sub-urban highway lined with villas and country seats. When it left the Alban hills there was a bad patch through the Pomptine marshes, which was not properly repaired until the time of Trajan. Its old terminus was Capua, but a branch ran to the great port of Puteoli and the coast lands under Vesuvius. From Capua it continued to Beneventum where the Via Latina joined it, and thence through the Campanian vineyards, from which came the Falernian and Massic wines, to Tarentum and the hill-pastures of Calabria. The branch to Brindisi was, as we know from Horace, nothing to boast of, and it had to wait for Trajan to be ranked among the good roads. The Great North Road, the Via Flaminia, left the city by the Porta Flaminia and ran north through the corn-lands of Etruria and across the Apennines to Ariminum (Rimini), where in 27 B.C. Augustus had set up a triumphal arch to celebrate his remaking of the highway. From Ariminum it branched into two, one following the Adriatic coast to Aquileia, the gate of the north-east, while another, the Via Aemilia, skirted the base of the Apennines, crossed the wide valley of the Po, and led to Gaul and the North by the Alpine passes. The Via Salaria ran north-east from Rome through the Umbrian hills to the Adriatic, and the Via Aurelia by way of Pisa and Genoa was the coast road to Gaul. These were the main arteries, the *routes nationales*, but there was a multitude of lesser roads threading every part of the peninsula. The face of Italy was never more smiling than at the beginning of the principate. What are now wild glens in the Apennines had then their hamlets and man-ors, the sea-shore was lined with country houses, and for nine months in the year the dreary wastes of the Cam-pagna were white with sheep.

II

Let us attempt a bird's-eye view of the diverse lands on which the Augustan peace lay like a summer noon. Assume a cultivated Roman at the turn of the century, who had the leisure and the means to make a tour of the known world. From the Princeps he had a permit to visit forbidden countries, like Egypt, and from his bankers he had traveller's cheques which would be cashed by their agents in the most distant places. Let us follow his itinerary. Naturally he first turned his eyes to the East.

In the third week of July the north-west wind made Brindisi a busy harbour, for it was the season for exporting the wool from the Calabrian sheep-runs. To the voyager eastward the first sight of the mainland was the white temples of Nicopolis (Prevesa), the city founded in memory of Actium on the northern horn of the Ambracian gulf. This was a prosperous place, since Augustus had settled a Roman colony there, and the inhabitants of impoverished Aetolia had thronged to the new foundation. For the rest, the first impression was disappointing. Zacynthus was still well-wooded, but the cities of Cephallenia had gone, and Lysimachia on the mainland was in ruins. But Patrae (Patras) on the south shore of the Corinthian gulf was another bustling Roman colony, an Augustan foundation for the X and XII legions, and thither many of the citizens of the older Achaean towns had migrated. It had a brisk linen industry, and as a port held a strategic position for trade. At the head of the gulf, Corinth, re-established by Julius, had a similar advantage, and was by far the most flourishing of Greek cities. Beyond the isthmus the shores of the Saronic gulf presented a melancholy sight. Megara was in decay, and Athens was no longer queen of the Aegean. The soil of the Attic plain, never rich, was now wholly worked out,

like some of the old tobacco lands of Virginia today, and
tillage was everywhere giving place to coarse pasture.
There was still some traffic in what had once been a famous mart: honey from Hymettus and marble from Pen-
telicus, though the new Carrara quarries were decreasing
Italy's demand for the latter. The chief luxury exports
were bronzes for the decoration of the rich Roman houses.
Athens had become a museum-piece, a place to visit on the
grand tour for the sake of its ancient glories, and also a
university town for those who sought a more elaborate
course in philosophy than that afforded by the Roman
schools. The glory had departed from Hellas, for its principal export had long been its citizens. As traders, teachers, physicians, the Greeks were scattered throughout the
empire, making fortunes in a hundred crafts, and the little
country was left shabby and dispirited. Our traveller, if
anything of a philhellene, must have left the Piraeus with
few regrets.

A very different sight met his eye when the Etesians
had carried him past the Cyclades and Rhodes to where
the tall pharos of Alexandria kept watch over its shallow
seas. Here was a city of many races and tongues, and
among its half-million inhabitants [1] were Egyptians,
Greeks, Anatolians, Persians, Sabaeans, and a multitude
of Jews. Its great sea harbours, and the network of cross-
channels linking up all the mouths of the Nile, were
crowded with shipping from every port of the world, and
the canal through the Bitter Lakes to Arsinoe on the gulf
of Suez gave the city a water outlet to the East. Its broad
streets were lined with shady colonnades, and everywhere
there were noble public buildings, such as the Museum,
that staff college for learning, and the great Library which
was one of the wonders of the world. Conspicuous above

---

[1] Diod., XVII, 52, 6; he gives the free population as 300,000; cf. Marquardt, *Röm.
Staatsverwaltung*, I, 297.

the harbour was the new and splendid temple erected in honour of Augustus, to which all Egypt brought votive offerings.[1] There our traveller was at home, but strange to his eyes were the Egyptian shrines where animal-gods were worshipped with exotic rites. He found himself among a motley people, cultivated, excitable, avid of new things, speaking familiarly of the remotest lands, for to their city came trade routes from the uttermost places. They would talk readily of art and letters, but especially of commerce, for commerce was the breath of their being. From Alexandria were shipped not only the huge corn cargoes for Rome, but porphyry and serpentine, bricks of a special quality, red and grey granite, paper made from papyrus, alum and dyes, and from its workshops a variety of manufactured articles — fine linens, metal-work, jewellery, and the most delicate glassware. But above all, the city was the emporium to which came the products of Arabia, India and even China, for transport to the West. Spices and drugs, gums and perfumes, rare gems, ivory, tortoiseshell and gossamer silks filled its sweet-smelling warehouses.

When our traveller, having had his fill of the capital, passed south through the maze of waterways to the Nile valley, he found himself in a natural sanctuary. Egypt was defended on the north by the Delta, and on the other sides by a waste of sand, and through it ran the great river which was its life. To the south, beyond the first cataract of the Nile, lay the kingdom of Ethiopia, which was only a loose alliance of desert tribes, while from the east and west no danger had to be feared. Nevertheless the land was fully garrisoned, for Rome dared run no risks with her granary. Forts like peel-towers commanded all the points of vantage. The vital problem, then as today, was the protection of the irrigation system, which before

[1] A second temple to Augustus as 'Saviour' was erected at Philae.

Actium had fallen into decay. Augustus enlarged and improved the canals and dykes,[1] and by selling some of the royal domain-land encouraged the peasant proprietor. The *fellahin* in their mud huts had the advantage of more equitable taxation and complete security.

Egypt to the traveller was fascinating in itself, but still more as the frontier post of the mysterious East and the fabulous South. In its streets he could meet men who had ventured far into the unknown. Some had gone beyond the land of the Ethiopians and brought back tales of the snow mountains where lay the springs of Nile.[2] From Coptus (Quft) on the river a little below Thebes a carefully guarded road ran eastward, by which in six or seven days caravans could reach the port of Myos Hormos (Kosseir) on the Red Sea. This was the route for that part of the merchandise of the East which did not travel by Arsinoe and the canals, or by the great road which led by Petra to Syria. Under Augustus this merchandise had grown into a regular traffic. In the time of the Ptolemies, Strabo tells us, not twenty ships a year passed the strait of Bâb-el-Mandeb, while now that number was six times multiplied.[3] The goods which reached Myos Hormos were partly the gums and spices of Arabia, but still more the produce of India and the Far East. Some time about the turn of the century a sea captain named Hippalus [4] discovered the tremendous fact of the periodicity of the monsoon, and ships, instead of hugging the coast, could now sail direct to the mouth of the Indus, starting at the summer solstice and returning to Alexandria the following February. Roman money circulated in India, Roman and

---

[1] He greatly increased the amount of cultivated land, so that a rise in the river of 12 cubits at Memphis was as good as 14 cubits before. Strabo, XVII, 1, 3; Suet., *Div. Aug.*, 18.

[2] 'mercatores qui ulteriora Aethiopiae scrutantur.' Pliny, *N. H.*, VI, 173.

[3] II, 5, 12.

[4] For Hippalus, see *Periplus*, 57; Bunbury, *Hist. of Anc. Geog.*, II, 351.

Greek cults reached its shores, a temple of Augustus was erected in Mysore, and Indian traders were common in the streets of Alexandria. Within a century India was to become, after Italy, the chief producing ground for the empire.[1] She sent Rome luxuries, while Rome's return cargoes were the same as those of later exploiters — wine, and cheap articles produced in mass. The traders did not stop at the Malabar coast; they rounded Cape Comorin, they visited Ceylon, they began to push into Malaya, and they were presently at the confines of China, though Chinese goods still came mostly by the overland routes to the Black Sea or the Tigris valley. They ventured south also, in search of ivory and gold, to Zanzibar and Mozambique where the Sabaean Arabs had preceded them. No city in history, not even Venice in the Middle Ages, can have matched Alexandria for travellers' tales.

The coast road from Egypt to Syria has some claim to rank as the most famous of all the roads of history. Up and down the seaward levels had marched the great armies of Egypt and Assyria, while the Jews looked on fearfully from their barren hills. From Sennacherib to Mark Antony that strip of plain had been the gate in which empires clashed. It was a route for trade as well as for arms; and now, under the Augustan peace, the caravans from Egypt hugged the shore as far as Gaza, where there was an important road junction. One branch went east through the Idumaean country to Petra in the desert, one went north-east to Jerusalem, and the main branch continued north through the plain of Ascalon. This last was in turn subdivided in the plain of Sharon; the western road followed the coast by Caesarea, Tyre, Sidon and Berytus (Beirut) until it reached Seleucia, the port of Antioch; the eastern crossed the hills of Ephraim to the

[1] Pliny, *N. H.*, xxxvii, 203.

plain of Esdraelon, where it sent off a branch to Damascus, and continued thence down the valley of the Orontes to Emesa and Antioch.

Syria had produced in the past a notable breed of sailors, but now its ports were merely the doorway to the great cities of the interior. Of these, Jerusalem among its hills owed its fame to its religion and its stubborn people, but the others were marts of high importance. Antioch, which could be reached by water from Seleucia, was second only to Alexandria in commercial repute. Situated in a flower garden, it was a city of palaces, whose streets at night were lit artificially like a modern capital, and whose houses had water laid on indoors, a place of exchange for the merchandise of East and West, the nearest point to the Euphrates, and the focus of a network of trade routes. Damascus, watered by the snows of Lebanon, was like-wise a garden-city, set in the midst of orchards, an emporium, but also the home of many crafts and industries. From it caravans journeyed to the Euphrates through the wonderful city of Palmyra, whose wealth was already a legend in Rome. To Antioch and Damascus came a large share of the overland traffic from India, and far in the South the fortress city of Petra, on its cliffs above the Nabatean sands, received much of the produce of Arabia. The Roman peace became less solid as it stretched east-ward. There was a multitude of quarrelsome princelings, and, as has been well said, the map of Syria was like the map of eighteenth-century Germany. The *bedawin* of the desert were troublesome neighbours even when they ceased to be nomads, and beyond the Euphrates lay Parthia with its ill-defined frontier. Rome under Augustus had never less than four legions as a garrison, a garrison which at any moment might become a field force, besides auxiliary troops in peel-towers to watch the Euphrates crossings. Though it was defended by the sea in the west and the mountains in the north, and in the east and south by deserts, Syria was never, like Egypt, an enclosure of settled peace. The traveller felt behind its prosperity a certain lack of ease, and its luxury was the habit of men to whom life must always be something of a gamble.

Of that prosperity there could be no question. To one coming from Egypt, where in late summer the air hung languid above the brimming water-furrows, the Syrian atmosphere, even in the flats, seemed tonic and aromatic. The heat was great, but it braced the traveller. As soon as the deserts were passed, evidence of wealth met him on every hand. At Berytus, which was a colony of Agrippa's and remained the most Roman part of the land, the vineyards and flax plantations were famous; Sharon was a garden; Tyre and Sidon were still the home of the purple dyes; the valleys were rich in crops, and even in the Judaean hills the pockets of good soil produced abundantly; the great cities were hives of industry; every harbour was packed with shipping; the numerous roads were crowded with convoys, including strings of camels from beyond the deserts, which seemed strange to the Roman eye. The Syria of today has small resemblance to the Syria of Augustus. Then it contained perhaps ten million people; strategically it was one of the most vital parts of the empire, and it was the greatest of manufacturing centres. Districts which are now barren were then productive, for the soil had not been overworked and there was no lack of water. The great forests, found now only in patches on Lebanon, were then widespread, so that the streams ran full and the rains came in due season. An elaborate system of canals and reservoirs irrigated what today are wastes of sand. Recent excavation has revealed the fact that the country northeast of Palmyra, which is now without human dwellings, had then twenty-four temples, and pastures which bred the most famous horses in the world.

Syria was not the easiest of Augustus's problems. There was Judaea, a volcano in periodic eruption, and the exposed frontier towards Parthia. The wealth of the cities needed constant guardianship, and that duty fell wholly on Rome. The natives were not a warlike race, and the opinion of the Roman soldiery on them may be judged from an inscription scribbled on a boulder, 'The Syrians vile folk.' [1] They had much the same repute as the Jews today, that of men who would go anywhere and do anything in the way of business, the commercial traveller *in excelsis*, and we find their tracks in the remotest northern and western parts of the empire. In Rome, as Juvenal complained bitterly, the Orontes had flowed into the Tiber.[2] Syria was the forerunner of Venice and Genoa in acting as middleman between East and West. But the Roman, wintering in Antioch or Damascus, learned that there was another characteristic of the people. The country was practically tri-lingual, with Latin, Greek and Aramaic, but, except in Berytus, the specific Roman culture made little headway. The Hellenic and the Semitic strains had intermingled, and had produced their own intellectual activity and a quick interest in liberal studies. The minor arts flourished; Syrian actors and musicians were plentiful in the west, and Publilius Syrus fifty years before had introduced the mime to Rome. From the little town of Gadara had sprung Meleager, the poet of 'The Garland,' Menippus the Cynic philosopher, Theodorus the rhetorician, whose lectures at Rhodes were attended by Tiberius, and Philodemus, who was the teacher of Virgil. Sidon, a century earlier, has produced Antipater, whose epigrams adorn the *Greek Anthology*. Posidonius, the fashionable Stoic professor in Rome, had been a Syrian; indeed that philosophy drew from the East some of its

---

[1] οἱ Σύροι κακὸν γένος, — quoted by Charlesworth, *Trade Routes of Rom. Emp.*, 56.
[2] III, 62.

chief exponents, for its founder, Zeno, was a Semite. This appetite for the things of the mind was to continue for centuries and to influence profoundly the thought of the empire, in science and philosophy, in religion and law, in prose and poetry. Of Syrian blood were Iamblichus and Heliodorus, the first novelists; Lucian the satirist; Nicolaus the historian; Porphyry and Iamblichus the Neo-Platonists; the jurists Ulpian and Papinian; and a host of Christian fathers, orthodox and heretic.

The traveller, returning from Syria to Rome when the spring sailings opened, had a choice of routes. The ordinary plan was to take ship from Alexandria. Or he might go overland through the passes of the Taurus across the tableland of Anatolia to some port on the Black Sea, and thence by water to Thessaly, and the eastern terminus of the Via Egnatia. Or, if he had ample leisure, a coasting vessel would take him up the shores of Asia to Byzantium. To the average Roman there was little attraction about the second route. It was safe enough, since the buffer states of Commagene and Armenia were flank guards on the east; but the road led over a high plateau, which at the best was monotonous and dusty. The coasting voyage, on the other hand, took him into a land made classic by literature and history, and among islands and cities which he revered as the cradle of civilization.

Anatolian roads had not attained the perfection reached in the later empire. Asia Minor was primarily a littoral studded with cities, some of which exploited a considerable hinterland. It was a peaceful province and was therefore under the Senate's charge, and Ephesus seems to have been the principal seat of government, with Pergamum as a close rival. Each city was allowed to retain its ancient constitution, which gave it self-government, and all, having suffered much in the civil wars, were enthusiasts for the new empire and zealous in the cult of 'Roma et Augustus.' [1] Rhodes was no longer the metropolis of the eastern Aegean; Ephesus, Smyrna, Cyzicus, Pergamum and Miletus were more important, and inland municipalities like Thyateira, Sardis and Laodicea acted as feeders for the sea-borne commerce. Once the 'royal road' to Persia had followed the Maeander, but now Syria had taken its place as the gate of the East. The river valleys, both those debouching on the Aegean and on the Black Sea, were highly cultivated, and from the hill country came the finest wool, but only the coast lands were homogeneous; from the rich plains of Pamphylia the traveller going inland entered Pisidia, a land of half-savage mountaineers, and the hardy Galatians had little in common with the soft Lydians. The peninsula, once a bridge between East and West, had now lost most of its strategic importance, but it was fast winning a new prosperity. Along with Cyprus it produced almost every known mineral, all the precious metals, and a wide range of gems. To Italy it sent wine and oil and dried fruits, and a variety of fine timber; but its main industry was textiles — Coan silks, Milesian woollens, carpets and blankets, and dyed fabrics from Laodicea. Every port was a busy centre, since for the first time for centuries the land had honest government and peace.

The traveller observed another thing. Asia was composed of layers of old civilizations, Ionian, Hellenic and Hellenistic, and its culture remained permanently Hellenic. Latin was the official tongue, but Rome, even less than in Syria, imposed upon the land her modes of thought. The temples of Augustus were dutifully served, but they could not compare in splendour or fame with an old shrine like that of Artemis at Ephesus. There were only two Roman colonies, Alexandria in the Troad and Parium on the Pro-

[1] See W. H. Buckler, 'Auguste, Zeus Patroos,' in *Rev. de P.* (1935), 177–88.

pontis; no town had the Latin citizenship; there was no attempt at romanizing, except a half-hearted effort to exalt Ilium, or Troy, as the cradle of Rome. The Roman visiting the gleaming cities on the Aegean realized that here, rather than in Greece itself, the Hellenic tradition survived, and felt himself in a land more foreign in many ways than Syria or Egypt.

If time allowed, and our traveller, before completing his last homeward stage by the great Macedonian highway, ventured north from Byzantium, he found himself in a very different world. Vines and olives gave place to fir trees, the merchantmen of the south to fishing smacks, and the sunlit Aegean to the grey waters of the Euxine. On the northern shore lay the little Bosporan kingdom, which farmed the rich black soil of the steppes and supplied the nearer cities of Asia with corn. It was the furthest outpost of Rome's authority, for west of it lay the Scythians of the Crimea, and east and north the Sarmatian tribes, outliers of the great nomad peoples of Central Asia. The traveller in the Bosporan capital heard uncouth names like Iapyges, Roxolani, Alani and Aorsi, which were to be only too familiar to his grandchildren, and knew that he was very near the edge of the world.

III

The visitor to Africa took ship at Puteoli in the bay of Naples, the busiest port in Italy, and one of the chief industrial towns, for to it the iron ore from Elba was brought for smelting, and its potteries produced the red-glazed Arretine ware. Carthage was his destination, the famous city which the fears of republican Rome had kept derelict, but which Julius and Augustus had very wisely re-founded. It was already the chief of African centres and rapidly regaining its ancient wealth. Its crafts were glass-blowing and dyeing, but its main importance lay in the fact that it was the harbour from which African agricultural products were shipped. Of these products corn was the chief, and the export was already drawing up fast on Egypt. Wheat in Africa was said to give up to four times the yield of the same grain in Egypt and Sicily. Every eye-witness agreed on the richness of the soil; to Horace Africa was pre-eminently the 'fertile land,' to Columella 'abundant in corn' and to the elder Pliny the 'chosen home of Ceres.' Farming was conducted on novel methods, for the hillsides were terraced, and at different levels had palms and orchards, olive-yards, vegetable gardens and wheat-fields.

The people were mainly Berbers, though there were various colonies of Roman veterans, and a certain admixture of the old Punic population. The city dwellers were a docile race, who gladly acquiesced in the rites of 'Roma et Augustus'; but they clung, too, to their ancient gods, and in most cities there were temples to Baal and Tanit. Only one legion, the III Augusta, was required to keep order and watch the frontier. The old province of Africa, the modern Tunisia, was now but a small part of the Roman sphere of influence, which stretched for a thousand miles west to the Atlantic. Augustus took Numidia, which roughly corresponded to what is Algeria today, from its king Juba and annexed it to the province, while in return he gave Juba Mauretania (Morocco) and all the western lands. Juba was an enlightened ruler, and he made his capital, Iol Caesarea, a centre of industry and learning, developed the sheep-runs in the mountains and the forests of ebony and citrus, exported wild beasts for the Roman circus, and created a flourishing trade in purple dye. Africa under Augustus had the old province as its heart, with the coast-lands of Cyrenaica to the east and the Numidian plateau to the west, and beyond the latter the protected realm of king Juba. There was no definite southern frontier except the line of forts which looked out on the Sahara. A network of roads linked Carthage and the ports with rich valleys like that of the Bagradas (Majerda), and a trunk road followed the coast to Cyrenaica and ultimately to Egypt.

The problem before Rome was to draw the nomad tribes of Numidia and Mauretania to habits of settled life. For this purpose bounties were offered for the reclaiming of marsh and bush land, and apparently with success; for tillage began to take the place of pasture, and the farmers came together into little towns, very much as in Picardy today. Presently these towns were to expand into cities, which in the later empire had their full complement of temples, baths and amphitheatres built of the yellow African marble, like the Tunisian Bulla Regia and the Algerian Timgad. To keep the peace there was a constant frontier bickering with the mountaineers of Morocco and Saharan tribes like the Garamantes and the Gaetuli. But in the main it was a quiet and contented land, and a proof is that it turned its eyes to distant horizons. There were settlements on the western coast of Morocco, and Juba's navy sailed past the Pillars of Hercules and discovered the Canaries, bringing back from them hunting dogs and a new legend of the Happy Isles. The quick Berber mind, leavened by Roman and Punic influences, turned readily to intellectual interests. In time Africa was to furnish the *beau idéal* of the cultivated Roman, like the grandfather of Septimius Severus and the elder Gordians. It was to produce men of letters like Fronto and Apuleius, jurists like Silvanus Julianus, scholars like Florus and Aulus Gellius, a theologian like Tertullian, and in St. Augustine one of the major influences on human thought.

Spain is physically a southern land akin to Africa, for

it is only at the Pyrenees that the damp mossy woods begin which are the true mark of the North. Her southern frontier in Roman days was not the straits of Gibraltar, but the Moroccan uplands, and with the Riff unsettled the wealth of Baetica was insecure. That was why Augustus planted settlements on the northern and western Moroccan coasts, one at least of which was actually under a Spanish governor. The farmers of southern Spain imported rams from Africa, and there was a constant coming and going between the two countries, ferries plying from Lixus to Cadiz and from Tingis (Tangier) to Belo. Consequently the traveller was wise, if he wished to survey the western half of the empire, to make a circuit dockwise and reach Spain from its natural complement.

It was the oldest Roman province in the West,[1] and it had taken the longest time to conquer. The reason for this was partly its natural formation and partly the character of its people. Spain was a land with a rich coast fringe, and inland a high plateau, rising in the south and north-west to considerable mountains, and cut into by long, awkwardly placed river valleys. Communications, except round the coast, had to climb in and out of glens and cross and recross steep ranges. Geographically the country was dislocated, and composed of more or less isolated pockets of habitable land. There were many rivers, some of them with long courses and navigable for a considerable distance — the Ibrius (Ebro) and the Sucro (Jucar) on the east, the Baetis (Guadalquivir) and the Anas (Guadiana) on the south, and the Tagus and the Durius (Douro) flowing to the Atlantic; but they made highways only for their own valleys. The country was divided into the semi-tropical south, the high and arid central plateau, the long-settled Mediterranean coast, and

---

[1] The Spaniards spoke a slightly archaic Latin, since the tongue had been so long in the country. A parallel is the French of the Canadian *habitants*.

in the north and north-west a wild tangle of mountains.
The population took the colour of their surroundings. The
basis was Iberian, a stock probably of Berber origin, mixed
with, but not dominated by, a Celtic element. These Ibe-
rians were shepherds and hunters on the plateau and in the
mountains, and bold sailors on the western coast, and they
were never as fully romanized as the Gauls. The Basques,
who represent them today, were even in the fourth century
A.D. to the Roman Prudentius 'bruta Vascorum gentilitas,'
and they still retain their ancient independence. The
natives were split up into so many little tribes — Pliny
mentions thirty-four of them in Tarraconensis alone —
that they could not unite against an invader, but the
difficulty of their country made it necessary to reduce them
step by step. There was no single nerve-centre at which
a conqueror could strike. That is why the subjugation
of Spain was not completed until the time of Augustus
and Agrippa, and they found it no easy task. Along the
coast there was a marvellous racial variety — Roman
colonists, imported Italian workmen, relics of all the sea-
farers who had ventured to Spain from the Minoans to
the Carthaginians, but elsewhere the Celto-Iberians were
the Spanish people.

The first step of Augustus was political, the redistribu-
tion of the governments. The republican two had been
Hither and Further Spain. He took Baetica (Andalusia)
from the latter and made it a separate province under the
Senate. He made a new province of Lusitania (Portugal),
and added to it the north-west territories, Galicia and
Asturia, and all the rest he comprised in the huge government of Tarraconensis. Then he set himself vigorously
to road-making. Three roads entered Spain from Gaul —
one in the west by Roncevaux to Pampeluna, one over the
central Pyrenees to Caesaraugusta (Saragossa), and one,
the Via Domitia, at the eastern end. These he continued

as arterial roads through the country to the southern and western coasts. They were real engineering feats, for they had to cross high passes and involved much difficult bridging. He also completed the great circuit of coast highways; in this respect Spain was the opposite of Gaul, for there the roads radiated outward from a centre, while in Spain the importance lay in the periphery.

He did much, too, in the way of building new cities and amplifying old ones at strategic points in the interior, cities which should dominate the new roads and be centres of Roman influence. Examples are Asturica Augusta (Astorga) in the north-west, Saragossa on the Ebro, Emerita (Mérida) on the Guadiana, Italica in the plain of the Guadalquiver, and Tarraco (Tarragona) which rose in terraces above the blue Mediterranean. Mérida, the residence of the governor of Lusitania, impresses one even more than the aqueduct at Segovia or the bridge at Alcantara with the audacity of the Roman genuis. The V and X legions, which defeated the Asturians, were settled in 25 B.C. by Publius Carisius in a new city on the Gaudiana, which was meant to be not a mere frontier military post but a Latin capital and a model of Roman life.[1] Otho and Vespasian added to its population and curbed the Gaudiana, which Prudentius describes as 'viridante rapax gurgite,' but they did not enlarge the city, and Mérida was wholly an Augustan foundation. It had a bridge of sixty arches a kilometre long, which carried the road from Hispalis (Seville), an embankment against flooding of sixty-six bays, three aqueducts, a huge reservoir four miles off, a circus and an amphitheatre. Mérida was born in the purple, for its maker was Agrippa. From it ran north the second greatest of Spanish highways, by

[1] Rostovtzeff's view (*Soc. and Econ. Hist. of Rome*, 547) that the Augustan foundation was only a small garrison town, which was later added to, is refuted by recent archaeological research.

way of Salamanca and Zamora to Castile and Aragon and
the sea. In the eighth century the Arab invaders were
amazed at its splendour: 'one would think,' they cried,
'that men had come together from all the world to found
this city'; and still over the squalid modern *pueblo* broods
the mighty shade of Augustus.

To the Romans Spain seemed the richest of their possessions. Legends were rife of its extraordinary wealth,
and it was rumoured that in Baetica the horses had silver
mangers. It had few crafts and manufactures, but it had
everything else. The coasts and the valleys produced wine
and oil, wheat and flax, fruits of every kind, and esparto
grass for the Italian cordwainers, while the ports had a
busy traffic in pickled fish and sauces. Spanish honey, too,
was famous. But its main wealth was its minerals, which
soon came to be a monopoly of the imperial house, Livia
herself owning large mining properties. In these it was by
far the richest part of the empire. Phoenician and Cartha-
ginian adventurers had first prospected the land and sunk
shafts, and even in the time of Polybius the silver mines
in Roman hands employed forty thousand men. The chief
mining centres were the southern sierras and the mountains of the north-west. Spanish silver and lead were the
best on the market, and there was also alluvial gold, tin,
iron and copper, mercury and cinnabar, and the only
known mica vein in the world. Spain was to Rome what
Peru was to Spain itself in the sixteenth century, an almost
fabulous Eldorado. The methods of extracting and handling the ore had reached a high pitch of development; in
the Rio Tinto fields today one may see deep Roman
shafts sunk without explosives through solid quartz, and
Roman slag with so low a percentage left of copper as to
amaze modern metallurgists.

The traveller in the coast lands marvelled at the overflowing riches of the soil, but he marvelled still more if he

penetrated to the interior and saw the long strings of mules laden with ore on the mountain paths, and at night the glow of furnaces among remote sheep-walks. Spain in Roman hands was prospering beyond doubt, but the process of romanization was slow. The three legions quartered there kept the peace; the worship of 'Roma et Augustus' was observed in the chief cities, and an altar at Tarraco was the Spanish counterpart of the great altar at Lyons. But the old Iberian and Celtic deities did not lose their devotees,[1] and the Spaniard was not as ready as the Gaul to take on a Latin veneer. For that reason, perhaps, he made the better soldier. The men from the uplands were soon to be the backbone of the legions and to furnish the best auxiliary corps; nor was the race which invented the Moorish, and therefore the Norman, arch lacking in original talent. The south, indeed, speedily adopted new fashions, and Baetica became, like the Narbonese, more Roman than Rome. Cadiz, for example, could boast five hundred members of the equestrian order, a number equalled by only one Italian city. It was the most prosperous epoch in Spanish history, and the life of the country gentlefolk in the settled parts was as pleasant and varied as anything that Italy could show. There was a wonderful breed of horses, necessaries and luxuries were alike cheap, the gardens were rich in fruit and flowers, and the hills stocked with game, though rabbits were a nuisance to the sportsman.[2] The Roman influence was to spread slowly but surely, and whereas in 27 B.C. the names on the inscriptions are uncouth things like Magilo and Bodecius, two centuries later they are Antonii and Flavii.[3] From Spain were to come many of the chief figures in imperial

---

[1] These native gods were often identified with members of the Roman pantheon, and we find Jupiter Ahoparaliomegus, Mars Cariociecus and Proserpina Ataecina.

[2] See the account of the elder Seneca, *Controv.*, XVI, 22.

[3] *C. I. L.*, II, 2633, quoted by Arnold, *Studies of Roman Imperialism*, 156.

literature, Lucan and the two Senecas, Martial, Quintilian, Pomponius Mela and Columella, and famous emperors like Trajan and Hadrian.

We have seen that Augustus from the beginning of the principate gave special attention to Gaul, making new territorial divisions, holding a census of the people, and providing for the defence of its eastern frontier. It was the special charge of his house, for in seven miraculous years Julius had carried the eagles from the Mediterranean to the North Sea and from the Rhine to the Atlantic. Strategically it held a vital position in the empire; it paid as much in taxation as Egypt; it provided the army with the best cavalrymen and the best horses. It was of all the provinces the one which a leisured Roman was the most likely to visit. Our traveller, on his western tour, would naturally enter it from north-east Spain by the Via Domitia and Nemausus (Nîmes) and Arelate (Arles). The other routes were by sea from Ostia to Massilia (Marseilles), for those for whom the gulf of Lyons had no terrors, or by the great coast road along the Riviera. This last was the favourite, for it was kept in good order, since it was one of the busiest highways in the empire. He who journeyed by it could see something of those valleys of the western Alps which Augustus had brought into the Roman peace, and the tall monument on the hillside above Monaco which commemorated that achievement.

The Narbonese, or southern Gaul, was, as a province, older than Julius's conquest. It combined what is today Provence, Languedoc, Dauphiné, part of Savoy and a corner of Switzerland. As compared with the rest of Gaul its organization was urban, for it was above all things a country of splendid cities. Each city had attached to it a territory which had once been the possession of the local tribe, and that territory was an integral part of the civic life. Its ports were famous trading centres to which the merchants of all lands resorted; every acre was intensively cultivated, chiefly for the vine and the olive, and it exported its wines as far afield as Ireland. The Narbonese had indeed little kinship with the rest of Gaul, being, as the elder Pliny said, more like Italy than a province. Its inhabitants were drawn from many races, and, being rich, were pacific and if anything over-civilized, though in the future it was to produce fighting men like Agricola, and an emperor like Antoninus Pius. The doubts sometimes cast upon Gallic fortitude may be taken to apply to this warm and habitable southern land.[1]

Very different were the three northern provinces, where the Celtic strain ran pure, and a poorer soil and a sterner climate imposed harder conditions of life. The men were taller than the small-boned Romans, often fair in colouring, and their garb was sleeved coats and trousers as befitted a race of horsemen. Their organization was tribal rather than territorial, but they left their mark upon the soil, for they founded most of the towns and villages of the France we know today. But they were a society, never a nation, or, more accurately, a group of societies.[2] Left to themselves they wasted their strength on futile clan battles, and it needed the strong hand of Rome to impose that unity which means prosperity. Their temperamental difference from the Romans made them admire what they could not originate, and they remained consistently loyal to the empire. Indeed they invented for themselves a pedigree which linked them to Italy, and the Aedui and the Arverni claimed to be of Trojan blood.[3]

[1] Cf. Tac., *Ann.*, XI, 18; *Hist.*, IV, 76; *Germ.*, 28.

[2] 'Celticism has left only possibilities of nations. It survives only in the foundations of our western Europe, and has made hardly any contribution to its super-structures.' HUBERT, *The Rise of the Celts*, 15.

[3] 'Arvernique ausi Latio se fingere fratres
        sanguine ab Iliaco populi ——'
                                    LUCAN, *Phars.*, I, 427–28.

In Celtic Gaul Rome encouraged the formation of cities, but the country was never urbanized, for on the wide downs and beside the slow, reedy rivers there was always a multitude of little villages and scattered farms. The division between town and country was never absolute. The people retained their old customs and devotions, their old dress, and, in the country parts, their old speech. Alesia was still a traditional sanctuary, and the ancient goddesses of springs and hills and woods, the Matres, were still the popular objects of worship, though, as time went on they tended to become confused with the Mediterranean deities. The mass of the people were craftsmen, shepherds and farmers — stock-farmers principally, since the pasture was better than the tillage. The olive and the fig would not grow north of the Cevennes, and the vineyards were poor, so beer, not wine, was the popular drink.

The land was well adapted for communications. The long deep rivers, Rhone and Saone, Moselle and Seine, Loire and Garonne, had made the Gauls a nation of boatmen; [1] and since their craft were of shallow draught they could navigate a multitude of lesser streams, so that with easy portages goods could be sent by water throughout the land. There must have been fair roads even before the Roman conquest, or Hannibal and Julius could not have moved their armies at the pace they did. Augustus took the whole road system in hand, and with Lyons as the centre instituted five great trunk highways. One went down the Rhone to Marseilles and continued east and west along the coast; one ran south-west through Aquitania to the port of Burdigala (Bordeaux); one ran north by the Seine valley to the Channel shore; one led by the camps on the Rhine; while the fifth went by Besançon across the Jura, and so over the Alps to Italy. Lyons was the key to the Roman control. It was the true capital, and like-

[1] Hannibal found and made use of Gallic boats on the Rhone at Avignon.

wise the link between south and north. As the emporium
for Gallic trade it became immensely prosperous, and in
A.D. 64 it could contribute no less than forty thousand
pounds when Rome was ravaged by fire. Carriage roads
had now been constructed across the Alps by the Great
and Little St. Bernard passes, and by Mont Genèvre, and
of these Lyons was the terminus; it thus became the point
where Italy made its closest contact with the premier
province.

The mineral wealth of Gaul was inconsiderable, but in
all kinds of agricultural and industrial products the country was pre-eminent. We have seen the sub-tropical riches
of the Narbonese; elsewhere the produce was chiefly
pastoral, the sheep on the downs, the cattle in the plains,
and the swine in the forests. Gallic wool was of the best
quality, and there was a great export trade in hams and
cheeses, pickled meats and sausages; carrots, a new luxury
in Rome, came from the north; and the elder Pliny records
that in his day geese — for the sake of *foie gras* — were
driven all the way by road from Belgium to Italy. But
the chief wealth was industrial. The Gaul was an expert
workman and the crafts seemed to have been small family
businesses. The chief trades were weaving, glass-blowing
and pottery. At first the Arretine ware had been imported,
but it was not long before the Gallic potters imitated it
and improved on it, and so captured the market of the
world. It was the same with glass; soon Egypt and Syria
could not compete with the products of this northern land.
One reason for this success was the forests, which provided
cheap and plentiful fuel for the furnaces.

Gaul was also the gateway to the unknown, for to the
east lay the Germanies, and to the north Britain. The
latter, in the time of Augustus, was not a part of the empire, but its native princes were on good, though distant,
terms with Rome; there was a considerable traffic between

its shores and Gaul, articles of luxury being exchanged for metals, both base and precious, corn, hides and slaves, and, adds Strabo, 'very good hounds.' The traveller, who by way of Reims and Soissons reached Boulogne, saw beyond the Channel spectral white cliffs and felt himself very close to the ultimate mysteries. For he had heard in Gaul strange tales of ghost ferries which bore the souls of the dead over those grey seas to their last home.[1] In Boulogne harbour, too, he could meet sailors, who in their coasting smacks had gone east into the Baltic and north past the Norway capes, and could speak of an ocean curdled like milk and great bearded sea-monsters with ivory fangs.

One other part of the empire was open to the traveller, the land between the Danube, the Adriatic and the Aegean. Leaving Rome by the Via Flaminia he reached Aquileia, which was the gate of the north-east segment of the frontier. There the roads met which crossed the eastern Alps and served Rhaetia and Noricum and Pannonia. It was the base for the armies which were engaged in the frontier wars along the Danube. It was the emporium for the trade of the lands which today are Tyrol, Bavaria, Austria, Serbia, Bulgaria, Roumania and Transylvania, a trade mostly in the hands of the great merchant house of the Barbii. It was the southern terminus of the Amber Road,[2] by which amber was brought from the Baltic through the domains of a hundred savage tribes, to be fashioned in Aquileia for export into necklets and *bibelots*. Trade had followed the eagles and goods were beginning to enter Italy from the north-east, furs and hides and salted fish from distant places like south Russia and Scan-

---

[1] Procop., *Bell. Goth.*, IV, 20; Claudian, *in Rufin.*, I, 123-28.

[2] Under Augustus the Amber Road was made easy as far as the Danube. Later it was more fully explored, and seems to have run from Carnuntum (Petronell) on that river, up the valley of the March to upper Silesia; then by way of Kalisz and the Prosna to the Vistula valley and the coast. Pliny, *N. H.*, xxxvii, 45.

dinavia. Travel was easy down the Save valley to the Danube, and Rome held all the southern shore of the latter river. But beyond that lay the unsettled lands. Along with the Germanies this was the most difficult part of Rome's frontier, and the legions had often to stand to arms. Noricum had its industries, Moesia had good farming land, and Pannonia exported metals, besides bears for the amphitheatre from its gloomy forests; but the day was still far off when the Danubian basin was to rise — and with it northern Italy — to a spectacular prosperity.

IV

We must picture the empire of Augustus as primarily the coastal belt of the Mediterranean watershed, and the western lands looking to the Atlantic. Many inland territories had been added, but these were the glacis of the fortress rather than the fortress itself, and often an embarrassing glacis to develop and keep in order. Beyond was the twilight of the little known, thickening into a darkness which no explorer had yet dispelled. There lay the wild lands and the legendary peoples. Adventurers now and then disappeared into the gloom and returned with wonderful tales, like those expeditions recorded a century and a half later in the lost work of the geographer Marinus, when the Ethiopian desert was traversed and a Roman general crossed the Sahara to a mysterious tropic kingdom. Roman eyes turned most anxiously to the northern frontier, for the pressure of famine in Scandinavia was driving tribes with uncouth names across the Baltic, and something in Central Asia — tribal convulsions or the desiccation of the land — was forcing unnumbered hordes down upon the slender defences of the Euxine. It could be only a matter of years until the tide beat against the actual Roman breast-work. The Scythians had been always familiar to Rome, as to ancient Hellas, as a generic name for the dwellers in the north-eastern plains: but now this name began to articulate itself, and men spoke familiarly of the monstrous blond Roxolani; and the Getae whose cavalry fought in the heavy phalanx of Iran, and whose god was a bear on a mountain peak; and the Dacians who built great forts of squared stone; and the Sarmatians who were ruled by women, and who rode on swift small horses, wore scale armour, and bore painted arrows in scarlet quivers. Of the Parthian menace Rome had long been cognizant, but these northerners were a new enemy. They were still little more than names, but they were steadily creeping nearer, and already the frontier posts had exchanged shots with their vanguard.

The urge of the advancing tide was also felt in the north-west. If a man stands today on the bank of the Rhine facing the Taunus hills he is looking to a land which was never settled, or fully conquered, by Rome. Rome in the days of Augustus knew little about it, believing that it was all a deep, dark forest, to which she gave the name of Hercynian, stretching illimitably towards the sunrise. But she felt its influence and dreaded it, and laboured to devise some bulwark for her gentler Gaul. In his latter years Augustus had to face the first blast of the storm which was ultimately to overwhelm his empire.[1]

[1] The details in this chapter are taken principally from Strabo, Tacitus, Diodorus Siculus, the elder Pliny, Josephus, Plutarch, Columella, and the later geographers — the author of the *Periplus maris Erythraei*, and Ptolemy. I have also drawn largely upon Mr. M. P. Charlesworth's *Trade Routes and Commerce of the Roman Empire*, and various writings of Rostovtzeff, Tenney Frank, F. Cumont, and Jullien.

V. THE SHADOW IN THE NORTH

(A.D. 6–12)

Communi fit vitio naturae ut invisis, latitantibus, atque
incognitis rebus confidamus vehementiusque exterreamur.

CAESAR.

Out of the North
All ill comes forth.

Northumbrian Proverb.

THERE was one problem of empire for which Augustus
did not find even a provisional solution, the problem of
the frontier. We cannot be certain about the policy of
Julius. Undoubtedly he intended to conquer Parthia and
push the Roman border in the East beyond the Mesopo-
tamian plain. If he had lived and had been ten years
younger he might have attempted also to make of Germany a second Gaul. But these would have been conquests, not frontier adjustments. Julius was a great soldier,
and a soldier, even when he is a statesman, is always
tempted to practise his art.

After Actium Augustus had no wish to increase the
Roman territories; he had far too heavy a task before
him in administering them within their present confines.
His aim was to find a border-line which could be easily
and economically defended, and if in the quest for a
scientific frontier he was compelled to enlarge their bounds
— an enlargement of which he boasts in the *Res Gestae* —
this was by accident and not by design. His problem was

that of Britain on the north-west border of India, to create a system, whether by a garrisoned frontier or by buffer states, which would give reasonable protection to the civilized lands under his rule. From the start he regarded the Danube as the natural boundary — perhaps Julius had bequeathed him the precept — for it not only gave him a river line, but, as we have seen, it safeguarded one of the great strategic overland routes of the empire, that from Aquileia to Byzantium. It is more difficult to see his reasons for the extension on the West, since the Elbe was no easier a river to defend than the Rhine. The simplest explanation is that he desired to shorten the frontier and get rid of an awkward angle. The Elbe and the Danube between them made a logical northern border, which must also include the mountain quadrilateral encircling Bohemia.

It was a policy for which much can be said, but, as Augustus and his successors found, it had no finality. Before A.D. 6 Roman influence had crossed the Danube, and Dacia, the present Transylvania, was a submissive neighbour since the downfall of Burebista. It may be that Augustus's plan had by this time been widened in scope and included the conquest of Dacia, which Trajan later achieved, as well as the control of Bohemia. Such an extension would have given Rome the whole of the Danube basin. But the search for a scientific frontier on this side of the empire was a fruitless business in the absence of either of the great boundary lines of nature, the sea or an unscaleable mountain range. If the eagles marched to the Elbe why not to the Vistula? And the Vistula would have been no abiding line, for it could be turned on the north. Some have argued that the failure to annex and civilize the German plain led to the ultimate downfall of the empire, since that plain was a re-entrant angle in the imperial defences, a wedge could be used to split them, a corridor and a place of meeting for the hordes from the North and East. But, even if this geographical fact had been grasped by Augustus, such an enterprise might well have seemed to him beyond the power of Rome, cumbered already with so many duties. And the probability is that it was not grasped, for his information about the plain was sketchy; he thought of it as merely swamp and forest, and he could not have divined the peril which was slowly moving from the Asian steppes.

I

In 9 B.C. Drusus had reached the Elbe. From 13 to 9 B.C. first Agrippa and then Tiberius had been engaged in annual campaigns with the Pannonian tribes of the Save and the Drave, and had conquered all the valley of the former river between Siscia (Sissak) and Sirmium (Mitrovitza), and advanced the frontier to the Danube. In his last campaign Drusus had attacked the Marcomanni in the Main valley, and one of their princes, Marbod (Maroboduus), fearing encirclement by Rome, persuaded his tribe to move eastward and occupy the hill country of Bohemia. There he speedily acquired power and prestige, and was on the way to found for himself a kingdom which would have endangered Roman interests on the Danube. Hitherto he had been on friendly terms with Rome, but she could not permit a second Pyrrhus to appear on her border, so some time before 2 B.C. L. Domitius Ahenobarbus led an army from the Danube to the Elbe. About the same time another army, marching up the frontier between Bohemia and Dacia, isolated the former country on the east. The result of a series of campaigns, of which the records are scanty, was that in A.D. 6 Rome was in a position to begin the conquest of Marbod and the Bohemian quadrilateral.

Tiberius, on his return from Rhodes in A.D. 4, had to hasten to the Rhine frontier, where Ahenobarbus had been having trouble with the Cherusci. He advanced as far as the Weser and received the submission of all the north-west German tribes, wintering somewhere near the head of the Lippe. Next year he crossed the Weser, defeated the Langobardi, and was joined on the Elbe by his fleet, which had sailed round by Jutland. The way was now prepared for the conquest of Bohemia. His plan was that he should march north from Carnuntum on the Danube, while Sentius Saturninus should move eastward from the Rhine to join him by way of the Main valley. Large forces were available, three legions on the Rhine, two in Rhaetia, five in Illyria and three in Moesia, and it is probable that the actual expeditionary force was twelve legions, or some sixty thousand men.[1]

Tiberius and Saturninus had almost reached their meeting-place when ominous news came from the south. The Pannonians had risen; all Illyria was aflame. Tiberius acted like the good soldier he was. He succeeded in getting word to Saturninus bidding him return to the Rhine, for no man knew how the fire would spread. To Marbod he offered peace and recognition as king and friend of Rome, and the leader of the Marcomanni wisely accepted the terms, for he was statesman as well as soldier.

The primary cause of the insurrection seems to have been the requisitioning of supplies and the enrolment of recruits for the Bohemian war before the Dalmatian and Pannonian peoples had realized the Roman strength. Their conquest was too recent, and they had learned something of Rome's ways without understanding the weight of her hand. The first outbreak was in the south among the Dalmatians, where a certain Bato raised at Sarajevo — ominous name — the standard of revolt, massacred

[1] See, however, Syme in *J. R. S,* (1932), XXII, 25.

Roman merchants and overpowered the slender garrisons. It soon spread to the Pannonians in the lower Save valley, whose leader was another Bato. They closed in on Sirmium, the principal Roman centre, and the situation became highly critical. In the east there was a chance of the rising setting all Thrace and the Balkans afire. In the west the road was open to Italy, for the rebels had only to cross the Julian Alps to be within a day's march of Aquileia. Moreover they were formidable fighting men, for many had served as auxiliaries, and had acquired the Roman discipline.

Tiberius kept his head. He completed his compact with Marbod, and in the early autumn marched south from the Danube, sending ahead the governor of Illyria, Messallinus.[1] The two Batos had revealed the old weakness of barbarians, an incapacity for concerted action. The Dalmatian had wasted time attacking Salonae (Salona) and raiding as far south as Apollonia. The Pannonian, with a wiser instinct, had hurled himself on Sirmium, but he was too slow, for Caecina Severus, the new governor of the new province of Moesia, was able to come up in time to save it. Meanwhile Messallinus had fought his way to Siscia, and five legions guarded the road to Italy. The gate had been closed just in time. The position now was that Tiberius held the keys of the west and north, Siscia and Sirmium, but everything south of the Save was in the enemy's hands. Siscia was secure, but Sirmium was in jeopardy, for the Pannonian Bato held the mountain north of the city. Rhoemetalces, the Thracian king, came to its assistance, but could not dislodge the besiegers, and, when presently Caecina Severus had to return to his own province to ward off Dacian attacks, on the Thracians fell the difficult task of preventing the fall of the city by harassing with a small force a powerful enemy. Tiberius realized

[1] A son of Messalla Corvinus.

that this was an affair not of one great battle, but of a slow wearing down of his opponents by famine and attrition. The pride of power which had conceived the Bohemian expedition had vanished utterly, and far into A.D. 7 the situation was a dangerous stalemate.

In Rome the anxiety was intense. She had become accustomed to easy conquests and had regarded all the land south of the Danube as securely under her rule. Now not only were Dalmatia and Pannonia in revolt, but the Dacians were marching, Thrace was not too safe, and at any moment the smouldering embers in Germany might burst into flames. She suddenly discovered that she was trying to hold a great empire with inadequate forces. There were no reserve legions which could be spared from the West, and the most that could be done was to recall veterans to the standards and to raise volunteer companies, chiefly among liberated slaves. Something could be got from the East, but that would take time, and meanwhile there was the vital point of Sirmium in peril, and the army of Moesia, busy with its own urgent tasks, unable to relieve it. To add to his anxieties Augustus had a famine on his hands, and so straitened were Rome's finances that he was compelled to impose new taxes, to suspend official banquets, and cut down the public games.

During A.D. 7 Tiberius at Siscia continued his Fabian policy. Sirmium was the key, but Sirmium could not be relieved until Caecina and the army of Moesia were reinforced. Bitter words were spoken of him in Rome; it was rumoured that he was spinning out the war so that he might be hailed as a saviour; but he refused to alter his plans. He divided his army into contingents, to occupy strategic points and clear special districts, thereby keeping the Dalmatian rebels from cultivating the soil and replenishing their commissariat. He would not think of a pitched battle until he was ready for it. Before the end

of the year the Moesian army, reinforced from the East,
could muster five legions as well as auxiliary troops,
under Caecina and Plautius Silvanus. The two Batos had
now joined hands, and, while still holding the high ground
north of Sirmium, endeavoured to stop the western march
of the Romans up the Save. At a neck of firm ground,
where the road crossed the Volcaean Marshes, there was
fought at last a field action, which narrowly missed being
a Roman disaster. With a better intelligence service, and
with troops trained to the difficult country, the two Batos
all but succeeded in surprising the Romans while in the
act of forming camp. The Thracian cavalry broke, and
many of the auxiliaries were routed, but the legions held
their ground and beat off the enemy. Caecina and Silvanus were free to join Tiberius at Siscia, where there
was now a huge concentration. Germanicus, the young
son of Drusus, a quaestor for that year, had arrived with
reinforcements, and Augustus himself was at Ariminum
to watch the campaign; he knew the country, for forty
years before he had captured Siscia. Tiberius now disposed of a force consisting of ten legions, with eighty regiments of auxiliaries, the Thracian cavalry, and an unknown number of volunteers and veterans from Rome.
He controlled the valley of the Save and was able to
deploy these armies on a wide front; he himself at Siscia,
Silvanus at Sirmium, and Caecina guarding the Moesian
border.

The long campaign was nearing its end. The next year,
A.D. 8, the Pannonian Bato despaired of his cause and went
over to Rome; but he was captured and slain by the
Dalmatian Bato, who fomented a fresh Pannonian revolt.
He in turn was defeated by Silvanus and retired southward
into the Dalmatian hills. Next year came the final 'mop-
ping up.' Tiberius was able to visit Rome and consult with
Augustus, while Germanicus succeeded in capturing three

important Dalmatian fortresses. On his return to the field, the commander-in-chief organized the final operations. The consular Aemilius Lepidus entered the country from the north-west and Silvanus from the north-east, while Tiberius and Germanicus followed Bato and ran him to earth in a rock fortress near Salonae. The Dalmatian leader surrendered on terms, and was imprisoned at Ravenna. The three years' war was over.

It was the most serious military problem which Augustus had to face, for it touched the empire at a vital point. The loss of Illyria would have made a dangerous fissure between East and West. Moreover, the Dalmatian and Pannonian revolts revealed a certain mismanagement in provincial administration which must have given the Princeps food for thought, for it was in defiance of the spirit of his rule. 'You Romans,' Bato told Tiberius, 'have yourselves to thank for it, since to protect your sheep you send not dogs or shepherds, but wolves.' As it was, Illyria became an integral part of the empire and formed a secure base for the development of the Danubian provinces. Three centuries later it produced great emperors and the best of the legions. The campaign is the chief title of Tiberius to military fame. He made no mistake, but, eschewing melodramatic short-cuts, in spite of the clamour from Rome, he broke the enemy by the only methods possible — starvation, attrition, and a slow, deadly scientific envelopment. He kept, too, his motley forces in good discipline and good temper, for he treated his men humanely, fed them well, and took exemplary care of the sick and wounded. The rebellion, which may be described as the Batonian war [1] put an end to all grandiose schemes of expansion to the north. Augustus was well content that the frontier should be the Danube.

[1] This name is actually found in an inscription. Dessau, 2673. The narrative given above is a reconstruction from most imperfect authorities — Dio, LV, 29-34, LVI, 11-17; Vell., II, 110 *sqq.*; Suet., *Tib.*, 16.

II

For the moment Tiberius enjoyed in Rome a mild popularity. His victory was duly acclaimed by Senate and
People; he was given the title of Imperator and award-
ed a triumph, while the young Germanicus was granted
the triumphal insignia and the right to be consul before the
legal age. That was in the early autumn. But while
the man in the street was discussing the latest details
of the Illyrian campaign and the secretaries of Augustus
were estimating its cost, news came from Germany which
turned the modest satisfaction of the capital into terror
and shame. Roman arms had met a second Carrhae.[1]

Rome's eyes had always looked anxiously to the North.
Gaul, before the conquests of Julius, had been largely an
unknown land, and being unknown it was feared. At any
moment out of those northern wilds might come a new
torrent which no second Marius could stem. Now Gaul
was a docile and familiar country, and its place as a *terra
incognita* had been taken by Germany. Pytheas, the
Greek from Marseilles, had journeyed to Britain in the
fourth century B.C., and had given the world the names
of 'Thule,' which perhaps was northern Norway, and
'Teutones.' Polybius knew of a German people near the
Danube estuary, and Posidonius, who continued his history, first distinguished the Germans from the Celts and
the Scythians. But in the age of Augustus there was little
detailed knowledge, and the writers of the first century
A.D., like Pomponius Mela, the elder Pliny and even
Tacitus, while they realized the distinctive character of
the German races, had no real understanding of the land
or the people. A certain number of denationalized Germans lived west of the Rhine, but for the country to the
east of the river there was only the news brought back by

[1] On the exact date of the German disaster see Rice Holmes, II, 174-76.

Drusus's soldiers and by bold merchants who had penetrated its recesses. As a consequence a bleak picture had
been constructed in the Roman imagination. Germany
was one vast domain of swamp and forest, a nine days'
march from north to south, and of incalculable extent from
west to east. Rains and mists blew over it at all seasons,
and there were no easy avenues of approach, like the open
downs and the wide shallow vales of Gaul. Rome had
heard of the forest-dwellers in the Taunus, the Harz and
the Teutoburger Wald, the forerunners of the Franks and
the Thuringians; she had heard, too, of wild races who in-
habited the sandy plains south of the Baltic, and of wilder
folk in the frozen lands beyond that sea. So she thought
of the country as a nightmare, and of its peoples as the uttermost barbarians in habit and creed.

Some of her picture was true. Throughout the Middle
Ages the Taunus and the Harz had about them an aura
of the uncanny as the last haunt of the primeval gods.
The Romans, accustomed to open country and long pro-
spects, feared the great forests, so vast that a man might
march all day without seeing the sun, and so dense that a
squirrel could travel for leagues without having need to
touch the ground. Moreover, the trees there were not the
kind they knew. In the western parts there were oak and
ash and elm, but the further one went the blacker the
woods grew, until there was nothing but the inky darkness
of pines.

The people were like their dwelling-place. They did not
live in compact towns, but in villages such as can be seen
today in Scandinavia, where the cottages straggled over
a wide extent of country, and all around lay the shaggy
mat of the forest. In the nearer woods they herded their
droves of swine, and further afield they hunted deer and
bear and bison. The hunters lived by themselves in clear-
ings; they were the Men of the Mark, the chief warriors,

a foreshadowing of the feudal squires. There were no temples for their dark divinities, only sacred groves, such as that described by Adam of Bremen, and sacred trees — maypoles for festivals, but also dule-trees, where swung outlaws and captives of war. Such trees were dedicated to Wodin, their chief god. Their theology was what we should expect from men living among the glooms and broken lights of the primeval forest, hearing strange noises in the tree-tops when the thunder crashed, and awful voices in the wind. Wodin had a special sanctuary, somewhere between the Elbe and the Oder, and to him alone were human sacrifices offered. No man, as Tacitus tells us, might enter that sanctuary without a chain about his neck to show his submission to the god. There was a second holy place on the island of Rügen, where Nerthus, the Earth-goddess, was worshipped; once a year she was brought in procession to the mainland in a car which, like the Ark of the Covenant, none but the priests might approach.[1] There were other divinities; the Thunder-god, Thor, the deity of the plain man; Tyr the Warrior; Frey, the god of fertility, who gave good harvests; and Balder, the young Apollo of the North. But the real divinity was the forest itself, for it was out of the forest trees, the ash and the elm, that the old gods had fashioned the first pair of human beings. Their Olympus was a bright country in the sunset, Asgard, from which the rainbow made a bridge to earth, and to which, after death, went the spirits of the good and brave. There was dark cruelty in the faith, but there was also profundity and beauty, and centuries later, in the Elder Edda, it was to blossom into high imaginings.

The forests were also the home of magic. There was a race of wise women, like the Norse Völvas, gigantic beings who appeared to men in dreams. Drusus had met one

[1] Tac., *Germ.*, 40.

of them who foretold his death. There were also the maids of Wodin, the Valkyries, who rode through the night skies to choose the slain in battle. The peasant, returning home in the twilight, heard the wild swans whistling overhead and felt himself in the presence of the unseen. It was a land where portents crowded in on everyday life, and Rome, hearing the rumour of them, knew that the North was very near the brink of things. For there, as Tacitus believed, the noise of the dawn could be heard, and the light of the sun's setting lingered on till its rising, so that there were no stars. 'Illic usque tantum Natura.' In such a domain of magic the legions were not fighting with man only, but with the princes and powers of the air.

During the Pannonian revolt there had been an ominous quiet on the German frontier. The commander of the Roman army was P. Quintilius Varus, who had been governor of Syria in 6 B.C. Varus seems to have been more of the courtier than the soldier, though the disaster which he suffered may have led the Roman historians to depreciate him unfairly; in Syria he feathered his nest so successfully that in two years he raised himself from poverty to opulence; his steady preferment may have been due to the fact that he married a great-niece of Augustus.[1] He was unaccustomed to administrative work in a wild country, and had assumed from the easy success of Tiberius before his arrival that Germany could be treated like any other Roman province. Accordingly he levied taxes on the Syrian model, was tactless in his handling of the tribes, and refused to heed the warnings of those of his officers who had some knowledge of the land. He had under him five legions and a mass of auxiliary infantry and cavalry. Three of the legions he led in person and two were in charge of an experienced soldier, his nephew,

[1] Claudia Pulchra, granddaughter of Octavia and niece of the young Marcellus.

Lucius Asprenas. Of the discontent among the tribes, especially the Cherusci, he seems to have had no inkling.

Germany east of the Rhine was held by isolated Roman posts, and by one strongly entrenched garrison at Aliso on the Lippe. In September A.D. 9 Varus was at his summer camp on the west bank of the Weser (near the modern Blomberg) in the territory of the Cherusci, and was about to start back for his winter quarters, Vetera Castra near Xanten on the Rhine. The Cheruscan chief, Sigimerus, had a son Arminius, who had served in the Roman army and won Roman citizenship.[1] To him there came the dream of freeing his countrymen from the Roman yoke. His father, also a Roman citizen, refused to join in the project, and sent a warning to Varus. But Arminius, who had brought the neighbouring tribes into the plot, had the ear of the Roman general, and at dinner the night before his departure told him of trouble among the Chauci and the Bructeri which he would do well to suppress on his way to the Rhine. This meant a circuitous route to the north-west in difficult country, where Arminius had prepared an ambush. Some of the loyal Germans warned Varus that the tale was false, but they were not believed. Arminius and his fellow conspirators were actually entrusted with certain detachments from the legions, which they declared they needed for the escort of the supply trains they had undertaken to furnish.

Next morning Varus set out in stormy autumn weather, accompanied by women and children and great quantities of baggage, for his journey was not a punitive expedition but a mere shifting of quarters. Arminius and the conspirators accompanied him for some way until he was well into a land of thick forests. There they left him, in order, as they said, to assemble the tribes to help in quieting the

---

[1] According to von Rohden (*Pauly-Wissowa*, II, 1190) the German name Hermann has no connection with Arminius.

alleged revolt. Varus found himself in a pathless country where his troops had to hew their way through a mass of undergrowth, and in many places to build causeways for the waggons to move. He found another thing. As if by the touch of unseen hands great trees would topple down to his left and right and behind him. They had been already cut half through in the German fashion, and before the Romans knew it they had an abattis on every side of them. Suddenly from behind the tangle came flights of arrows and javelins, and they realized that the enemy was upon them, and that this enemy was Arminius himself.

Varus was doomed from the start, for he had sent out no scouts and had made no provision for supports, as Julius had done when he had a like experience in his war with the Nervii.[1] He swung round and tried to make for the fort of Aliso, burned his waggons, and that night struggled out to more open ground. But next day he was again forced into the forest, and in a deluge of rain the doomed column wrestled through swamps and undergrowth, blinded by the storm, crippled by falling trees, and all the while exposed to the enemy's sharp-shooters. On the third day the end came.[2] A cavalry regiment tried to cut its way to the Rhine, but failed. Varus and many members of his staff took their lives. A few legionaries escaped, some died fighting, but most surrendered and were crucified or beheaded as offerings to the gods. It was a repetition on a greater scale of what had befallen Sabinus and Aurunculeius Cotta in the Gallic revolt sixty-three years before, but there was now no Julius to snatch vic-

[1] *de bell. Gall.*, II, 17, 22.

[2] The actual site of the disaster was probably in the Teutoburger Wald somewhere between Osnabrück and Detmold; but no topic has given rise to more speculation among scholars from Melanchthon to Mommsen and E. Meyer. The different views (and also the question of the site of Aliso) have been examined by Rice Holmes, II, 164–74.

tory from disaster. Arminius had meanwhile slaughtered
the legionary detachments which he had borrowed, and
now every Roman post east of the Rhine fell to him, except Aliso. There a good soldier was in charge, one
Lucius Caedicius, who first beat off the enemy attack, and
then on a dark night cut his way out, and led troops,
women and children safely to Xanten. For a moment it
seemed as if the conqueror might sweep into Gaul, but
Lucius Asprenas hurried down from Mainz with the two
legions that remained of the army in Germany, and the
Rhine was secure.[1]

The affair of the Teutoburger Wald was a heavy blow,
not only to Roman pride, but to the whole new frontier
policy. It had been due not to cowardice, for the legions
died bravely, but to rashness and ignorance. Rome had
misunderstood the nature of Germany, and the uncertain
tenure which mere military demonstrations in force gave
her over a proud people. The chief blame rested not on
Varus but on Augustus and Tiberius. Arminius was a
tribal, not a national, leader, for the Germans were even
less than the Gauls a nation, and Tacitus, in his desire to
exalt the repute of Germanicus, has made of him a more
grandiose figure than is warranted by the facts. But he
was beyond doubt a brilliant guerilla commander, though
he does not rise to the heights of Vercingetorix, the great
opponent of Julius. The rest of his story is soon told.
After the death of Augustus the young Germanicus was
given the German command, crossed the Rhine, and, while
Caecina Severus moved up from the south in support,
dealt with the Chauci and Cherusci. He won various
small successes, but he did not subjugate the land, and,
in spite of his eight legions, he did not conquer Arminius.
But he avenged in Roman eyes Varus's disgrace, and bur-

---

[1] The authorities for the disaster of Varus are Vell., II, 117 *sqq.*; Tac., *Ann.*, I, 58
sqq., Germ., 37; Dio, LVI, 18 *sqq.*

ied the Roman skulls which he found fixed to the trees
in the sacred groves. The stand of Arminius against Germanicus was a finer performance than his conquest of
Varus. His fate was that which seems to dog all tribal
leaders, for in A.D. 19, when he attempted to make himself king of the Cherusci, he perished by the jealousy of
his kinsmen. Similar was the destiny of Marbod, who has
been rightly called the first statesman in the history of
the German race. He had shown his wisdom by making
peace with Tiberius at the outset of the Pannonian revolt,
and by refusing an alliance with Arminius when the latter
sent him the head of Varus. Presently he found himself
in the field against Arminius, and, though he held his own,
his kingdom began to crumble. Rome refused him help,
being not averse to see the fall of one who had given her
much anxiety. His end was exile at Ravenna for eighteen
melancholy years.

The consternation in Rome made his Pannonian triumph impossible for Tiberius and sent him post-haste to
the Rhine. He did not yet know the extent of the German revolt, but he realized that, but for the waste of time
over the siege of Aliso, Arminius might have been across
the Rhine and ravaging the fields of Gaul. It was not the
only time in history that an enemy's entanglement with
a fortress has saved the situation. But on his arrival he
found things less bad than he had feared. He refused to
attempt the recovery of the lost ground, and contented
himself with strengthening the Rhine garrisons. The three
lost legions — XVII, XVIII and XIX — were not replaced, but remained a gap in the army list; and the lost
eagles were not recovered, so Arminius could boast that
Roman standards remained hung up in the German
groves.[1] Extemporized corps of veterans and volunteers

[1] Tac., *Ann.*, I, 59.

were hurried to the Rhine to join the forces of Asprenas, and presently other legions were added from Spain and Illyria, so that that frontier was held by no less than eight [1] — a precaution which was the measure of the Roman fears. In A.D. 11 Tiberius had a summer camp a little east of the river, but, neither then nor in the following year, did he attempt any reprisals. Late in A.D. 12 he returned to Rome to celebrate his delayed Pannonian triumph, leaving to Germanicus the wardenship of the marshes.

With Varus perished the policy of frontier expansion into which Augustus had drifted. He now realized that to extend Roman territory to regions which it required an army to hold, was a burden which the empire could not support. It would involve the employment of auxiliary troops on a dangerous scale, and an expenditure which would disorganize his whole scheme of finance. Moreover, there was the risk that Rome, by such an advance, might weld what were still separate tribes into a nation. So with the cordial assent of Tiberius he fell back upon his old frontier conservatism. It was the one great check which he had met in his career, and it cut him to the heart. For a time he let his hair and beard grow in token of mourning; for the few remaining years of his life he fasted on the anniversary of the calamity; and he was often heard to cry, as if the words were unconsciously wrung from him, 'Varus, Varus, give me back my legions!' [2] The legend of Rome's invincibility had been shattered.

Yet Rome had had many defeats in her record, and there must have been a special reason for the profound impression made by the German disaster. The explanation is that she was now faced with something which she

---

[1] These seem to have been I, V, XX, and XXI in lower Germany, and II, III, XIV, and XVI in upper Germany. See Syme, *J. R. S.* (1932), XXII, 29.

[2] Suet., *Div. Aug.*, 23.

did not understand, which she could not assess, and which she therefore feared and magnified. An enemy like Parthia was a formidable but intelligible thing, which could be beaten if it were worth her while to take the necessary trouble. But this menace from the North was intangible and evasive, with a mystery about it which unnerved the clear Roman mind. In the later campaign of Germanicus, Caecina saw the ghost of the dead Varus beckoning to him out of the marshes, and the tale is a parable of the Roman mood. Upon a civilization, essentially urban and of the South, fell the awe of those wild things of the North which in the end destroyed it.

VI. THE CLOSE

(A.D. 12–14)

> I am an old and solitary man,
> Mine eyes feel dimly out the setting sun,
> Which drops its great red fruit of bitterness
> To-day as other days, as every day,
> Within the patient waters.
>
> BROWNING, *Soliloquy of Aeschylus.*

I

WHEN in the beginning of A.D. 13 Tiberius at last celebrated his triumph for Pannonia and Germany, Augustus had completed his seventy-fifth year. His span of life had far exceeded those of Alexander and Julius. By a strict and temperate regime a body, naturally frail, had been preserved to a great age, but now infirmities were crowding fast upon him. Rheumatism crippled his limbs, his poor circulation made him feel cold acutely, and he was easily fatigued. For a little the tragedy of Varus had prostrated him, and, though he had recovered his spirits, it was plain to those around him that his vital force was ebbing. The Princeps had become a very old man.

In those last years he seems to have felt his loneliness. His daughter and granddaughter were in exile, and his only surviving grandson was half an idiot. There was no one of his own blood to succeed him, and this he was apt to lament with the sad monotony of age. He was beginning to turn more and more to his stepson, Tiberius, to write him affectionate letters, and to worry about the chances

of his smooth succession. There were several others who
might make a bid for it; Lucius Arruntius, for example,
and Asinius Gallus, and Marcus Lepidus — all unsuitable;
he must see to it that there was no mishap.[1] His mind,
too, turned back on his long career, reviewing every detail
of it, and he set himself to complete a summary of his
work which he could leave as his testament. He had long
been busied with this, and now he brought it up to date.
It would be published everywhere, so that he who ran
might read what he had done for Rome and the empire,
for he knew well that when the lion was dead the dogs
would bark again.[2]

He could still transact business, but he had to husband
his strength. He could no longer go regularly to the
Senate-house, so he did most of his work in his own rooms
at the Palatine, with the help of Tiberius and his privy
council, and the Senate decreed that the decisions thus
arrived at should have all the force of a senatorial order.
He kept a close watch on finance, and he did not forget
his old ingenuity; for, finding that his tax on bequests
was unpopular, he proposed to replace it by a levy on
lands, houses and commission-agents, with the result that
the Senate hastily confirmed the original proposal. In A.D.
13 he accepted a renewal of his imperium for another ten
years, while the tribunician power was continued for Tiberius; a law was also passed giving the latter equal rights
with his stepfather in the command of the armies and
the government of the empire, and empowering the two
to conduct a census together. The census was duly held,
and was concluded in May A.D. 14 with a solemn purifica-

---

[1] Tac., *Ann.*, I, 3.

[2] His defence was a recital of things done, *res gestae*, against the charge that his work
was trickery achieved by bribes; cf. Tac., *Ann.*, I, 2. 'Militem donis, populum annona,
cunctos dulcedine otii pellexit.' The original is lost, but copies exist at Ancyra in Galatia (in Latin) and at Apollonia in Pisidia (in Greek), and fragments of another at Antioch in Pisidia. See Hardy's ed. of *Mon. Anc.*, Introd.

tion in the Field of Mars. Augustus was too ill to read
the customary vows, and left them to Tiberius. During
the ceremony strange things happened. An eagle circled
round his head, flew to Agrippa's tomb and perched on
the first letter of Agrippa's name, as if to warn the Princeps that he must soon follow his great marshal. A flash
of lightning obliterated the first letter of 'Caesar' on a
statue of Augustus on the Capitol; now 'aesar' in Etruscan meant a divinity and 'C' stood for 100, and the au-
gurs prophesied that within one hundred days he would
join the gods. Moreover, there was an eclipse of the sun,
and meteors in the sky foretold the death of princes.
The mind of Rome was attuned to marvels and Augustus
accepted the omen. He had already deposited his will with
the Vestal Virgins, and he now put the finishing touches
to his political testament. He had wound up his account
with the world.

For long he had been feeling the burden of age and sick-
ness, and a melancholy satiety with life. He had dared so
much, schemed so much, toiled so much, and now he was
at the end of the road. The writing of his testament had
given him a momentary satisfaction, but it was soon
dimmed as one dreary day of weakness succeeded another.
Milton's words in *Samson Agonistes* might have been his:

> So much I feel my genial spirits droop,
> My hopes all flat: Nature within me seems
> In all her functions weary of herself.

His one comfort lay now, as ever, in work. He struggled
to finish the census, the last of his imperial duties, but
the pleasure had gone out of achievement though the obligation remained. As he reviewed his career he saw the
shades rather than the lights, the immense, almost super-
human labours which to his present weakness seemed
monstrous in the retrospect.[1]

[1] Corneille has caught his temper:
'J'ai souhaité l'empire, et j'y suis parvenu;

But, his final official tasks completed, his mood seems to have changed. The hour of release was near and his spirit was suddenly enlarged. He welcomed the thought of death with a kind of gaiety.[1] He would take a last holiday and see again that happy south Italian land which he had always loved. He would revisit the home of his forefathers.

That holiday was in accord with the tenor of a sane and strenuous life, the proper 'falling close' to a great epic. Tiberius had certain matters to arrange in Illyria, and the Princeps resolved to accompany him as far as Beneventum on his way to Brindisi. He set out from Rome with Livia and a large suite, and came by the Via Appia to the little coast town of Astura on the bay of Antium, where the river of that name twined through woods to the sea. There Cicero, when the loss of Tullia drove him from Tusculum, had purchased a small villa looking across the marshes, where he spent his days planning a shrine for his dead daughter.[2] At Astura the company joined the imperial yacht, and, since the state of the wind compelled them to embark by night, Augustus caught a chill in the bowels; so it was in weakness and discomfort that he coasted down the lovely Campanian shore, where fifty-eight years earlier he had met his mother and made the decision which changed the course of the world. He was greatly cheered by what happened at Puteoli, where the yacht put in. The crew of a corn-ship from Alexandria greeted him in white raiment with incense and garlands, praising him for safeguarding their lives and occupa-

---

Mais en le souhaitant je ne l'ai pas connu.
Dans sa possession j'ai trouvé pour tous charmes
D'effroyables soucis, d'éternelles alarmes:
Mille ennemis secrets, la mort à tout propos,
Point de plaisir sans peine, et jamais de repos.'

[1] See on this point the remarks of W. Weber in *Princeps, Studien zur Geschichte des Augustus* (1934), 9 *sqq.*   [2] *ad Att.*, XII, 19, 36.

tions.[1] This was the kind of tribute he loved, and he gave forty pieces of gold to each of his attendants to be spent on Alexandrian wares.

His health improved and he passed several days at his villa in Capri, that fortunate isle where land and water make the fairyland of a dream. A boyish gaiety returned to him, as if he had rid himself of the burden of the years. He gave dinners to his friends and many gifts, compelling the company to dress fantastically, Romans in the pallium and Greeks in the toga. He entertained a band of young athletes who were training for the Greek games at Naples, and joined in pelting them with fruits and sweetmeats. He invented bad Greek verses, and puzzled one of Tiberius's learned astrologers by demanding from what poets they came. He made jokes about Capri, calling part of the island Apragopolis, the Land of Do-nothings, because of the laziness of its people. Whenever his complaint ceased to trouble him he was in a mood of youthful high spirits.

Capri had given him rest, but when he crossed to Naples he overtaxed his strength and brought back his illness. He was unwilling to disappoint honest folk who desired to compliment him, so he sat through the whole of a blazing Campanian day watching athletic games which had been established in his honour. Then he continued his journey to Beneventum, where he said goodbye to Tiberius. It would seem that he now felt his weakness increasing, for he set out at once on his return journey. But at Nola, eighteen miles from Naples, he became gravely ill and was compelled to halt. There he was put to bed in a villa of his family, in the very chamber where, when he was five years old, his father had died. It was clear to his attendants that his days were numbered, and a mes-

---

[1] 'per illum se vivere, per illum navigare, libertate atque fortunis per illum frui.' Suet., *Div. Aug.*, 98.

senger was sent post-haste to recall his stepson. Tiberius arrived in time to spend some hours with him, and to receive his last words of counsel.

It was the month of August, his lucky month which bore his name. On its nineteenth day he had entered upon his first consulship, and that was to be the day of his death. His mind was clear and he was free from pain, except for the swift ebbing of strength. He had finished his course and he faced the end with a gentle dignity. Homer had always meant much to him, and he may have found comfort in that line which is the quintessence of peace: 'The night is at hand, and it is good to yield to the night.' [1] His friends gathered about him, and he asked them whimsically if they thought that he had been a good actor in the comedy of life. As Julius had quoted a tag of Menander before crossing the Rubicon, so he quoted a verse from a Greek play:

> Since well I've done my part, then, gentles, pray
> Applaud, and send me with your thanks away....

He was left alone with Livia. For a moment his mind wandered into a nightmare, and he cried out something about young men carrying him off. He recovered himself, and sent for a mirror, had his hair combed and his sagging jaw put straight. He asked about a child of Drusus who was ill, and then, feeling the coming of death, he endeavoured to kiss his wife, murmuring 'Farewell, Livia; live mindful of our marriage.' He died in the arms of the one being left to him in the world to love. [2]

---

[1] νὺξ δ' ἤδη τελέθει· ἀγαθὸν καὶ νυκτὶ πιθέσθαι. *Iliad*, VII, 282.

[2] Suet., *Div. Aug.*, 99 *sqq.*; Vell., II, 123; Dio, LVI, 30 *sqq.*; Tac., *Ann.*, I, 5 *sqq.*; Pliny, *N. H.*, VII, 150; Plutarch, *de garrulitate*, 11. There is some baseless scandal in Tacitus and Dio which is examined by M. P. Charlesworth, *A. J. Phil.* (1923), XLIV, 145–57.

II

The days were too hot for travel, so the body was carried by night along the roads to Rome. The magistrates in each little city had charge of it in turn, and each night it lay in the local court-house. Nola sent the dead Princeps to Naples, Naples to Cumae, Cumae to Formiae, and Formiae across the Pomptine marshes and the Latin plain to Bovillae among the Alban hills. The grape-gatherers, coming home from the vintage, saw the mourning procession setting out on its night's journey, and at dawn the workers in the olive-yards saw it reach its daily resting-place.

Bovillae, twelve miles from the capital, contained the family shrine of the Julii, the proud race which claimed descent from the Goddess of Love. There, as was fitting, the principal ceremonies began. The equestrian order, which had been Augustus's special care, had obtained from the consuls the privilege of now taking charge of the body, and the deputation of knights was headed by an odd, vacant youth, Claudius, the son of the elder Drusus, who was one day to be emperor. The journey from Nola had taken the better part of a fortnight, and it was now early September. That night the cortege set out on its last stage along the Appian Way. It entered the sleeping city by the Porta Capena, passed through the hollow between the Caelian hill and the Palatine, and crossed the ridge beneath the Esquiline till it reached the palace, where the body was laid in the vestibule.

Next day the Senate, summoned by Tiberius, met to arrange the funeral. The magistrates had discarded their purple-bordered togas, and Tiberius and his son Drusus were in sombre black. A great wave of sorrow and regret had passed over Rome, and many novel proposals were made to honour the dead. One was that his life, from his birth to his death, should be officially known as the Augustan Age, and so entered in the calendar. The Princeps had left explicit instructions for the ceremonial on the same lines as the funeral of Agrippa, and these must be followed. The will, drawn up the previous year, was brought by Drusus from the care of the Vestal Virgins, and, according to custom, was read by an imperial freedman. There were large bequests to Livia and Tiberius, and huge donations to the Roman populace. Then Drusus read various testamentary memoranda, a statement as to the army and public finance, notes of advice to his successor, and the summary of his life's work, which we call the *Res Gestae*. It was a solemn moment, for these were the last words of Augustus to his people.

Then came the funeral. The coffined body was laid beneath a couch of gold and ivory, which was draped with coverlets of purple and gold. Above, on the couch, so that all men could see it, was a wax image of the dead man in triumphal garb. The procession was formed, other images of Augustus in gold being borne behind the bier, as well as images of his ancestors and kin, and of famous Romans like Pompey. Only Julius was not there, for Julius was a god. The mourners descended from the Palatine to the Sacred Way and thence to the Forum, the heart of Rome; past the temple of Vesta and the dwelling-place of the Vestals; past the new temple of Castor and Pollux, rebuilt by Tiberius in honour of Drusus, and the well where the Twins had watered their horses; past the temple of Janus to the Rostra, where so much of Roman history had been made. At the Rostra the cortege halted, and Drusus delivered the customary funeral panegyric on the virtues of the dead. At the temple of Divus Julius, Tiberius pronounced a second eulogy, of which Dio has a paraphrase.[1] It dealt chiefly with his official work, his

[1] LVI, 35-41.

devotion to the state, his public economy and private
liberality, his love of candour and honest speech, his
supreme administrative gifts. There was no rhetoric in
the speech, but much sober fact; its tone was that of the
Res Gestae, and it was such a tribute as Augustus would
have approved.

The procession moved on in the hot September noon,
while crowds choked the streets and covered every house-
top. It passed under the Capitol and the shining new
temples which Augustus had built, and through the Triumphal Gateway to the Field of Mars, where, beyond the
bend of Tiber, loomed the great dome of the imperial
Mausoleum. All Rome followed it, senators and senators'
wives, the equestrian order, and the praetorian guards.
The body was laid on a pyre, and on the pyre, as a last
tribute, the citizens cast the decorations which they had
won in war. Then centurions applied the torches. As
the flames mounted an eagle was released and soared sky-
wards, a custom drawn from the ancientry of the East,
and a symbol that the soul of the Princeps had ascended
to Heaven.... Slowly the great concourse departed, but
Livia remained for five days on the spot. On the sixth
day, accompanied by some of the chief men of the equestrian order barefoot and ungirded, she collected the ashes
and placed them in the Mausoleum, which held the mortal
remains of Octavia and Marcellus and Agrippa.

On the 17th of September the Senate formally declared
that Augustus now ranked among the deities of the state.
An ex-praetor, one Numerius Atticus, swore that he had
seen him ascending to the skies, and was well rewarded
for his vision.[1] Temples were decreed to him in Rome and
elsewhere, and priests and festivals assigned to his cult.
His image on a gilt couch was placed in the temple of
Mars, and the house at Nola, where he died, was made
holy ground.

[1] Dio, LVI, 46.

The news of his death was soon carried by the official posts to the uttermost parts of the empire. To the armies it meant little; they had taken the oath to him, but it was Tiberius who, for the past decade, had led them in the field. The peoples, who from the Loire to the Euphrates were worshipping him as a saviour, had a moment of alarm as if the foundations were cracking. But they comforted themselves, reflecting that Augustus was a god and that gods do not die. They redoubled their offerings to one who was not only divine but had now joined his fellow divinities. . . .

The child, whose birth we have seen in Bethlehem that winter night when Quirinius had ordered a census of Judaea, was now out of his teens, and pursuing his trade of carpenter in Nazareth, where he had taken over Joseph's business. He had accompanied his parents to the solemn festivals in Jerusalem, and had won something of a name for his skill in expounding the Jewish scriptures in the local synagogue. He was commonly known as Jesus of Nazareth, but sometimes as the Son of Mary. When not working at his trade he was given to long wanderings, for, though he was friendly to all, he loved wild nature and solitude. When the news of the death of the master of the world came to the Galilean hills, and the neighbours were troubled lest this should mean the end of the Augustan peace and an orderly empire, he did not seem greatly concerned, for his thoughts were on a different peace and another empire. Sixteen years later he was to proclaim a kingdom mightier than the Roman, and to tell of a world saved not by Man who became God, but by God who became Man.

III

The career of Augustus may be likened to a high plateau approached by a long, steep and perilous ascent. For fifteen years his feet were on the crags, and for forty-three he surveyed the world from the tableland. In the first stage his problem was how to win supreme power, and in the second how best to use it. His character remained the same throughout his life, in the sense that the qualities which enabled him to outstrip his rivals were those which made it possible to remould the world — iron self-command, infinite patience, and an infallible judgment of facts and men. Few have ever entered upon a more apparently hopeless task than Augustus when, in his nineteenth year, he left Apollonia, and few have ever won a more triumphant success. For years he led a life of unremitting physical toil and mental anxiety combined with miserable health — no small test of fortitude. Close-lipped, tenacious, cautious and yet intrepid, he is amazing, but he is not attractive. The earlier Augustus is the Industrious Apprentice raised to the highest power, the Eldest Son of the fairy tales, whom nothing will keep from his heritage. He lived in constant peril, but his prudent days had none of the glamour of adventure. He took desperate risks, but only after meticulous calculation. He is the least romantic of great men.

When Actium was fought and won he revealed the same qualities, but they were given a new direction and tempered by something of which hitherto there had been few traces. The common *arriviste* is apt to find himself lost at his journey's end. He does not know how to use what he has gained. The very gifts which made him formidable on the road keep him puzzled and uncertain at the goal. Here — on the side of character — lies the marvel of Augustus's career. A cold, self-contained youth was exchanged for a genial maturity; he who had held himself apart became the friend of all the world; what had appeared to be a devouring personal ambition was transmuted into an anxious benevolence, a selfless care for the vast oecumene of which he was the head. To 'pietas' and 'gravitas' were added 'civilitas' and 'clementia' and 'providentia,' and between them they made up a complete 'auctoritas.' These latter qualities he had always possessed, but they had been necessarily frostbound during the bleak years of struggle and frustration. The miracle was that they did not die, but, when at last the sun shone, could break into blossom and fruit.

His character, as I have said, was adequate to his powers of mind, a thing unfissured, four-square, simple, wholly intelligible. He had most of the major virtues which Aristotle enumerates, but especially he had *phronēsis*, that practical wisdom which is the proper attribute of the ruler. Here we are faced by something far from simple. We have seen its results in the system of government which he created; it will be well to look into it more closely, for it is in this respect that he excelled other men.

His inspiration came from Julius. What that inspiration was we can only guess, for there was little time allowed the conqueror of the world to make his thoughts explicit. The mind of Julius, so far as we can read it, was the mind of a dreamer joined to the temperament of a soldier. He believed that, just as he had beaten his enemies and brought a great part of the earth under his sway, so he could mould to his will the civilian life of the world. His penetrating vision saw the ultimate needs of the empire, but he underestimated the difficulties in the way of meeting them, the tardiness of the process by which human nature can be accustomed to a new mode of life. Had he lived he might have gone far in the path he had marked out, but no lesser man could equal his pace.

With the cardinal article of his faith, that the old Republic could not govern an overseas empire, Augustus agreed; but on four points, as we have seen, he revised his policy. Julius would have made the frontier secure by fresh conquests in the East and North; Augustus, aware that he was not a military genius, hesitated and compromised. Julius aimed at an hereditary monarchy which should have something of the sanctity of the eastern and hellenistic thrones. To this the empire was to come in the end, but Augustus realized that the time was not ripe for it, and that republican sentiment was still a force to be reckoned with. Julius was a bold iconoclast about republican forms which had survived their usefulness; Augustus sought to cherish whatever of these forms could be made to work, that there might be a decent bridge for tradition-loving Romans between past and present. Lastly, Julius stood for the ideal of a universal imperial citizenship, an ideal which was one day to be realized, and which was to be the chief imperial cement. There is evidence that Augustus would have accepted this as an ultimate purpose, but he saw that for the moment his task was to restore to Italy prestige and self-confidence, since Roman citizenship would be valueless without an authoritative Rome. Who shall say that in these matters he did not judge wisely?

He was a builder whose concern was with things, not fancies. He could appreciate a far-reaching plan, but towers and adminicles must wait for the deep foundations. He had his preferences like other people, but he brought them always to the test of plain reality. Julius had been a dreamer; Augustus admired, examined and discarded many of his dreams. There were dreamers in plenty in Greece and the East; his sharp practical logic saved the world both from oriental extravagance and the sterile mysticism of the philosophers. He had none of the dangerous fanaticism which is to be found in men so diverse as Machiavelli and Calvin, an exaggerated view of the sanctity of the state; he would give the state the sanctity

which belonged to it and no more. He was free from
egalitarian whimsies, a malady from which the ancient
world did not greatly suffer; he did not believe in that
degeneration of democratic theory which imagines that
there is a peculiar inspiration in the opinions of the ignorant and a singular nobility in the character of the penniless. But he had equally no belief in a crude authoritarian-
ism; he would have assented to Aristotle's definition of the
purpose of the state — that it originated for the sake of
life and was continued for the sake of the good life.[1] He
sought not only to give every class a modest comfort, but
to assign it a function in the community.

This doctrine of function was no new thing, for it derived from the Greek philosophers,[2] and at the time was
accepted by most thinking men; but after Augustus it had
to wait for many centuries until it was revived as a principle of democracy. We must be careful in using this last
term, for it has acquired a flavour today which would
have been incomprehensible to the ancient world. Of the
familiar democratic technique certain parts, like the representative idea, were in the circumstances impracticable.
But one democratic essential — government by discussion — Augustus would fain have established. He sought
to make the Senate, constantly refreshed from below and
therefore in a sense representative, a true consultative
assembly, whose decisions the Princeps must accept or
refute by argument. He would have applauded, too, the
definition of Pericles: 'Our constitution is named a democracy because it is in the hands not of the few but of the
many. Our laws secure equal justice for all in their private disputes, and our public opinion welcomes and honours the best in every branch of achievement, not for any

---

[1] *Politics*, I, 2, 8.

[2] *e.g.* Plato's conception of justice as each man doing his proper task (τὸ τὰ αὑτοῦ
πράττειν), and Aristotle's definition of health as a 'harmony of functions.'

class reason, but on grounds of excellence alone.'[1] The Republic had been a close oligarchy; the empire brought a large new recruitment to the public service and endeavoured to give to the humblest a modicum of civic interests.

Augustus had notable advantages. He had to deal with the stubborn reactionary, but he was little troubled by the foolish progressive. The voice of the revolutionary was stilled; Rome had had too much of him and craved above all things for order and decorum. Nor did he suffer from the minor intellectual, the man whose talent is for a cheap disintegration. Rome did not want the atomiser; her one desire was to escape from chaos. Moreover, the sophist was everywhere at a discount when men were seeking a positive faith. Callicles and Thrasymachus were rare types even in the academies. Plato three centuries before had put them out of business and they had not recovered. Lastly, Augustus was free from intellectual pride. He was not dogmatic, but content to feel his way modestly, and when he blundered to retrace his steps. And he did not overrate himself or his achievements. Like Ecclesiastes, he could rejoice in his labour, and yet admit that much of it was vanity and its reward vexation of spirit. He had his task which must be done without thought of the price. The mainspring of his life was the Stoic precept: 'We also must be soldiers, and in a campaign where there is no intermission and no discharge.'[2]

We have already seen flaws in the great structure, which were to widen into breaches. The chief was that he laid too heavy an administrative burden on his successors. Not all his ingenuity could devise a means of making the empire fool-proof, and the state suffered when its head was a dolt or a degenerate. That was on the executive side; a graver blemish was that it did not bring the gov-

[1] Thucydides, II, 37, 2. [2] Seneca, *Ep.*, LI, 6.

erned into any close organic relation with the government, and therefore prevented the growth of political capacity and true citizenship. But from this, as we have seen, there was no escape. Self-government had been possible in the small city-state, but no method had been found of applying it to a larger unit; indeed, it may be questioned whether in the full sense such a technique has yet been discovered.

For the rest, the Augustan constitution remains one of the major products of the human intelligence. It was a whole into which the parts fitted smoothly, but both whole and parts were elastic and capable of swift adaptation to unforeseen conditions. It was elaborate, but that was necessary, both because of its origin and its purpose. Augustus succeeded to a lawless world. Now lawlessness cannot be got rid of merely by a strong hand. Penal and repressive measures, unless they are woven into a fabric which fits the social body, will remain external applications and not internal remedies, and will sooner or later issue again in lawlessness. Civilization is always a matter of delicate adjustments, a conspiracy and a construction. The cure for anarchy is a hierarchy.

Elaboration was needed, too, because of the vast range and variety of the new duties of government. Augustus did not unduly reverse the institutions which he created, or put too high a value on any mechanism for its own sake. He was less a slave to a panacea than we moderns, who are apt to credit some type of constitution, some economic dogma, some international apparatus with a plenary power of salvation. But he recognized the truth that a complex task demands a complex technique. It should be remembered that Plato, the foe of the mechanical, in the *Laws*, which he wrote in extreme old age, and therefore as his final testament, provides for the state a perfect jungle of minute regulations.

To most minds the Roman experiment lacks the charm of certain earlier polities. In the Rome of Augustus we cannot look for the free grace and simplicity of the Athens of Pericles. That is inevitable. Any large-scale organization must lose some of the merits of its rudimentary beginnings. Quantity will have a coarsening effect on quality. In the *Protagoras* [1] Plato describes a gathering before dawn in the colonnades of an Athenian house, where young men met to talk philosophy, and old Prodicus, still in bed and wrapped in a sheepskin, discoursed in his deep rumbling voice. Such a scene has a morning freshness which will not be found in the most perfectly equipped of universities. But quantity was of the essence of the problem which faced Augustus, since his task embraced the known world.

There is no merit in an empire as such. Extension in space does not necessarily mean spiritual advancement. The small community is easier to govern, and, it may well be, more pleasant to live in. If its opportunities are limited its perils are also circumscribed. But the alternatives which confronted him were empire or anarchy. He must make an oecumene of the world or let it sink into chaos. What he achieved was a polity so reasonable and so well adjusted that it continued for centuries, and in its fall left behind it massive foundations on which men are still building. The Athenian empire lasted for fifty years at the most, and the stupendous creation of Alexander the Great for less. What has been the fate of succeeding imperialisms? That of Spain endured on the grand scale for little more than a century; that of Napoleon for a decade; the British Empire is less than two centuries old, and in its present form is a thing of yesterday. In the brief span of recorded history empires have had a shorter life than many monarchies, theocracies and even republics. The

[1] 316 *sqq.*

Augustan alone reached a venerable age. In the coming of Christianity it had to face the greatest of all historic convulsions, but such was its potency that it weathered the storm and influenced profoundly the organization of the Christian church.

The true achievement of Augustus is that he saved the world from disintegration. Without him Rome must have lost her conquests one by one, and seen them relapse into barbarism or degenerate into petty satrapies. The wild peoples of the East and North would have ante-dated their invasions by centuries. Without him a parochial Rome would have assuredly been destroyed by eternal civil war. Without him the great traditions of Hellas and Palestine would have been choked by debris, the night of the Dark Ages would have fallen sooner, and our civilization today would have lacked its most precious spiritual foundations. He gave the world a new and rational way of life. Also — and this was not the least of his bequests — he preserved for it two great Roman ideals which were in danger of perishing, one of character and one of government. It was owing to him that a succeeding emperor could write: 'Let the God which is within thee be guardian of a living being, manly and of ripe age and engaged in state affairs, a Roman and a ruler, who has taken his post like a man waiting for the signal which summons him from life, ready to go.' It was the inspiration of Augustus which enabled a poet three centuries later to pay a tribute to Rome which wise nations have taken as their creed:

> Alone she gathers to her bosom those
> Whom late she vanquished; citizens, not foes,
> She calls them now. Their conqueror they proclaim
> Mother, not mistress. So her general name
> Enfellowships mankind, makes fast, with bands
> Of love devout, the far-off daughter lands,
> That, whereso'er we range, 'tis all one race —
> Debtors to her by whose peacemaking grace

> No place is strange but everywhere a home —
> One world-wide family all akin with Rome.[1]

It is due to him that the Roman concepts of public duty and service are still a living force among us. Historians have denied him the name of genius which they grant readily to Alexander and Julius and Napoleon; but if it be not genius to re-make and re-direct the world by a courageous realism and supreme powers of character and mind, then the word has no meaning in human speech.

The wheel of birth and death moves inexorably in that sphere of man's activity which is concerned with government. Constitutions come into being, flourish, wither, and descend to an unlamented grave, only to be later revived, acclaimed and again rejected. Nothing lives continuously, but nothing wholly dies.

> Multa renascentur quae jam cecidere, cadentque
> quae nunc sunt in honore.[2]

The work of Augustus was for centuries too much the accepted background of their life for men to question or assess it; it was taken for granted like the equinoxes and the seasons. In the Middle Ages, under the name of Octavian, he became a cloudy figure of necromancy. But now, at the second millenniary of his birth, scholarship has enlarged our knowledge of him, and the problems he faced have a livelier interest for us, since they are not unlike our own. History does not repeat itself except with variations, and it is idle to look for exact parallels, but we can trace a resemblance between the conditions of his time and those of today. Once again the crust of civilization has worn thin, and beneath can be heard the muttering of primeval fires. Once again many accepted principles

[1] Claudian, *de cons. Stilich.*, III, 150–60. The translation is by my friend the late Professor J. S. Phillimore of Glasgow.

[2] Hor., *Ars Poet.*, 70–71.

of government have been overthrown, and the world has become a laboratory where immature and feverish minds experiment with unknown forces. Once again problems cannot be comfortably limited, for science has brought the nations into an uneasy bondage to each other. In the actual business of administration there is no question of today which Augustus had not to face and answer.

If his 'magna imago' could return to earth, he would be puzzled at some of our experiments in empire, and might well complain that the imperfections of his work were taken as its virtues, and that so many truths had gone silently out of mind. He had prided himself on having given the world peace, and he would be amazed by the loud praise of war as a natural and wholesome concomitant of a nation's life. Wars he had fought from an anxious desire to safeguard his people, as the shepherd builds the defences of his sheepfold; but he hated the thing, because he knew well the deadly 'disordering,' which the Greek historian noted as the consequence of the most triumphant campaign. He would marvel, too, at the current talk of racial purity, the exaltation of one breed of men as the chosen favourites of the gods. That would seem to him a defiance not only of the new Christian creed, but of the Stoicism which he had sincerely professed. True he had been sparing in his grants of Roman citizenship, but that had been for a temporary purpose, since the heart of the principate must be first made strong if the blood was to circulate freely to the members. From the Elysian Fields he had watched the development of his empire and had come to see the wisdom of Julius's liberalism, for had that empire not drawn much of its strength from the non-Italian stocks, in philosophers, poets, emperors and soldiers?

But chiefly, I think, he would be perplexed by the modern passion for regimentation and the assumed contradiction between law and liberty. To bring order out of anarchy he had been forced to emphasize the first, but he had laboured also to preserve the second. His aim had been to keep the masculine vigour of the republican character, and to cherish likewise all worthy local and provincial autonomies, for he recognized that the empire depended upon men, and that men to be of any account as citizens must have a decent measure of freedom. He would sadly admit that the machine which he created had been too strong for Roman liberties, and that in its grip the Roman character had lost its salt and iron. Being too much governed, men had forgotten how to govern themselves. But in the centuries since his death he had observed that the world had discovered certain methods of which he had not dreamed, and that it was possible for greater numbers than he had ever ruled to live a life which was both orderly and free. With the disappearance of slavery and the spread of education the constituents of society had changed, and self-government need not be mob-government. Here lay a path to the solution of what had been his gravest problem, and he would be amazed that men should so light-heartedly reject it. And when this expert in mechanism observed the craving of great peoples to enslave themselves and to exult hysterically in their bonds, bewilderment would harden to disdain in his masterful eyes.

THE END

INDEX

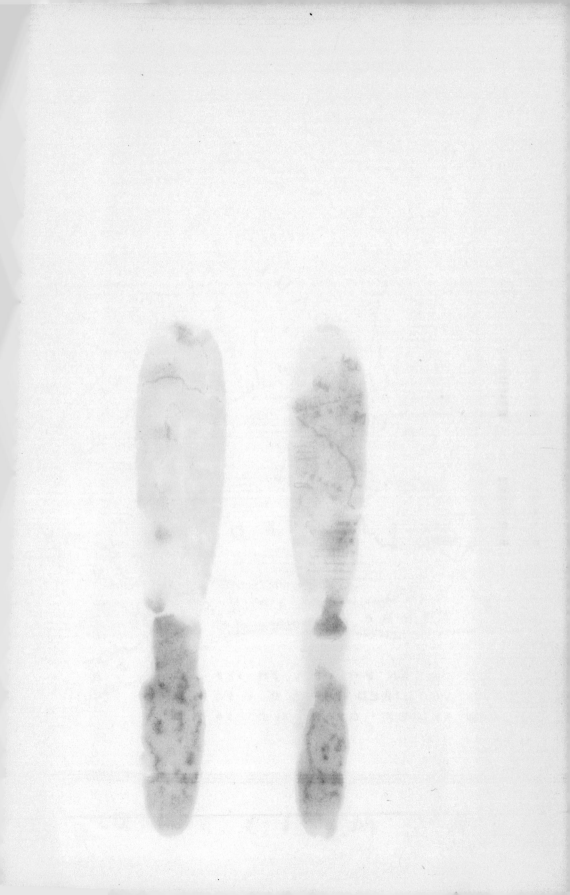

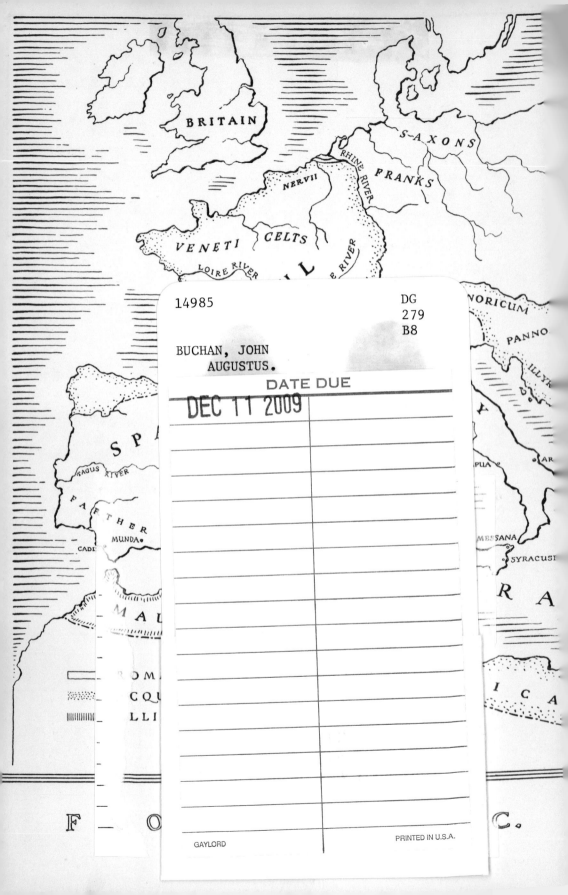